ACTING IS BELIEVING
A BASIC METHOD
SEVENTH EDITION

This one's for Julia, the third of the three Js.

ACTING IS BELIEVING
A BASIC METHOD
SEVENTH EDITION

CHARLES MCGAW
LATE OF THE GOODMAN SCHOOL OF DRAMA
A SCHOOL OF THE ART INSTITUTE OF CHICAGO

AND

LARRY D. CLARK
DEAN, COLLEGE OF ARTS AND SCIENCE,
UNIVERSITY OF MISSOURI — COLUMBIA

HARCOURT BRACE COLLEGE PUBLISHERS

FORT WORTH • PHILADELPHIA • SAN DIEGO • NEW YORK • ORLANDO • AUSTIN • SAN ANTONIO

TORONTO • MONTREAL • LONDON • SYDNEY • TOKYO

Publisher	TED BUCHHOLZ
Editor-in-Chief	CHRIS KLEIN
Acquisitions Editor	BARBARA J.C. ROSENBERG
Developmental Editor	CATHLYNN RICHARD
Project Editor	JULIET GEORGE
Production Manager	JANE TYNDALL PONCETI
Art Director	BURL SLOAN

Cover Image: Linocut by Stephen Alcorn, created for *The HBJ Anthology of Drama* (1993) and dedicated to Tiberio Antinori.

ISBN: 0-15-501584-2

Library of Congress Catalog Card Number: 94-073547

Address for Editorial Correspondence: Harcourt Brace College Publishers, 301 Commerce Street, Suite 3700, Fort Worth, TX 76102.

Address for Orders: Harcourt Brace & Company, 6277 Sea Harbor Drive, Orlando, FL 32887-6777. 1-800-782-4479, or 1-800-433-0001 (in Florida).

Printed in the United States of America

9 0 1 2 3 4   039   10 9 8 7 6

PREFACE

It's hard to believe that it is time once again to introduce a new edition of *Acting Is Believing*. Think of it! The Seventh Edition. Charles McGaw's brilliant interpretation of the turn-of-the-century techniques—developed by Stanislavski and extended by others who worshiped the great Russian actor and director —has stood the test of time like no other version of this system. I remain honored by my association with this "classic" acting text.

The book retains its four-part organization, opening with an introductory section "Preliminaries," and a glossary of the language of the theatre. From there, the text moves on to discuss "The Actor Alone," "The Actor and the Play," and "The Actor and the Production." For the Seventh Edition of *Acting Is Believing* I have continued the approach I took for editions five and six: clarify the syntax, update the examples, rearrange the material in instances where practice indicates a better way of doing things, and integrate wherever possible new approaches to teaching acting that are compatible with McGaw's original blueprint. He defined his fundamental philosophy succinctly in the Preface to the Third Edition when he said

> The book maintains that, while a not quite definable something called talent is necessary for success, basic acting consists in performing a number of specific tasks about which there is no mystique. These tasks are likely to demand a good deal of hard work. *Acting Is Believing* is intended to serve talented students who are willing to work hard.

I hope the Seventh Edition still serves the same intent and maintains the same uncomplicated formula for learning how to act.

Once again, I need to acknowledge the help of more people than space provides the opportunity to thank. Reviewers of the new edition included Julie Gagné, Valencia Community College; Victoria Parker, Portland State University; and Jane Saddoris, West Chester University. Also, I must pause to give my strongest appreciation to two important women in my life: (1) my Executive Staff Assistant, Marla Applebaum-Wilcox, who cheerfully calls the same person for the fifth time to see why I haven't yet received the permission I requested for the photograph or the excerpt; and (2) Yvonne, my spouse of now more than forty years, who has the uncanny ability to read this manuscript as if she had never seen it before, providing me with invaluable insight and relentless attention to detail. I appreciate the professionalism of the former and the loving support of the latter.

Larry D. Clark

CONTENTS

ACTING IS BELIEVING
A BASIC METHOD
SEVENTH EDITION

PART 1
PRELIMINARIES

CHAPTER 1

TRAINING YOUR TALENT: AN INTRODUCTION

"Acting is believing": what a simple definition, yet how complex the concept. Nevertheless, there it is—a challenge, a goal for your study and practice. To train as an actor is to train your ability to believe, to become able to exist in your believed but imaginary circumstances as if they were real, to command the technique to relate to other believers as if they were who they pretend to be, and to possess the tools to transmit clearly and artfully your beliefs to an audience.

No single appropriately comprehensive definition of acting exists. In fact, throughout this book we will be trying to understand what acting is. At one level, we can say that acting is behaving as if things that are *not* real *are* real, a broad definition that covers even the make-believe games of childhood. At this level, depending to a degree, of course, on the quality of his[1] imagination, almost every child becomes an accomplished actor and relishes his opportunities to perform. So long as he acts, as most children do, only for his own benefit and for others who are participating in the make-believe game, he is remarkably relaxed and natural, totally in control of his part of the performance. When he tries to perform for spectators, however, he often gets his first negative review. Becoming self-conscious, he is accused of "showing off," thus demonstrating his inability to solve one of the basic problems confronting anyone who proposes to act in the professional sense of the word—the problem of establishing the proper relationship between the actor and the audience.[2]

A little later in life, everyone gathers experience in acting in another context and for another purpose. These performances, which we may suitably term *social acting,* will vary, depending on the circumstances and the intention of the actor. Described at times as good manners, at times as "little white lies," and at other times as downright deceptions, these performances can vary from cordially receiving guests whom one has no desire to see, to disguising a splitting headache so a companion's pleasure will not be ruined, to pretending ignorance that a surprise party is being planned, to trying to palm off the often-repeated excuse of having had to work late at the office when one has actually been out on the town. Notice that social acting involves a dimension missing from childhood games. Here one deliberately shapes a performance for the benefit of someone else (in many cases for an audience of a single individual), and success follows only if the performer can convince the audience that what is not real is real. Almost everyone develops some degree of skill at this level of acting, but failure can be instantaneous and devastating if one's behavior is so transparent that the audience is not "taken in."

Further evidence that acting skills are a part of our everyday life is evident in instances where we talk so vividly about events we have observed or

In recent years, many colleges and universities have committed their programs to producing new plays, always a challenge and thrill for the actor. This scene is from the University of Missouri-Columbia Black Theatre Workshop's prize-winning production of *Strands,* written by Eric Wilson, directed by Clyde Ruffin, scenery by Patrick Atkinson, lighting by David Raver, costumes by Clyde Ruffin. (Photo courtesy of the University of Missouri-Columbia Department of Theatre.)

participated in that our listeners share to some extent the quality of the original experience—which is to say we can tell these stories with some degree of dramatic effectiveness. And most of us attempt on occasion to mimic the speech and behavior patterns of others—even the sounds and movements of animals and machines. All of us also enjoy sharing the performances of others and stimulating them to more complete and graphic portrayals than they could muster without our help. This natural human capacity to perform, listen, react, and affect the performance of others is at the heart of the actor's art.

These rudimentary experiences are frequently all the actors bring to school, college, or community theatre productions; and when intermingled with general intelligence and a director of some skill and imagination, they provide the basis for a certain level of success. Indeed, repeated experiences under such conditions can produce actors of considerable overall ability. But the person who aims to perform consistently at a level of professional competence needs more thorough and demanding preparation. Performing a major role requires talent and technical skills fully as great as those necessary for a professional pianist to perform a major concerto, and this talent can be developed and these skills acquired only through long and intensive training.

Today, more than ever before, such training is necessary. A very informative handbook for the serious student of acting says:

> In the old days ... actors without formal training were the rule. Now [they are] definitely the exception. Training in the art and craft of acting is a virtual necessity for a successful career, and if you are hired at first without it, you will need it thereafter.[3]

During those "old days," fledgling actors received their training by working as walk-ons and bit players in stock companies or by touring road shows, learning their skills in schools of very hard knocks. At a time somewhat later, one hears of young aspirants who were able to descend on Broadway or Hollywood and find employment, if not fame, merely on the basis of their charm, physical attractiveness, or unique personality.

Those days are over. Stock companies have practically disappeared. The number of touring shows has been reduced greatly, and employment with those that remain is certainly not available to untrained actors. Today, the theatre, the motion pictures, and television afford the aspiring actor an extremely competitive market, in which thorough training is necessary for even moderate success. For the first time in history, most of our professional actors at least began their training in a college or university.

Furthermore, the best opportunities for stage actors today are often in regional theatres employing permanent or semipermanent companies. These theatres usually offer a mixed repertory of classics and modern plays that require actors with range and versatility. In the past several decades, the growth of these theatres, alternative theatres, children's theatres, theatres associated with colleges and universities, conservatories, and community theatres has given both actors and playwrights many opportunities to practice their profession away from the boom-or-bust syndrome of Broadway and from the major production centers for motion pictures and television.

Even so, it is still commonplace for acting teachers to announce to their students that "there are no jobs" in acting. It is true that within Actors' Equity members earn, on the average, less than $10,000 a year (and included within that average are several actors who make more than $2 million annually!). Nevertheless, the best acting students are those who are so irrepressibly committed to this ephemeral and often heartbreaking career that they persist in trying it against all odds.

Furthermore, all who study acting know that the skills a student acquires in an acting class have many applications beyond the perimeters of professional theatre.[4] First, studying acting and drama gives a better understanding of oneself and others. Second, creative dramatics, theatre for the aged, and the application of acting skills to the "human potential" movement in psychology provide new opportunities for the actor to put his training to work. Moreover, increased leisure time and the recent emphasis on fitness, healthy diet, and meditation open interesting employment opportunities to trained actors willing to put their skills to other than a theatrical use. People trained in theatre successfully populate all sorts of jobs, but especially those requiring effective communicators with the ability to listen carefully and understand or evaluate a role other people are attempting to perform.

ACTING WITH PROFESSIONAL COMPETENCE

Although everyone acts and in a simple way achieves some measure of success, the talent and skill involved in game playing and social acting fall far short of that necessary for professional accomplishment in the theatre. The successful stage performance is a carefully planned feat of artistry that communicates with the greatest possible effectiveness a viable interpretation of the meaning of a particular play to an audience. Rather than a casual world in which actors behave impulsively in chance events, the stage is a world of controlled design in which all the parts of the pattern serve to illuminate a purpose, usually that of a playwright as interpreted by a director. Of course, inspiration and spontaneous responses can be an exciting part of the art of the theatre, and we will talk about that later. But, from the beginning, students of acting must realize that acting is not doing what "feels natural," that spontaneous responses are most valid (and most likely to appear) after careful preparation, and that inspiration comes as a result of hard work, not as the stimulus for it. Tyrone Guthrie, one of the most eminent of twentieth-century directors, wrote:

> drama is absolutely and elaborately prescribed, and the greatest acting contains a minimum of spontaneous invention and a maximum of carefully calculated effect repeated with only minute variations at every performance of the same part. Dramatic performance, therefore, is concerned with repeating a series of intelligibly prescribed actions in order to form an intelligibly prescribed design.[5]

To list some of the more important characteristics of good acting, we may say that it is:

1. *Analytical:* demonstrating careful study, understanding, and appreciation of the playwright's meaning. (We attempt to underscore this important aspect of acting throughout *Acting Is Believing,* but take it up in particular in Part III, "The Actor and the Play.")

2. *Interpretative:* expressing faithfully this meaning in terms of the actor's experience and imagination. (Part II of *Acting Is Believing,* "The Actor Alone," is designed to provide the actor with the capability to unleash these valuable tools.)

3. *Formalized:* creating a visual and oral form that will make the meaning comprehensible to others and will have intrinsic artistic value. (The last three chapters of Part III focus on creating a basis for and communicating an effective interpretation of a play.)

4. *Projectable:* having dimension, energy, and clarity that can communicate the meaning to an audience of a certain size occupying a certain space. (The chapters mentioned in number 3—especially those labeled "Interpreting the Lines" and "Speaking the Lines"—also deal with this aspect of acting.)

5. *Repeatable:* having enough permanence that the actor can effectively repeat the performance over a period of time. (Part III, "The Actor and the Production," delineate tools for coping with this portion of the actor's work.)

All we have said thus far makes acting appear to be incredibly complex and demanding, and indeed it is. Nevertheless, if a person possesses the proper motivation to succeed, we can state the remaining essential qualities of a successful actor quite simply. Remember them as the two *t*'s: talent and training.

Talking about talent is easy, but defining it precisely is extremely difficult. It frequently appears to be unrecognizable in its undeveloped state, because biographies of many actors of great prominence tell how they were advised early in their careers that they had no potential for success. Certainly, talent must not be confused with being stagestruck or "screenstruck." Many such people are absolutely without it and are attracted to the profession of acting only by the most superficial elements of "show business."

Perhaps the best way to define talent is to delineate the qualities of a successful actor. A successful actor has a body and a voice capable of dramatic effectiveness. He is a person with a great desire, perhaps a great need, to share experiences with others. Often more vulnerable than the average person, he reacts strongly and deeply to both criticism and praise. He is perceptive of the world about him; he has an unflagging curiosity about the human condition; he sees, hears, smells, touches, and tastes intensely. He is sensitive enough to other people that he can appreciate and understand their modes of behavior, even though they may be quite different from his own. His vivid imagination

The theatre can have a therapeutic effect when plays are performed in prisons, hospitals, and at demonstrations. In these photos, teacher/director Richard Klepac uses acting techniques with a class of mentally retarded students. (Photos by Jeff Taylor.)

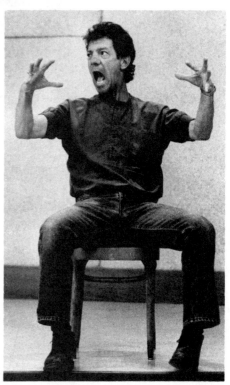

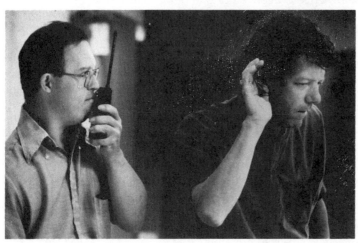

allows him to project himself into other periods and other places. He has enough intelligence to comprehend a playwright's purpose and to understand how the character he is playing relates to it. He has enough courage and self-confidence that he is not afraid to reveal his inmost thoughts and feelings on a public stage. His keen histrionic sense tells him what is and what is not interesting to an audience.

A person with these attributes will probably be considered "talented," and he has a good chance to be able to learn to act. Without all these, he faces an uphill struggle.

Training, the second *t,* is the method by which talent is developed. It requires time, tenacity, patience, hard work, and self-discipline. Enthusiasm, a striving for perfection (although it can never be achieved), and a willingness to work cooperatively with others all are important. In fact, as necessary as abundant talent is to an actor's chance for success, it can be a trap in the early stages of his development if it tempts him to get along with a minimum of effort. Before he knows it, persons of lesser talent but with uncompromising discipline and a better attitude will be accomplishing more. If you are starting your training with the idea that acting is just fun and games, beware: You will soon be disappointed and discouraged.

To arrive at an understanding of what an actor's training involves, we can divide the process into six parts.

1. *Cultural development:* an important and inadequately emphasized aspect of the training process. Uta Hagen says, "To be more than an adequate or serviceable actor, it takes a BROAD EDUCATION in the liberal arts."[6] The material from which the actor draws is the entire realm of human knowledge and experience. He cannot afford to be ignorant of historical or contemporary events, linguistics (especially foreign languages), literature, music, visual arts, or the history of the theatre and drama. An actor without access to such accumulated knowledge is deprived of one of his richest sources.

2. *Internal training:* learning how to control and to make effective use onstage of his sensory and emotional responses.

3. *External training:* the development of his body and his voice as responsive and expressive instruments. Voice production, speech, and movement are the actor's principal tools.

4. *Interpretative training:* learning how to read a play, to analyze its structure, and to discover its total meaning.

5. *Rehearsal techniques:* learning how the actor prepares for rehearsals at home; how he works at rehearsals during the various stages in the preparation of a play for public presentation; how he relates to the other actors, the director, the stage manager, the production staff; and how he observes the principles of rehearsal ethics and discipline.

6. *Performance skills:* learning how to prepare before a performance; how to relate to, and to share the play with, the audience; how to maintain energy, tempo, and rhythm; and how to keep repeating a performance without losing its original effectiveness.

A performance at the Delacorte Theatre in Central Park. Free Shakespeare in the park is a tradition in New York City as well as in other cities across America. Actors performing outdoors must contend with wind, rain, and the noise of airplanes passing overhead. At the Delacorte, Shakespeare fits naturally into the pleasant "picnic" setting of the park, and enthusiastic audiences line up for their tickets hours before the play begins. (Photo by George E. Joseph.)

With the exception of cultural development, which must come as a lifelong commitment to expanding one's knowledge of and sensitivity to literature and the arts, these processes roughly comprise the order of presentation of the material of this book. One must be cautious, though, about thinking of acting as a step-by-step, logical process. Good actors never stop honing their abilities in all these areas. Students should always be careful not only to bring the skills and understandings of previous lessons to bear on their current exercise, but also to continue a regimen of practice and exploration that expands their abilities to perform the skills they are accumulating. Good actors never cease to study and practice their basic skills, just as accomplished musicians devote a tremendous portion of every day to practicing the foundations of their technique.

Actor training cannot be accomplished simply from studying a book but requires the guidance of able teachers, coaches, and directors. Since theatre is a highly cooperative endeavor, working with others in exercises and in scene study is essential. After acquiring the basic skills, the student should be given an opportunity to work before an audience, preferably first in a laboratory situation and later under conditions that approximate those in the professional theatre.

Good acting, then, does not result from some God-given knack that enables special people to perform instinctively. Rather, it ensues from the practice of certain skills that can be learned if one has the aptitude and the determination to do so. Once mastered, these skills provide the actor with an external and an internal technique for performing a role by executing a series of specific tasks. When these tasks are harmoniously and artfully integrated, they help reveal the purpose of the play as interpreted for a particular production. Only then can acting be said to be "good," no matter how "beautiful" it may have looked or sounded nor how "exciting" the event itself may have been to an audience. Only then will "acting" and "believing" become synonymous.

True, great actors have about them an aura, a personal magnetism, sometimes described as "star quality." They have a "stage presence" that compels attention and makes an audience want to watch them and listen to them. It is important to note, however, that even these people at the beginning of their training spent an important period of time concentrating on developing the same basic skills that form the essence of this text. In book after book, biography after biography, this simple fact becomes abundantly clear: Good actors work hard, train hard, and take their work seriously. They know that great achievement can come only after practicing their technique so frequently and so thoroughly that it becomes a natural part of everything they do.

The final goal of the great actor is to have the audience believe completely in the reality of the performance.

What part should a textbook play in the complex task of training an actor? It should organize your study in a logical progression; it should create an awareness of recurring problems and suggest solutions, thus guiding you toward technical proficiency; and it should provide you with useful practice exercises. No text can be comprehensive, and this one, while not ignoring any aspect of the acting process, focuses on the development of internal and interpretative skills.

This book proceeds from the fundamental belief that the student actor begins his training with self-exploration. The tools you will use as an actor, while they may be sharpened by practice and stretched by learning and exercise, are present within you even as you read these words.

This important truth constitutes the essential difference between acting and other arts. The painter works with pigments and canvas, the sculptor with clay and stone, and the pianist with keys that control hammers on strings, but the actor is his own instrument. He communicates with an audience by playing upon his own voice and his own body, which we shall call the actor's *external resources*.

The need for the actor to develop a well-trained voice and body should be obvious. A musician forced to perform on an inferior instrument is at a disadvantage. And an actor is at a similar disadvantage if his muscular and vocal control are not all that they could be. In fact, the training of the actor's voice and body as an instrument occupied almost the exclusive attention of acting teachers until well into the current century.

Today's theatre practice demands that this training—as essential as it is—be accomplished in conjunction with other studies and exercises fundamental to the actor's development. A fine speaking voice and a well-coordinated body in themselves do not make an actor, any more than possessing a Stradivarius makes a violinist. Along with the instrument, the *how* by which the artist reaches his audience, must come the *what*. The primary task of the actor is to create an imaginary character behaving logically in circumstances provided by the playwright and interpreted by the director, and the raw material for accomplishing this task we shall call your *"inner resources."* They will join your voice and your body as the fundamental bases for the study of acting.

The need for inner resources surfaces the moment you start to think seriously about performing a role in a play. Suppose you have been cast in a part that requires you to enact the funeral rites for a native of Bandjarmasin. If you are like most untrained actors, you will go to your first rehearsal without a clue about what to do when you get there, perhaps already visualizing a storm of applause on opening night, after which hundreds of spectators murmur that you "have it in you" to be a great actor.

In fact, arriving at such a moment will come only after an arduous journey in which you systematically discover what you "have in you" that might help you bring to life on the stage a native of Bandjarmasin engaged in the solemn ritual of disposing of his dead. The chances are ten to one against your ever having heard of the place, to say nothing of your having a familiarity with its customs. Once you realize you must create an unambiguous character in these unfamiliar circumstances, despite your overwhelming lack of knowledge about either of them, you will probably experience a sense of defeat. How could you possibly perform, or indeed even imagine, an action that you could be certain would be truthful to this character?

You have now encountered the world of the actor at rehearsal. All actors face the same dilemma when they prepare to perform a role in any play, no matter how common or how exotic the situation and the setting. Your goal as a student of acting is to be able to bring to the rehearsal a method of studying the role together with the tools that will enable you to access the necessary raw materials for creating and performing it. These raw materials, simply put, constitute the accumulation of your own experience.

Your inner resources, then, are comprised of everything you have done, seen, thought, or imagined in your lifetime. Your actions onstage are limited to these resources. For the role in question, you will need to find elements in your inner resources that will allow you to create and believe in the circumstances of the unfamiliar character from Bandjarmasin. Just as you are dependent on your voice and body to carry out your actions, you are also dependent on your inner resources to tell you what actions to carry out.

Fortunately, your resources are not confined to what you have personally experienced; they also come from reading, observing, seeing plays—from countless sources. And a part of talent is the ability to deepen and extend experiences in the imagination.

The need for inner resources is not confined to exotic and unlikely dramatic circumstances. For instance, let us suppose you have been cast as Shakespeare's Romeo or Juliet, and that the scene for rehearsal is Act III, Scene 5, sometimes called the second balcony scene. To illustrate the current point, we need only recall the chief facts of the situation. Romeo and Juliet are the son and daughter of two powerful and wealthy families who have long been bitter enemies. Having met by chance, they have fallen deeply in love and have married secretly. Within an hour after their marriage, Romeo, involved in an outbreak of the ancient enmity, has killed Juliet's cousin and has been banished from his native city of Verona. There appears to be no hope of happiness together as the young couple say farewell in the dawning light.

What an exciting prospect to play one of these famous lovers! You have now learned that you must be prepared to explore your own inner resources before you can possibly create a character in whose behavior you, the other actors, and the audience can believe. But how do you know what inner resources to explore? How can you begin to match your own experience with that of the character? You begin with the script, first discovering the physical actions the character must perform. The process of defining and using these actions is the first topic we shall take up—right after we learn to begin speaking to each other in the special language of the theatre.

1. Wherever the generic *he* appears in this book, it is naturally to be taken to mean *he* or *she*. It is also traditional in the theatre to refer to both male and female stage performers as actors, but when referring to female performers, we occasionally use the term actress. It should be clear to even the most casual observer that women and men make equally gifted actors, directors, playwrights, and producers.

2. Throughout this book, the term *professional* should be understood to mean a highly developed level of competence, not necessarily an actor who makes his living in the theatre.

3. Robert Cohen, *Acting Professionally* (Palo Alto, CA.: Mayfield Publishing Company, 1975), p. 26.

4. For instance, *Acting Is Believing* is referenced in that portion of a popular textbook on trial practice for lawyers that discusses the importance of communicating a clearly defined **intention** during examination and cross-examination of witnesses.

5. Tyrone Guthrie, *New York Times,* August 28, 1966.

6. Uta Hagen, *A Challenge for the Actor* (New York: Macmillan Publishing Company, 1991), p. 36.

NOTES

CHAPTER 2

LEARNING THE LINGO

Time out! Acting is believing: to believe is to understand, and in addition to comprehending everything possible about the play, the actor must also understand the theatre, both as a profession and as a place to work. Like every profession, the theatre has its own special vocabulary. Partly technical, partly slang, much of it is standardized on the English-speaking stage. Actors must be familiar with this language, just as mechanics must know the names of their tools or surgeons the names of their instruments.

Since your teacher will want to speak to you in the special vocabulary of the theatre while you are working on your classroom exercises, and since you will find this special shorthand invaluable when talking to your exercise partners, we shall discuss these terms at this time. Your teacher will identify what portion of the lexicon of the stage that you will need immediately. The remainder will be reserved for the time when you are actually working with a director in a play.

Refer to this section often as your work progresses. This list of terms is not exhaustive, but good theatrical dictionaries are available, and one or two are listed in the "Additional Sources" section of the Bibliography at the end of this book. For convenience, we have grouped the selected terms into categories.

STAGE DIRECTIONS

Blocking The director's arrangement of the actors' movements on stage with respect to one another and the stage space. Some of the purposes of blocking are to tell the story, develop characterization, set mood and atmosphere, and create suspense. The term *blocking* is also often used in two additional ways: as a synonym for *covering* (see definition) and as a term for situations in which actors find it psychologically difficult or even impossible to remember a line or perform a required action.

Stage right The actor's right as he stands onstage facing the audience.

Stage left   The actor's left as he stands onstage facing the audience.

Downstage   Toward the audience.

Upstage   Away from the audience.

Below   Toward the audience. Same as "downstage of."

Above   Away from the audience. Same as "upstage of." (An actor who walks *below* a piece of furniture walks between the furniture and the audience; an actor who walks *above* a piece of furniture walks between the furniture and the upstage wall of the setting.)

In   Toward the center of the stage.

Out   Away from the center of the stage. (The direction to move *in three feet* means to move three feet closer to the center of the stage; to move *out three feet* means to move three feet farther away from the center of the stage.)

In order that a director may designate an actor's position onstage precisely, the acting portion of the stage is divided into fifteen areas.

STAGE AREAS

STAGE AREAS. These abbreviations stand for: up right, up right center, up center, up left center, up left; right, right center, center, left center, left; down right, down right center, down center, down left center, down left.

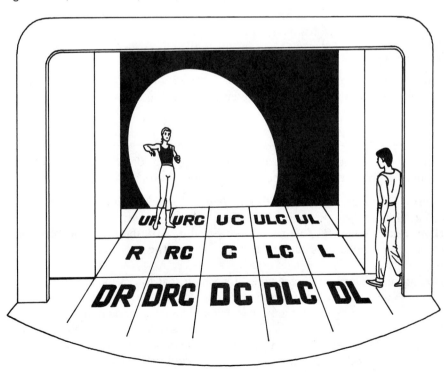

Onstage   The part of the stage, usually enclosed by the setting, that is visible to the audience in any particular scene.

Offstage   All parts of the stage not visible to the audience.

Backstage   The entire stage portion of the theatre building, in contrast with the auditorium, which is designated as *out front.*

Wings   Offstage space at the right and left of the acting areas.

BODY POSITIONS

Eight *body positions* designate the position the actor is facing in relation to the audience (see chart). All positions are designated by the degree to which the actor faces the audience.

Open   A position in which the actor is facing toward the audience, or nearly so. To *open* is to turn toward the audience. Since effective communication requires that the actor be seen and heard, he must—without sacrificing believability—keep himself as *open* as possible. Although there are many exceptions, you should follow these practices unless a reason exists for doing otherwise:

1. Play shared scenes in a quarter position.

2. Make turns downstage.

3. Do not cover yourself or other actors while making gestures or passing objects. In other words, use the upstage arm.

4. Kneel on the downstage knee.

Closed   A position in which the actor is turned away from the audience. To *close in* is to turn away from the audience.

ACTORS' POSITIONS IN RELATION TO ONE ANOTHER

Actors' positions in relation to one another are considered with regard to the relative emphasis each actor receives (see illustration).

Share   When two actors are both *open* to an equal degree, allowing the audience to see them equally well.

Give, take   When two actors are not equally *open*, the one who receives a greater emphasis is said to *take* the scene. The other is said to *give* the scene.

Upstaging   When one actor takes a position that forces the second actor to face upstage or away from the audience. Since the downstage actor is put at a disadvantage, *upstaging* has an unpleasant connotation and is generally to be avoided. You should take positions on the exact level of the actor with whom you are playing. Neither intentionally nor unintentionally upstage another actor unless you are directed to do so.

FULL BACK

THREE QUARTERS RIGHT

THREE QUARTERS LEFT

PROFILE RIGHT

PROFILE LEFT

ONE QUARTER RIGHT

ONE QUARTER LEFT

FULL FRONT

BODY POSITIONS

SHARED POSITIONS

GIVEN AND TAKEN POSITIONS

UPSTAGING

STAGE MOVEMENT

Cross   Movement from one area to another. When noting a cross in your script, the standard abbreviation is *X*.

Countercross   A movement in the opposite direction in adjustment to the cross of another actor. The instruction usually given is *counter left* or *counter right*. If only a small adjustment is necessary, the actor should make it without being told.

Curved cross   In crossing to a person or an object above or below you, it is necessary to cross in a curve so you do not arrive either upstage or downstage of the person or object. Sometimes called an **arc** cross. (Follow the solid lines in the illustrations.)

Cover (A)   When another actor moves into a position between an actor and the audience, thus obstructing him from view. Covering is usually to be avoided. Generally an actor is expected to observe these practices:

1. The responsibility is on the downstage actor. In other words, do not stand in front of another actor.

2. If another actor does stand directly below you, make a small adjusting movement.

3. Since a moving actor usually should receive attention, make crosses *below* other actors so you are not covered. This rule does not apply if the moving actor should not receive attention.

Cover (B)   A term used to define the speech or action invented by an actor to keep the audience from detecting a mistake.

Dress stage   A direction requesting the actors to adjust their positions to improve the composition of the stage picture.

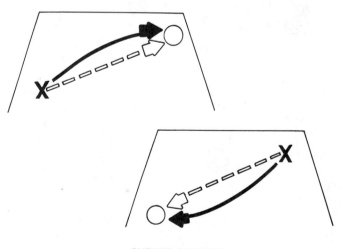

CURVED CROSSES

Small actions, such as smoking, eating, slapping, falling, telephoning, crying, using a fan, and tying a necktie are known on the stage as *business*.

STAGE BUSINESS

Business often involves the use of properties. *Props,* as they are commonly called, are divided into several categories.

PROPERTIES

Hand props   Small objects the actors handle onstage, such as teacups, letters, books, and candies.

Personal props   Hand props that are carried on the actor's person and are used only by him—such as watches, spectacles, and cigarette holders. An actor is usually responsible for taking care of his personal props during rehearsals and performances.

Costume props   Costume accessories used by the actor in executing business—fans, walking sticks, gloves, and handbags, for example.

Stage props   Objects for dressing the stage not used by the actors in executing their business. Vases of flowers, lamps, clocks, and bric-a-brac might be stage props.

Prop table   Tables that are usually placed offstage right and left to accommodate props the actors carry on and off the set. The property master and the stage manager are responsible for placing props on the tables, but a careful actor checks his props before each performance. It is the actor's responsibility to return immediately to the table all props he carries off the set.

Ad lib   Coming from the Latin *ad libitum* ("at pleasure"), the term applies to lines supplied by the actor wherever they may be required, as in crowd scenes or to fill in where there would otherwise be an undesirable pause.

LINES AND DIALOGUE

Aside   A line that the other actors onstage are not supposed to be hearing. The aside was a regular convention in plays of the seventeenth, eighteenth, and nineteenth centuries, but it is rarely used by modern dramatists.

Build   To increase the tempo or the volume or both in order to reach a climax.

Cue   The last words of a speech, or the end of an action, indicating the time for another actor to speak or act. An actor should memorize his cues as carefully as he memorizes his lines.

Pick up cues   A direction for the actor to begin speaking immediately on cue without allowing any lapse of time. Beginning actors tend to be slow in picking up cues, with the result that they often fail to maintain a tempo fast enough to hold the interest of the audience.

Pointing   Giving special emphasis to a word or phrase. An actor may also be directed to *point* a movement or a piece of business.

Tag line   The last line of a scene or an act. It usually needs to be *pointed*.

Telescoping   Overlapping speeches so one actor speaks before another has finished. It is a technique for accelerating the pace and building a climax.

Top   To "build" a line higher than the one that preceded it.

MISCELLANEOUS TERMS

Action   That portion of an actor's part in a play defined by the pursuance of a specific goal.

Adjustment   The technique that allows an actor to hold fast to the reality of his role while altering intentions or actions to fit the changing circumstances of the scene.

Affective Memory   A term Stanislavski used to indicate both sense memory and emotional recall.

Apron   The part of the stage that extends toward the audience in front of the curtain. Also termed *forestage.*

Asbestos   The fireproof curtain that closes the proscenium opening and separates the stage from the auditorium in case of fire.

Auditions   Readings of specific roles before the director to determine casting. In both the professional and nonprofessional theatre, plays are usually cast through auditions.

Back drop   (see **drop.**) The drop farthest upstage in any setting.

Backing   A drop or flats used outside an opening in the setting, such as a door or window.

Bit part   A small part with few lines.

Call board   A backstage bulletin board on which notices of concern to the actors are posted.

Character part   Contrasted to **straight part,** a role usually depicting an elderly, unusual, or eccentric individual.

Cheating   A term used without any derogatory meaning when an actor plays in a more open position, or performs an action more openly, than complete realism would permit.

Clear stage   A direction to leave the stage, given by the stage manager for everyone not immediately involved.

Company   A group of actors who perform together either in an individual play or for a season. Sometimes called a *troupe.*

Concentration   Giving complete attention to something. The ability to concentrate is a key part of effective acting.

Curtain call   The appearance of actors onstage after the performance to acknowledge the applause of the audience. Actors are required to remain in costume and makeup and to take the calls as rehearsed without variation. The term applies whether or not a curtain has been used.

Curtain line   The imaginary line across the stage floor that the front curtain touches when it is closed.

Dialogue   The lines spoken by the characters in a play.

Double   To play more than one role in a single play.

Drop   Any material, ordinarily **flown,** used as backing for a scene.

Ensemble acting   A theatrical presentation in which the stress is on the performance of the group rather than the individual.

Exit   To leave the stage; an opening in the setting through which actors may leave.

Extra   A small nonspeaking part: soldiers, townspeople, ladies-in-waiting, and so forth.

Flats   The canvas-covered frames that constitute the walls of a stage setting.

Flies   The space above the stage in which scenery is suspended. Such scenery is said to be **flown.**

Fourth wall   In an interior setting, the imaginary side of the room toward the audience.

Front curtain   A curtain closing the proscenium opening that hangs immediately behind the asbestos. It is usually used as the act drop.

Given circumstance   Any unchangeable fact that affects the playing of the scene.

Green room   A room located close to the stage, in which the actors may await entrance cues and receive guests after the performance.

Gridiron   A contrivance located in the flies for suspending scenery.

Ground plan   The arrangement of doors, windows, steps, levels, furniture, and so forth for a stage setting; also a diagram showing the arrangements. The director usually explains the ground plan at an early rehearsal. Each actor should draw the diagram in his script.

Improvisation   Spontaneous invention of lines and business by performers.

Indicating   Performing an action without an intention. *Indicating* is a derogatory term in psychologically motivated acting.

Intention   The character's real reason for performing an action.

Justification   The process by which the actor directs his imagination to believe strongly in the reality of each stage action.

"Magic If"   A term used by Stanislavski to describe the process by which an actor places himself in the given circumstances of the scene.

Motivation   Why the character acts.

ACTING AREAS IN ARENA

Mugging A derogatory term for exaggerated facial expressions.

Obstacle A physical or moral obstruction that hinders one from completing an *action.*

Pacing Although some directors attempt to distinguish between *pace* and *tempo,* for practical purposes they both mean the rate of speed at which the actors speak their lines, pick up their cues, and perform their actions—the length and number of the pauses. Pace is a subtle, and vital, element in a performance. Frequently heard directions are "Pick up the pace" or "The pace is too slow (or too fast)."

Places A direction given by the stage manager for everyone to be in his proper position for the beginning of an act.

Proscenium The wall dividing the stage from the auditorium.

Proscenium opening The arched opening in the proscenium wall through which the audience can see the stage.

Run-through An uninterrupted rehearsal of a scene, an act, or the entire play. In contrast is the "working" rehearsal, in which either the director or the actors may stop to work on details.

A production of *Juno and the Paycock* by Sean O'Casey at the Arena Stage in Washington, D.C. Arena theatres add a great deal of intimacy to the theatre-going experience and provide a challenge to actors, especially those who have acted only on proscenium stages. (Photo courtesy of the Arena Stage, Washington, D.C.)

Stealing A director may ask an actor to *steal;* that is, he wants a movement that will not receive the audience's attention. The term is also used to mean taking the audience's attention when it should be elsewhere. Scene stealers, either intentional or unintentional, are not well-liked in any cast.

Straight part A role without marked eccentricities, normally a young man or young woman. See **Character part.**

Strike The direction given by the stage manager to change the setting for another scene or to dismantle it at the end of a performance.

Subtext The actor's continuous thoughts that give meaning to the dialogue and the stage directions.

Trap An opening in the stage floor.

Try-outs Auditions.

Walk-on A small part without lines; an extra.

The interior of the Guthrie Theatre in Minneapolis. In this famous seven-sided, thrust-stage theatre, the stage is surrounded by the audience in a 200-degree arc. No seat is more than 52 feet from the center of the stage. Built in 1963, the Guthrie was designed by Sir Tyrone Guthrie and Tanya Moiseiwitsch. (Photo courtesy of the Guthrie Theatre.)

TERMINOLOGY FOR NON-PROSCENIUM THEATRES

Most terms in this list pertaining to stage movement or actors' positions in relation to one another were developed for the proscenium theatre. Recent years, however, have seen a pronounced movement toward *arena* or *three-quarter round,* or *thrust* stages, although such spaces are certainly as old as the theatre itself.

For staging in these spaces, acting areas are usually designated in one of two ways: according to the points of the compass or according to the hours of the clock. Thus, an actor may be directed to cross either to "northwest" or to "ten o'clock." Such terminology works well in an arena space, but the thrust stage, in which the acting area extends out into the audience in various configurations, calls for more ingenuity. A combination of the terminology used for the arena and for the proscenium stage will usually work for almost any space.

EXERCISE

Start a diary of other terms that have definitions particular to the theatre. Many such words are *italicized* in this text.

Communication is never easy, but you can make a good start on being able to converse precisely with your teacher and with your fellow students by learning to speak a common language. Gaining such a vocabulary is an integral part of learning to act, the goal of this entire book.

PART 2
THE ACTOR ALONE

CHAPTER 3

DISCOVERING THE PHYSICAL ACTIONS

A part of the definition of acting with which we began this book called for the actor to be able to exist in imaginary circumstances as if they were real. The first step toward achieving this goal is to discover the physical life of the character he is playing.

Think again about that exciting moment when you arrive at the first rehearsal of *Romeo and Juliet*. You are about to enter the personal world of these characters at a special dimension, and your first task as an actor will be to find out what they do. You will read the play more carefully than you have ever read anything before in order to discover what specific actions these characters carry out and what logical sequences these actions follow from the beginning to the end of each scene and from the beginning to the end of the play.

You will discover these actions, the basic raw material for performing your role, by studying carefully the play's *given circumstances*. In some cases your discovery of the facts of the script, with the help of your director, will provide enough material for a fully developed character. But more often the answers are only suggested in the play, and such is certainly the case with *Romeo and Juliet*. Your next step, then, is to search the facts you have discovered for *implications* that will add depth and believability to the raw material. Once you have firmly established the facts and understood their implications, you will be ready to augment the circumstances with material drawn from your own imagination. The latter aspect is significant, for it is how the actor places his unique interpretation on the role.

Creating this unique interpretation is one of the most exhilarating facets of acting. Unfortunately, this excitement can seduce the actor into rushing into that phase of his work before he has sufficiently completed his study of the script. The behavior of the character must always be firmly grounded in the facts of the play. Listen to the pertinent advice of Constantin Stanislavski, whose pioneering work for the Moscow Art Theatre at the turn of the twentieth century laid the foundation for much of our current acting technique:

> Let each actor give an honest reply to the question of what physical action he would undertake, how he would act (not feel, there should for heaven's sake be no question of feelings at this point) in the given circumstances created by the playwright.... When these physical actions have been clearly defined, all that remains for the actor to do is to execute them.[1]

Please take special notice of two important phrases in Stanislavski's lesson. He admonishes the actor to "act in the given circumstances created by the playwright" and declares that "there should be no question of feelings at this point." Recalling these two pieces of advice will serve the actor well during the entire creative process.

In Chapter 2 we defined "given circumstances" as the irreducible facts of the play. The search for them begins in the script, with a study of the dramatic elements of character, plot, dialogue, and locale. In most instances, the playwright uses these facts to tell the actor who the character is, what he says, what he does, and where and when he does it. At a later point in the rehearsal process, the given circumstances will also include directorial choices, stage business, costumes, and scenic environment; but mastering these elements is an aspect of acting that will be discussed in a subsequent chapter. For now, let us focus on answering four questions:

Who?
What?
Where?
When?

Each of these four "W's" (we will add an essential fifth in the next chapter) asks questions to which you must find unambiguous answers either in the text or in your imagination. Until these answers are clear, your acting, from simple exercises to complex characterizations, will at best be confusing and at worst be meaningless. The answers to the "W" questions generate physical actions, and these actions, when clearly performed, communicate the circumstances of the play to the audience. *Never embark on an acting assignment until you have specific answers to these questions.*

Your acceptance of the role of either Romeo or Juliet has committed you to act in the given circumstances of the play. Both these roles are specific characters created by a master dramatist. They are not you, just as they are not some movie actor, or popular singer, or the boy or girl next door. You will be expected to play the character the playwright has prescribed to the fullest extent that your experience and imagination enable you to understand the prescription. You have no choice, of course, but to play the role with your own body, your own voice, and your own live responses. It follows, then, that in seeking to discover the physical life of the character, you must always find a logical sequence of actions you can understand, that you can *believe* are *necessary*. The vital question is, "What would I do *if I were this character* in these circumstances?" To ask only "What would I do in these circumstances?" inevitably means that you play yourself rather than the character the playwright has drawn.

The actor uses the four "W's" to trigger his imagination, whether he is beginning to prepare a role or just about to step onstage. Each must be answered precisely and specifically. It is not sufficient, for example, for an actor in *When You Comin Back, Red Ryder?* to answer the "Where?" question with "in a restaurant." A more satisfactory response would be, "In a small, grimy, dusty diner in the New Mexican desert." The actors playing Jerry and Peter in *The Zoo Story* cannot sufficiently stimulate their imaginations by thinking of themselves "in a park." They must concentrate on being "in Central Park, near 75th Street and Fifth Avenue in New York, about nine blocks north of the Central Park Zoo." If the actor does not know enough specific details about the physical demands implicit in the "Where?" of the play, he must correct this deficiency during the rehearsal period.

The question "What?" (What has happened previously? What is happening in the play right now?) demands the same specificity. For instance, in *The Zoo Story,* Jerry is coming from the zoo and looking for someone to kill him. In the same play, answering "When?" with "the afternoon" is not acceptably specific. Does that mean twilight? Noon? Mid-afternoon? Similarly, the "Who?" question must not merely trigger thoughts of a saleswoman, a prince, or a second baseman, since these terms stand for an infinite variety of people. Consider, for example, the differing images conjured up by Prince Hamlet, Prince Valiant, and Prince Charles. Specific replies to all four questions will start you on the road to building a character's plausible, consistent behavior, and they are absolutely necessary if you are to *believe* in what you do.

Each of the four "W's" is not always equally important in every scene. Sometimes, for instance, logical actions growing out of "Who?" dominate the moment. At the beginning of *A Streetcar Named Desire,* when Blanche sneaks a drink before Stella comes home, she needs to do something with the glass. The physical action that the actress playing Blanche selects can merely get the audience on to the next moment in the play or can tell them a great deal about who Blanche is. In the original Broadway production, Jessica Tandy, standing in front of the kitchen sink, ignored the seemingly logical choice of rinsing out the glass. Rather, she shook it vigorously and replaced it in the cabinet. In this way, the preliminary picture the audience had probably formed of a delicate but fading southern belle was cracked, if not shattered.

As you perform the exercises at the end of this chapter, try altering the dominant "W" in the scene. Notice how each selection will offer a different range of choices of physical actions.

"Making physical actions your own" and "building on your own live responses" are important problems to be considered in later chapters. We are also postponing for the moment a thorough discussion of the actor's use of emotion, acceding to Stanislavski's warning that "there should be no question of feelings at this point."

It is true, of course, that feeling is an important part of acting. But feelings are unpredictable. You cannot directly act an emotion, nor can you call forth an emotional response *at will.* You must learn to begin with physical actions because they are tangible, controllable, and thus actable. You can always be comforted by the knowledge that you can carry out a series of actions whenever you *will* to do so. What is more, since physical actions and the way we feel about what we do are often inextricably linked, performing the needed actions in the given circumstances may bring forth the desired feeling. Stanislavski continued the passage quoted earlier:

> Note that I say execute physical actions, not feel them, because if they are properly carried out the feelings will be generated spontaneously. If you work the other way around and begin by thinking about your feelings and trying to squeeze them out of yourself, the result will be distortion and force....

But whether or not the physical actions generate an emotional response, the careful playing of them will realize the intention of the scene and accomplish the actor's primary responsibility. Success is not to be judged by whether or not emotion is aroused in the actor.

The references in the preceding paragraph to the actor's *will* introduce one of his most valuable inner resources. In attempting to solve his many, and sometimes complex, problems, the actor must search always for solutions that are subject to his will. He must find things to do that he can repeat whenever he wants to and that he can control.

COMMITTING YOURSELF TO ACTION

The will to action is one of the actor's most powerful inner motive forces, both on the stage and off. What he wills to accomplish in his search for the physical life of the character determines what he creates onstage. The strength of his desire to do these things determines how interesting his performance will be to himself and, to a large extent, how interesting it will be to his audience. The will to action is effective to the degree it is directed toward logical activity, supported by the given circumstances, and meaningful to the actor. It must also be capable of motivating strong desire. An essential part of any performance is the strength of determination with which the actor performs his actions. There is no place either on the stage or in the rehearsal room for halfheartedness or indifference. The actor must learn to commit himself without reservation to the action of his character. Doing so, he will find that this personal commitment is one of the principal generators of feeling.

Unfortunately, a commitment to strong will does not in itself sufficiently guarantee believability. The actor must also be made to recognize that, through lack of knowledge or taste or imagination, he can will, sometimes tenaciously, to do the inappropriate or illogical thing—a thing totally unsupported by the given circumstances. The result will be a performance that is at odds with the play.

Strong commitment to proper action must not be confined to performance. You must practice this wholehearted giving of your total being to what you are doing in every classroom exercise and every moment of rehearsal. Finding ways to focus your mind and your energy will help you to learn how to work and will sustain you as you keep studying and working. Such commitment is an important part of all creative talent.

EXERCISE

To illustrate what is meant by "exploring your inner resources" and "discovering physical actions," we talked about playing a native of Bandjarmasin or Romeo or Juliet. But these problems, involving a knowledge of exotic customs or an understanding of what you would do in a scene of emotional crisis, are too complex for beginning practice, so we shall start with a simpler exercise.

In Act I, Scene 2, of *The Miss Firecracker Contest,* by Beth Henley, Delmount is listening to the nervous and eccentric Popeye prattle on about one thing and another, including a recitation of common terms for groups of farm animals, such as "a gaggle of geese." As he listens, he eats a dish of vanilla ice cream, finally interrupting her with, "Oooh! Now the ice cream has given me a headache. Lord Jesus! A gaggle of geese! Oh, my head! My head!" He exits.

Here is an acting problem providing an opportunity to explore your inner resources for the purpose of finding the logical sequence of actions demanded by the given circumstances. If you had never suffered an ice cream headache or if you had never observed the behavior of anyone who had one, it would be impossible for you to solve this problem until you had enlarged your experience. You would have to investigate the nature of this occurrence to find out what actions would be truthful. Fortunately, an ice cream headache is not an uncommon occurrence, so it is relatively easy for you to find in your own experience what you would do if you were Delmount in this situation. You would take a bite of ice cream, start to swallow it, feel the sharp pain in your forehead, and try to stretch the muscles of the face and head to alleviate the sensation.

This is a simple but very real acting problem. Ignore the sex of the character and the context of the scene for the moment, and work on it until you can *believe your actions.* Here, as in all succeeding exercises, choose your actions so they constitute a definite dramatic structure. This means they should have a *beginning* (acquainting the audience with the problem), a *middle* (developing the problem), and an *end* (resolving the problem). Each of these three structural elements should be played clearly and precisely. In the early exercises the structure will be simple. In this exercise the beginning is Delmount's discovery that his head aches. The middle is stretching the muscles to restore a normal feeling. The end is his exit after his recovery, after he has solved his problem.

Plays are filled with situations like this one that require you to perform in such a way that you convince the audience you believe the actions you must undertake. Other examples are: Your foot goes to sleep; you try to keep from sneezing; you have a toothache; or, you try to keep from scratching an itch. Perform each of these actions as you exit the stage, drawing on your own experience until you can believe what you do, thus making your work as believable as possible to your audience.

Several times already, beginning with the title of this book, we have referred to "believing your actions" or to "creating a character in which you can believe." An actor must believe what he is doing, and his fundamental responsibility to the audience is to induce their belief in his actions. So the objective of the exercise is not to pretend you have an ice cream headache but is to make yourself *believe* you do *through the actions you take* to ease the sharp, throbbing sensation. Acting is literally a matter of make-believe, fueled by an attitude almost identical to that which comes naturally to children.

Children with their mud pies, their kings and queens, and their cowboy-and-Indian games provide for themselves a set of circumstances very similar to those given to the actor by the dramatist. They instinctively behave in whatever fashion their experience or imagination leads them to think is true to the imposed conditions. The pleasure they receive from the game is in direct proportion to their ability to give themselves over to what they are doing—in other words, to the extent they are able to believe their actions. As the game wears thin and their belief decreases, they invent new circumstances to stimulate further action. One child may propose: "Let's make believe the king wasn't really hurt when he fell off his horse but was only pretending. He did it so the prince would feel sorry for him and help him fight the Black Knight." A whole new sequence of actions is justified, allowing the child and his playmates to continue the game with renewed belief.

Of course, the throne is actually Father's dining chair. The king's crown is cardboard. The swords are blunt sticks ("Mother won't let us sharpen the ends because then they would be dangerous"). When the game is over, the precious crown that has been guarded so carefully is kicked to one side of the living-room floor. The children never think these things are real, yet while the game is on they treat these "props" as if they were true.

It is the same for the actor. During the day King Lear's robes hang limply on a hook in the dressing room, and the imperial crown lies unguarded on the prop table. But when the performance begins, if Lear is to convince the audience he is every inch a king, the actor performing the role must believe in the circumstances given him by Shakespeare, by the director, by the costumer, and by the scene designer as thoroughly as he believes in the actual world around him. "No half-belief," as Michael Redgrave said. "Belief...does not begin and end by an intellectual process, but...is so deep-rooted that it fires each movement, echoes in each silence, and penetrates beyond 'the threshold of the subconscious,' where it becomes creative...."[2]

BELIEVING YOUR ACTIONS ONSTAGE

None of this is to suggest that the actor is subject to a kind of hallucination that blurs his view of the surrounding reality and induces him to accept the pieces of glass in the crown as diamonds. He knows that the life of the character he is playing lives only in the imagination, and, like the children, he knows that the crown and the robes he will wear are not real. He knows, in short, that he is not actually King Lear. He is an actor, so toward all of these things he says: *"I will act as if they were real."* And this conviction in the truth of his actions enables him to believe also in the *truth* (not the *reality*) of the cardboard crown. If he loses his sense of truth, it will not be because the crown is not real but because he cannot believe his own actions in relation to it.

Learn this first axiom well: The best way an actor can evoke a feeling of belief in what he is doing is to concentrate on simple physical actions. Stanislavski frequently emphasized that "small physical actions, small physical truths and the moments of belief in them ... acquire a great significance on the stage...."[3]

SUSTAINING BELIEF

Once an actor learns to believe in the truth of his actions, sustaining that belief is a difficult and ever-present problem. He must work in front of an audience and in the midst of all the inevitable distractions of a theatrical production. He must be able to summon his belief on cue whenever he is required to perform. The slightest doubt as to the rightness or truth of what he or the other actors are doing is likely to upset him immediately. An actor who treats his crown like the cardboard that it really is can destroy the belief of a stageful of others, just as a cynical child can destroy the magic of the game by protesting he can't fight with "an old stick."

The actor may renew a wavering belief, just as the child does, by discovering new circumstances that will excite new actions. When, for instance, you need further stimulation in the exercise from *The Miss Firecracker Contest*, try introducing circumstances such as these:

Delmount is deeply in love with Popeye. He does not want his actions to make him appear foolish.

Delmount's speech and actions are a ruse to allow him to call for somebody to save him from Popeye's boring conversation.

Delmount wants Popeye to know that her tiresome conversation has somehow caused his headache.

Discovering additional circumstances helps to renew the actor's belief. When he asks the fundamental question, "*What* would I do if I were this character in this situation?" and finds the true answer, he is provided with fresh reasons for action.

EXERCISE

Continue to work on the problem from *The Miss Firecracker Contest*, carrying out the actions in each of the circumstances just given. Study the play to find suggestions for other circumstances that might alter the way Delmount performs these actions.

At this point you will find it useful to review what you have learned thus far about the way an actor works. Here is a summary:

1. The actor simultaneously develops his inner and outer techniques. His outer technique depends on a trained voice and body to provide an effective instrument for communicating the meaning of a play to an audience. His inner technique allows him to use his own life experience as a means of finding and understanding what that meaning is.

2. The actor's first step is to discover a logical sequence of physical actions the character he is playing would carry out in the given circumstances. He begins with physical actions because they are tangible and subject to his will.

3. To make these actions personal and, at the same time, to satisfy the intention of the dramatist, the actor asks: 'What would I do if I were this character in these given circumstances?"

4. Finding the answer to this question induces the actor to believe the truth of his actions, even though nothing in the character's imaginary world is real.

5. The actor must find strong reasons for these actions and commit himself wholeheartedly to carrying them out.

6. The actor's belief can be sustained and renewed by finding additional circumstances, true to the script, that stimulate fresh action.

7. Carefully chosen and clearly performed physical actions are one of the surest ways of communicating the play to the audience, which is the actor's primary function.

IMPROVISATION

In order to accomplish the exercises in this chapter and most of those in the remainder of the book, you will need to gain some skill in the actor training technique called *improvisation*. Improvisation as a method of learning, rehearsing, and performing has dominated actor training during the past several decades. Much of the theory underpinning this approach grows out of the research on games and play conducted by psychologists, anthropologists, and sociologists. The charm, and indeed the value, of the method lies in its ability to tap into your natural propensity to pretend, to make believe, to create, and to perform in a game of the imagination.

One reason improvisation has become such an important technique in actor training is that it places an emphasis on intuition and spontaneity. Viola Spolin, one of America's greatest proponents of improvisational acting, brought this aspect of the improvisational method to light when she wrote: "Spontaneity is the moment of personal freedom when we are faced with a reality and see it, explore it and act accordingly."[4] What better objective for a student who would learn the art of the actor?

Improvisations retain the quality of a game because their performance situation is not controlled by a playwright's words or a director/choreographer's scheme of movements. Actors are given the bare parameters of a situation and are left to perform the actions suggested by their physical involvement in the moment. Like everything related to acting, an improvisation must provide an actor with specific objectives that he must decide to accomplish in a specific way.

It is important for you to develop a sense of personal freedom and self-expression during improvisational exercises. The given circumstances of the exercise will limit to an extent the range of possible choices, but you must learn that there is no right or wrong way to perform it. Your teacher will serve as the master of the game, because he or she will possess a mature mastery of both the artistic and technical aspects of the theatre. You will bring your own insight, imagination, and experience to performing the actions; since they are your own, they cannot be known until you discover them and create them for your teacher and your classmates.

EXERCISE

As an introduction to improvisation, perform an imaginary "exit" scene. Play yourself and perform alone, but ask yourself the four "W" questions, just as you would if you were preparing a role from a play. Your teacher will provide the given circumstances of the scene. Examples might be:

(1) You exit because you have heard something that disturbs you.
(2) You exit because you are about to be late for an appointment.
(3) You exit because you have inadvertently entered a place where you are not supposed to be.

Early in their training, actors need to master a dependable method of working that will not only guide their study but yield practical results. Some would-be actors have a notion that practical effort, especially if it involves the use of pencil and paper, will dampen spontaneity and hamper creativity. This notion is ill-founded. Inspiration comes from conscious technical effort, and a talent that cannot be nourished by hard practical work is not very robust to begin with. Writing down thoughts stimulates further thinking, and practice carried on in the imagination can provide a solid theoretical foundation for a method of working that will sustain you throughout your career.

You now know how to discover the physical actions for your character in a given scene. Once you have done so (and this does require pencil and paper), you should list them. Your list of actions (and don't be afraid to number them) should form a sequence that is logical and appropriate for the character in the situation, and each action should be such that you are psychologically and physically capable of carrying it out. Your list for the following exercises should be short and not excessively detailed, as it will not be practical unless you can keep it easily in mind. It should, on the other hand, be complete—no gaps that make it difficult for you to go from one action to the next. Your imagination, stimulated by the given circumstances, will provide the necessary strong desire to accomplish the sequence.

Making this list is the first step of a practical technique that Stanislavski called "making a score of the role."[5] It is just a beginning, because much of the remainder of this book is devoted to finding ways of expanding and deepening the score. When completed, the score becomes a comprehensive working design of your role and will include your physical and psychological actions, your major and minor objectives, images, subtext, and line readings. Scoring a role provides three advantages:

1. The preparation of it forces you to dig deeply into the play and into yourself.

2. Augmenting it during rehearsal keeps you alert to the stimulation of the director and the other actors.

3. The existence of the score makes it possible for you to review your creative effort whenever you need to.

The score begins with simple lists of actions, and you should practice by deriving such lists for the exercise at the end of the chapter. The following is an example:

In *Of Mice and Men* by John Steinbeck, Lennie, a giant, childlike farmhand, sneaks a week-old puppy away from its mother and plays with it, even though he has been warned that it is too young to be handled. He kills the puppy and tries to conceal his mistake by hiding it in a pile of straw. (*Note:* This scene actually occurs before the curtain rises for Act III. As we shall see, some of the

MAKING A SCORE OF PHYSICAL ACTIONS

most profitable improvisation work an actor can do involves scenes that are important to the development of the play but that take place offstage.)

The Beginning: "Temptation and Anticipation"

1. Sneak into barn concealing a puppy.

2. Kneel on pile of straw.

3. Get comfortable on your heels.

4. Place puppy on straw in front of you.

5. Poke puppy with your finger.

6. Check to see if you have been followed.

7. Pick puppy up.

8. Hold puppy gently to your chest.

The Middle: "Ecstasy and Agony"

9. Laugh (speech and sounds are actions).

10. Hold puppy at arm's length in front of you.

11. Toss puppy in the air and catch it.

12. Feel puppy bite your finger.

13. Drop puppy.

14. Slap puppy with the back of your hand.

15. Hear puppy cry in pain.

The End: "Remorse and Cover-up"

16. Pick up lifeless puppy.

17. Try to shake puppy back to life.

18. Hear somebody approaching.

19. Hide puppy in straw.

Note that this score has been divided into structural units—a beginning, a middle, and an end—that will give the exercise form, clarity, and dramatic interest. Also, each of the units has been given a name suggestive of the essential quality and the basic reason for the series of actions. Choosing a right name for each part of the structure is an extremely helpful technique, as it unifies the actions and helps the actor understand the attitude of the character toward what he is doing. It also helps establish proper relationships with the objects he is handling and with other characters in the exercise or scene.

While the parts of the score should be closely related, progressing logically and inevitably from one to the other, the actor must clearly make a *transition* from one part to the next. Clear transitions bring each unit of the structure to a definite *terminal point* and start the new unit with a firmly positive *attack,* a new impulse manifesting itself in movement, gesture, or speech. Terminal points and new attacks make the structure evident and give both actor and audience a sense that the play is moving forward.

The beginning, middle, and end of a score of physical actions are not arbitrary but represent distinct components of the overall action. For example, the routine of the beginning must come to a complete end (terminal point) before the action of the middle can commence. The conclusion of an action like "getting comfortable on your heels" results in an instant of *stasis,* a momentary vacuum, a transition from which comes a strong impulse for new action—preparing to play with the puppy. Recognizing the terminal point of an action is essential to building a score of actions, and pushing off or attacking a new task gives the actor an opportunity to reinforce his belief in the human actions he is reproducing.

A sequence of individual actions can be distinguished further because each action will be influenced by the speed or pace of its environment *(tempo)* and by the internal performance pattern of the character *(rhythm).* Environmental influences are almost limitless, but some predominant sources of tempo are the prevailing mood, the weather, and other external circumstances, and even (or often especially) such artistic considerations as the placement of the action within a scene. The major sources of rhythm are within the character, and deciding on his or her rhythmic range is a consequential choice for the actor.

Since rhythm is such an important part of characterization, it is never too early to gain an understanding of it. In a recently published workbook for actors based on Stanislavski's techniques, Mel Gordon suggested:

> All human activity follows some rhythmic pattern, which can be felt by the actor and expressed physically. Every stage movement should be conceived in Rhythm. Also, each character has a private Rhythm. Finding the character's Rhythm is an essential key to discovering his personality.[6]

Once a character's rhythm is discovered, combining it with the proper tempo is a subtle process, yet one at which experienced actors often appear to be intuitively right. When they correctly sense what their characters are saying and doing onstage, correct *tempo-rhythms* are likely to come without conscious effort. In learning a technique, however, it is usually necessary to make a *conscious* effort before mastery of the technique produces *unconscious* results.

Because the two are so closely related, Stanislavski used the term *tempo-rhythm* to designate the combined rhythmic flow and the speed of execution of the physical action (including speech) in a given scene. Tempo-rhythms have a natural appeal to both actor and audience—an almost magic power to affect one's inner mood. This power is, of course, most evident in music. Recall the different moods created by your responses to a waltz, a piece of rap music, a military march, and a funeral march. Indeed, the popularity of rock is due primarily to the effect of its pervasive tempo-rhythm.

In the exercise from *Of Mice and Men,* make clear transitions between the units by using the technique of terminal points and new attacks. Then, experiment until you find an effective and distinct tempo-rhythm for the actions of each part. Be conscious of how it changes as you move from the actions of one part to those of the next. The tempo-rhythm may even change within a single passage. For example, in the sequence from *Of Mice and Men,* Lennie's tempo-rhythm will be dominated by a combination of the rhythm the actor chooses for Lennie's character as it is affected by the tempo of the circumstances of the scene—he fears he may be followed. Should Lennie hear a noise, the tempo-rhythm would change even if the activity he was performing had not been completed. A major change in the external circumstance will produce a major change in the tempo-rhythm.

Tempo-rhythm is ordinarily applied to the basic flow and speed of execution in each individual unit rather than to whole scenes of a play. In a sense, a scene's various tempo-rhythms add up to its overall pace. Scenes tend to have a pace that remains constant. The term *pace* refers to the speed at which the actors speak their lines, pick up their cues, and perform their actions.

To *pick up cues* does not imply that actors should race through a passage or scene. Usually, a director asks actors to pick up their cues to avoid the constant "line-pause-line" syndrome so common among new actors. In real life our communication with each other has a flow, and our pauses have a significance that a dramatist can only hint at in transferring the spoken word to the written page. Actors then translate the playwright's words back into the sounds and silences of real "speech."

Next is a second score of actions, taken from *The Effect of Gamma Rays on Man-in-the-Moon Marigolds,* by Paul Zindel. Beatrice, the mother, has been intimidated into staying home from a science fair assembly in which her younger daughter is a finalist. After arranging by phone the removal of an elderly boarder, she notices the children's pet rabbit and decides to destroy it. Study both this example and the one from *Of Mice and Men* until you can understand and apply the technique of scoring to your own work.

The Beginning: "Dawn of a New Life"

1. Slam phone down.
2. Burst into laughter.
3. Pour another drink.
4. Take drink to chair and sit comfortably.

The Middle: "Afternoon of Leftover Strings"

5. Accidentally hit rabbit cage with foot.
6. Examine cage and rabbit.

7. Rise and find a towel.

8. Pick up towel and throw over shoulder.

9. Get bottle of chloroform.

The End: "Evening of Final Resolution"

10. Cross to cage.

11. Pick up cage.

12. Take cage upstairs.

EXERCISE

Make and perform scores for several of the problems given here. Use pencil and paper; *write them out*. Remember that a score is a sequence of physical actions constituting logical and appropriate behavior in particular circumstances. Make the circumstances specific; find definite answers to the questions of *who, what, where,* and *when.* Choose actions that will communicate your meaning to an audience; that is, do not develop a habit of acting only for your own benefit. Your score should designate the beginning, the middle, and the end, and each of these units should have a suitable name.

After you have made the score, plan a simple arrangement of exits, windows, furniture, and whatever you need for the action, but let your imagination create as much detail in the environment as possible. Note that this detail provides a rich source for discovering physical actions. Give yourself actual or substitute objects (magazines, coffee cups, and so forth); do not try to pantomime nonexistent props. We will attempt this kind of sensory work later. Work by yourself in this exercise, but "hear" responses from the actors who are not there, as hearing and responding to other actors are vital parts of acting. Do not make up dialogue; use speech or sound only as necessary to call out or to release inner responses. Do not try to feel emotion. Do not try to be dramatic: Simplicity is one of the first (and one of the hardest) things to learn. All of these "do nots" are to make you aware that actors always work within a set of prescribed limitations. Only after limitations have been established can freedom be achieved.

Note the difference between this carefully planned improvisation and the spontaneous exercise suggested before. Perform each score many times. Technique is developed through repetition, and each repetition should stimulate your imagination to greater belief. It is not necessary in these exercises to realize all of the circumstances of the play; rather, the situations described should stimulate the actor to provide circumstances from his imagination.

(1) In *Coastal Disturbances*, by Tina Howe, it is August, and Leo, a lifeguard, gets ready for a day's work by doing his stretching exercises standing in the sand by his lifeguard's chair. Holly Dancer, a pretty young woman,

enters. The pace of Leo's exercises varies as he tries to attract her attention.

(2) On a sultry summer evening, Maggie, in *Cat on a Hot Tin Roof,* by Tennessee Williams, charges into her bedroom from the supper table to assess the damage one of her nephews has done with a hot, buttered biscuit to her pretty dress. She opens the curtains to allow more light in the room and decides to change her dress.

(3) In *Agnes of God,* by John Pielmeier, the young nun, Agnes, is lying on her back looking at the sun when it is transformed into a cloud that then becomes a vision of a lady. As the vision talks, holes appear in The Lady's side and hands, and Agnes tries to catch the blood that pours from the holes. (*Note:* Although Agnes tells this story to the psychiatrist, as we shall see later, it is extremely important that the actresses playing this role perform these actions as if the vision actually happened.)

(4) In *Beyond Therapy,* by Christopher Durang, Prudence is sitting at a table in a restaurant, reading *The New York Review of Books.* She scouts the patrons for her blind date, who she knows only from a description from a "Personals" ad. She spots a likely prospect, rises, and crosses to him.

(5) In *The Crucible,* by Arthur Miller, a Puritan farmer named John Proctor returns to his home in the evening, exhausted from having planted crops since daybreak. He puts down his shotgun, washes his face and hands, and eats his supper.

(6) In *Crimes of the Heart,* by Beth Henley, thirty-year-old Lenny MaGrath comes into her kitchen carrying a brown paper bag. Saddened because everybody has forgotten her birthday, she pulls a package of candles from the bag, retrieves a cookie from the cookie jar, takes a candle from the package, tries to stick it on the cookie, and finally sings "Happy Birthday" to herself.

(7) In *On Golden Pond,* by Ernest Thompson, Norman Thayer, in his sixties, arrives at his summer cabin in Maine. Slowly and lovingly, he rediscovers the covered furniture, photographs, and layout of the room.

(8) In *The Dining Room,* by A. R. Gurney, Jr., a furniture craftsperson, Paul, examines the dining room table and its chairs for weak joints, faulty glue, and loose supports.

(9) In *Death and the Maiden,* by Ariel Dorfman, Paulina Salas sneaks out to the terrace of her home, where she can overhear a conversation between her husband and a doctor named Roberto Miranda. Slipping as close as she can without being discovered, she recognizes the voice of the doctor as that of a person who previously raped her. She resolves to not let the doctor get away and slips unnoticed back into her bedroom.

(10) In *Lu Ann Hampton Laverty Oberlander,* by Preston Jones, the teenaged Lu Ann is left alone in the living room of their modest, small-town Texas home after her mother leaves for work. She turns on the radio, dances to the country-and-western tunes it plays, sneaks a smoke from a cigarette her mother has discarded, and then has to greet her brother and a stranger who arrive unexpectedly.

(11) In *Summer and Smoke,* by Tennessee Williams, Alma is an intelligent, tensely sensitive girl who has developed an abnormally reserved attitude toward young men. On an autumn evening she walks in the park, realizing that her prudishness has been responsible for her losing a brilliant young doctor with whom she has been deeply in love for a long time. She drinks from the fountain and quiets her nerves by taking a relaxation pill. When an unknown young man appears, she decides to make up for her past mistakes by attempting to attract his attention.

(12) In *When You Comin Back, Red Ryder?,* by Mark Medoff, nineteen-year-old Red is alone finishing his night shift at a truck-stop restaurant in an out-of-the-way New Mexico town. He plays the jukebox, smokes, and reads a newspaper but prepares to make Angel feel badly for being late when she comes to relieve him.

(13) In *Purlie Victorious,* by Ossie Davis, Purlie has involved Lutiebelle, a backwoods serving girl, in a scheme in which she will try to pass herself off as Purlie's educated and sophisticated Cousin Bee. After Lutiebelle has examined the beautiful clothes Purlie has bought for her to wear—slips, hats, shoes, nylon stockings—she picks up her own humble belongings and tries to escape.

(14) *Cloud Nine,* by Caryl Churchill, offers actors problems of playing across sexes and performing roles of many ages. In Act II, the role of Cathy, age 4, and played by an adult man, thoroughly explores a children's playground at a park, playing on and around all the equipment. Finally, she (he) picks up a toy gun and pretends to shoot people.

(15) In *The House of Blue Leaves,* by John Guare, eighteen-year-old Ronnie, wearing a heavy army overcoat and fatigues, has gone AWOL from the army and is trying to get into his home without waking his father. From his position on the fire escape, he reaches through the bars of a gate in front of a window, gets his father's trousers, takes a key from its pocket, unlocks the gate, comes into the room, relocks the gate, replaces the trousers, tiptoes to the icebox, takes out a box of milk, and is interrupted by somebody buzzing at the front door.

(16) In *K2,* by Patrick Myers, Taylor has been asleep on a ledge of an ice wall twenty-seven-thousand-feet up the side of the mountain. He slowly emerges from the mound of snow that has collected over him, stares at the bright sun for a long moment, then begins to dig into the mound around him in search of his buddy, Harold.

NOTES

1. Constantin Stanislavski, *Creating a Role* (New York: Theatre Arts Books, 1961), p. 201.

2. Michael Redgrave, "The Stanislavski Myth," *New Theatre 3* (June 1946): 16–18. "Copyright, 1946," quoted in Toby Cole and Helen Krich Chinoy, eds., *Actors on Acting,* new rev. ed. (New York: Crown Publishers, 1970), p. 405.

3. David Magarshack, "Introduction," *Stanislavsky on the Art of the Stage* (New York: Hill and Wang, 1961), p. 49.

4. Viola Spolin, *Improvisation for the Theater: A Handbook of Teaching and Directing Techniques* (Evanston, IL: Northwestern University Press, 1963), p. 4.

5. See Stanislavski, *Creating a Role,* pp. 56–62.

6. Mel Gordon, *The Stanislavsky Technique: Russia; a Workbook for Actors* (New York: Applause Theatre Book Publishers, 1987), p. 71.

CHAPTER 4

FINDING A PURPOSE

So far we have learned that the actor begins his task of believing by making a score of appropriate physical actions and learning to perform them honestly. We also know that it is counterproductive at this time for the actor to be concerned about how either he or the character "feels." Emotion is unquestionably a vital element of the actor's art, but it should not be sought directly. Even in scenes of tragedy, the actor is concerned with *action* rather than *feeling*. The question never is, "How would I feel if I were this character in these circumstances?" but rather, "What would I do?"

You should now know how to make a score of actions as the very first interpretative step in performing a role. You know each action must follow another in a logical sequence. You know your actions must be truthful, and you must believe each action is what you would do if you were the character in the given situation. Now we will learn how to make actions *purposeful*.

Whatever happens onstage must have a purpose, must serve some end beyond the accomplishment of the action itself. Moment by moment, the intent or meaning or significance of the performance, both for the actor and the audience, rarely lies in the action itself but in the purpose for which it is done. Even melodramatic actions such as loading a gun or mixing poison are not in themselves dramatic. We must know why, toward whom the lethal effort is directed. Clearly played for the right reasons, any number of simple, everyday actions—packing a suitcase, moving the furniture, lying down on the floor—may be dramatic.

So, to the four "W's" discussed in Chapter 3, we now add a fifth: *Why?* Answering this question gives the actor a reason to carry out the physical action. No lesson of more significance can be learned by the young actor. *Actions performed without a reason that is compelling to the actor and clear to the audience have no dramatic interest for either.*

Again, to discover "Why?" you look first in the dramatist's text, the place where all analysis begins. A careful reading should provide explicit reasons for most of the actions you have scored. If not, or if these reasons are unclear, you should follow the same procedure you followed with the other "W's." You turn next to what is *implied* by the text. (During this step the director usually becomes the chief interpreter for a particular production.) Finally, you seal the decision, make it personal, by drawing on your own insight and imagination.

Knowing how to make action purposeful is among the most valuable of all acting techniques. It allows you to believe more strongly in what you are doing as the character. It gives you a reason for being on the stage and thus relieves your tension. And it provides a principal means of conveying the import of the play to the audience.

In this book we are going to call the purpose for which you carry out your physical actions your *intention*. Others call it different names, a problem in terminology described interestingly by Robert Lewis:

> It has been called many things in many books and some people don't call it anything; but it is a process that is going on, if they are really acting. I myself don't care if you call it spinach, if you know what it is, and do it, because it is one of the most important elements in acting.[1]

"Spinach" might prove confusing, but *intention* is a term commonly used by actors and directors. By definition, an intention is "A determination to act in a certain way or to do a certain thing." So let's agree that *action* will mean the sequence of physical actions, the *what,* and that *intention* will mean the reason for doing them, the *why.* Put simply, *intention* is what you want, what you need to accomplish with your action.

The technique of executing simple physical actions motivated by a compelling psychological purpose ultimately became the basis of Stanislavski's approach, which he called the technique of psychophysical actions. Both simple and profound, the system empowers an actor to do knowingly onstage what he does spontaneously in life. Once mastered, it enables him to involve his entire physical and mental being in the performance of his stage tasks. Although good actors have always more or less consciously used this method, Stanislavski was the first to articulate it as a technique useful in *training* actors. Its effect on modern acting has been massive. Even such an innovator as Jerzy Grotowski, the renowned Polish director, called Stanislavski's work on physical actions one of the most stimulating influences he discovered during his exhaustive study of major actor-training methods.

STATING THE INTENTION

Return to the exercises in Chapter 3, and extend them by carrying out your actions to satisfy a clearly stated intention. This important step forces you to dig again into the circumstances. Once you have found the intention by examining both what the playwright gives you and your own experience, it is important for you to state it in a form that compels you to execute the action.

Here is the way it might work in the problem from *Of Mice and Men.* We have already made a score of physical actions and separated them into structural units, so we will add this circumstance, discovered by studying the script: Lennie is apprehensive and secretive about the puppy because his friend and protector, George, has repeatedly scolded him for being addicted to soft, furry objects and for being too rough with them—literally loving them to death. In addition to the physical action of playing with the puppy, we now have a psychological intention. Lennie is frightened that George will find him and scold him again, and so he must hide. We state the intention as "I must keep George off my back."

Stating and playing intentions in the problems from this exercise will be relatively easy. Mastering this early work will pave the way later for understanding the complex problem of "beats" and "super objectives."

EXERCISE

(1) Improvise on the score of actions from *Of Mice and Men* with the intention just given fast in your heart. And let your imagination work!

These improvisations are *not* to be seen as a game of "making up dialogue." Although you may need to speak in some exercises, making conversation is in no sense your objective. Your objective is *to realize a clearly defined intention through a logical sequence of actions*. Remember that speaking is an action. In life talk may be aimless, but onstage, the actor speaks only to help achieve his purpose. Lines, dialogue, speech (whatever term you prefer) must be conceived as actions employed to accomplish your intention.

(2) Carry out the same actions, but change your intention to "I want to punish George for scolding me." Keep firmly to this intention, even during the action of burying the dead puppy. Use your imagination to justify this intention.

Let's look at two more examples of determining actions and intentions from a script. In *When You Comin Back, Red Ryder?* by Mark Medoff, the scene is a diner in the desert of New Mexico in the late sixties or early seventies. Stephen/Red is a nineteen-year-old who wishes to escape the mundane world and become as famous as his movie hero. Angel, the waitress, is a few years older and accepts her life. She has a "crush" on Stephen and wants him to stay. In the opening scene, the conversation is about coffee, their names, and coupons, but Stephen/Red's intention is "I want to steer Angel's attention away from me," and Angel's is "I must force Stephen to pay some attention to me." This scene has many actions to be played, including reading a newspaper, drinking coffee, and eating a donut.

The Crucible, by Arthur Miller, deals with the famous witchcraft trials in Salem, Massachusetts, in 1692. The theme is the frightening effects of injustice and the misapplication of authority. John Proctor, about thirty years of age, is a hard-working farmer of independent spirit. His wife Elizabeth, also about thirty, has discovered that John had an adulterous affair with Abigail, a girl who worked for them and has since been dismissed. Abigail is one of the children bringing charges of witchcraft against innocent people, including Elizabeth. Earlier, she admitted to John that their allegations were not true. Elizabeth's Puritan ethic has magnified her husband's single infidelity into a situation of major proportions. At the opening of Act II, her intention is "I must make John go to Salem to expose and denounce Abigail." John's is "I must please Elizabeth and restore normality to my house."

DOING, NOT BEING

Note carefully the way an intention is stated:

1. It begins with "I want to …" or "I must …" to make the desire to carry out the physical actions personal and compelling.

2. "I want to …" or "I must …" is followed by an *active* verb because any statement of intention must germinate action. It must always be "I want to walk straight and steady." It must never be "I want to be drunk." It must be "I want to kick you downstairs." It must not be "I want to be angry."

Think always in terms of what you must *do,* not in terms of what you want to *be.*

One of the most common mistakes made by young actors is to attempt to act by *being* rather than *doing.* The actor who concentrates upon *being* drunk, *being* angry, *being* happy, *being* sad, or *being* afraid is thus certain to fail. Concern yourself, just as you do in actual life, with what you would do in each situation, not with what you would be.

When you are angry, your mind does not focus on being angry. Rather, you are concerned with the cause—the person or thing that has made you angry—and you may deal with the cause in any one of a number of ways. You may overlook it. You may seek release from your anger in some act of physical violence. You may forgive. You may plan some dreadful revenge. But certainly you are not saying to yourself, "I must be angry." You *do* something about the tricycle you have fallen over or about the person who has placed you in an embarrassing situation.

When you are frightened, you do not *want* to be afraid. Instead, you want to dispel your fear in some way. You may want to escape or to seek comfort from someone. You may want to calm your fears by turning your attention to something else. You may want to investigate the source of peril. You will want to do, not be.

A state of being is not actable because it provides nothing specific to do. It leaves the actor stuck with a general emotion, leading him into stereotyped movements and gestures—clenching his fists to show he is angry, putting his hand to his forehead to show he is thoughtful, or contorting the muscles of his face to show he is in pain.

Burning your hand may *be* painful. But you *want* to relieve the pain by applying salve, butter, cold water, or some other remedy. When a celebrity is pointed out in a crowd, you may *be* curious. But you *want* to secure a position where you can see to advantage. You may even want to get his autograph. To be in pain or to be curious is not actable. But to relieve pain or to satisfy curiosity is. You can easily carry out the actions of applying a remedy to your burned hand or of working your way into a favorable position.

EXERCISE

To realize more fully the importance of *doing* rather than *being* and of stating your intention with an active verb, work carefully on the following problems:

(1) Choose a word from the list to follow, and make it the basis for a series of actions. Do not let this instruction lead you into a trap. As you study the list, you should now realize that you cannot act any of these words. They describe effects. You must imagine a circumstance providing a reason for the *action that will produce the effect.* Then forget the effect, and concentrate on carrying out the action. For example, the following circumstance would provide an action for the word *cautious: You have just escaped from a war prison. In darkness, starved and exhausted, you are making your way across an area filled with booby traps. You find a knapsack that might contain rations.* State your intention as "I must work my way through the area without exploding a trap."

The following circumstance would provide an action for the word *spiteful: You have not been getting along with your roommate. You resent his constantly asking you to loan him money, so he can satisfy his extravagant taste for clothes. You return home to find he has "borrowed" money from your coin bank you were saving to buy a present for your sister. You take several articles of his new clothing, cut off all the buttons, and put them in the box where he keeps his coins when he has any.* State your intention as "I must get even with my roommate for his selfishness."

Now, look over the list, and select a word. Devise appropriate circumstances. Make a score of your actions. State your intention. Structure your score, and name each of the three units. Carry it out in an imaginative improvisation. Observe the instructions given for the exercises in the preceding chapter.

embarrassed	distracted
bashful	excited
frantic	exhausted
nervous	exasperated
terrified	disdainful
breathless	nonchalant

ruthless	tantalizing
spiteful	lethargic
awkward	bewildered
coarse	drunken
genteel	maudlin
cautious	violent
jealous	dazed
jovial	sickly
quarrelsome	apprehensive

All of these words come from playwrights' directions to actors in a single volume of modern American plays. They illustrate how dramatists (and often directors) ask for effects. Actors must be able to think of effects in terms of actions and intentions. A frequent comment to actors from directors is "Don't play the effect (even though he may have just asked for it), play the action!"

(2) Choose one of the following "everyday" actions. Create circumstances, and provide an intention you can endeavor to realize with unfeigned interest and excitement. Take, for example, polishing silver: You are in an antique shop in a foreign country. You discover among many dusty articles a blackened silver bowl that you think is the work of Benvenuto Cellini. Beneath the tarnish may be revealing marks. If you are right, the proprietor obviously does not suspect its origin. State your intention as "I want to get the tarnish off this bowl without attracting the notice of the proprietor."

Take, for another example, "walking five steps": You are in the hospital with a serious illness. You are very weak and short of breath. You are under strict doctor's orders to stay in bed. You decide to test your strength by walking a short distance to a chair. You reach the chair exhausted but convinced you are beginning to recover. State your intention as "I must start to use my muscles if I am ever going to regain my strength."

Now it is your turn. To solve the problem suggested by one of these "everyday actions," you need specific circumstances, a properly stated intention, a score of definite things to do, and imagination. Execute all physical actions precisely, clearly, and with complete commitment. Do not hurry them. Give them form. Observe all previous instructions.

looking through a window
opening a door
hunting for a lost ring
lying down on the floor
arranging furniture in a room
building a fire
feeding fish in an aquarium
drinking tea
wrapping or unwrapping a package
crawling on your hands and knees

packing a suitcase
washing your hands
picking flowers
walking five steps
digging a hole in the ground
acquainting yourself with a room you have never been in before
examining a bundle of clothes
waiting for someone to come home
hanging a picture
sitting perfectly still (Here your intention must justify the absence of
    physical action.)

Plays are filled with simple actions for which the actor must find intentions that stimulate his imagination and make the actions communicate the playwright's meaning.

WORKING AGAINST AN OBSTACLE

By now it must have become apparent that stated or implied in each intention has been an *obstacle*. Mined terrain is an obstacle to the successful escape from a prison camp. A shrewd antique dealer is an obstacle to picking up a Cellini masterpiece for a few *lire*. The interest in a play or scene (or in an acting exercise) lies in the possibilities it offers the actor to gain an objective against odds—odds sometimes so great that the struggle ends in defeat, either glorious or ignoble. Plays in which there is no struggle have little interest for either actor or audience.

As you crystallize each intention, ask "What is the *obstacle?*" or "What will make it difficult to accomplish the intention?" With no difficulty, there is no problem—no scene—no play! The obstacle, like the intention, may be either physical or psychological, internal or external. Internal obstacles always grow from the character's own personality and experience; external obstacles come from all other sources, such as societal expectations, other people, God, nature, laws—even such natural phenomena as the weather and the time of day.

Frequently the physical and psychological are so closely related that it is not possible, nor desirable, to separate them. The problem from *Of Mice and Men* is an example of this interrelation. The physical obstacle to Lennie's accomplishing his intention is that the puppy is not old enough to play with him. No matter how gently he treats it, he cannot show George his capabilities because the puppy is not yet trainable. The psychological obstacle is more complex. On a simple level, it is that neither Lennie's emotional nor his intellectual development is mature enough to comprehend the potential outcome of his action. He is a child in a very strong man's body; in fact, his great physical strength is one of the obstacles to his attaining the returned affection of the animals he needs so desperately. As he gratifies his longing to pet them, an ever-increasing desire for this gratification spurs him to handle them more and more roughly.

In the problem from *The Effect of Gamma Rays on Man-in-the-Moon Marigolds,* the obstacle is entirely psychological. The rabbit presents Beatrice with no difficulty. Instead, the obstacle is her own natural tendency to love her daughter rather than do anything to harm her.

In playing the latter scene, the actress—especially the beginning actress— would do well to concentrate on trying to find reasons to love her daughter, playing against the hate. Lennie should concentrate on what he is doing with the puppy, protecting it from pain after he has hurt it, searching for the extent of its injuries, and hiding it when he realizes it is dead. Note that his intention does not change through this sequence. At first, he wants to get George off his back by proving he can handle the puppy. When he is forced to abandon this strategy, he hides the dead puppy for the same reason. The psychological complexities of the intention and the character's strength of commitment to its completion give it varied textures at different moments during its performance, but the intention itself does not change.

Each character could play several other intentions. Selecting intentions is a large part of *interpreting* a role.

On the stage, as in life, psychological intentions and obstacles stimulate us to accomplish what we set out to achieve. A winner's motivation is nearly always psychological. The runner does not want simply to cover the distance faster than anyone else; she is motivated by desire to bring honor and prestige to herself and to the team and to win admiration and fame, perhaps by a determination to set someone right who said she could not do it. A man does not build a home just to complete the physical structure; he also wants to provide protection, security, and beauty for himself and his family. A proud collector would have a very special desire to get possession of a Cellini bowl. These illustrations from life suggest three important points for the actor:

1. Psychological intentions and obstacles can stimulate the actor's imagination more strongly than can physical intentions and obstacles.

2. The actor must make a personal commitment to overcome the obstacle and accomplish his intention. This commitment generates real feeling, and it is the actor's most dependable source of emotion.

3. The actor must feel the challenge physically as well as intellectually. A runner does not win a race by *wishing* to, *thinking* about strategy, or *feeling* victorious. Goals are achieved through purposeful *action.*

The beginning actor must pay particular attention to the importance of the obstacle. His psychophysical actions, if they are to have any dramatic interest, must be performed to overcome a counteraction that exerts a strong force against the accomplishment of his intention. He must not be indifferent to this opposition. Nonchalance toward the challenge of overcoming the obstacle, too common among student actors, will inevitably render a performance ineffective.

An even more basic error occurs when an actor fails to understand clearly what the obstacle is. Until he locates the obstacle, the actor cannot discover what means the dramatist has provided, either directly or by implication, for overcoming it. The actor will then be deprived of the only true and defensible stimulus for drawing additional strategies from his imagination.

Notice we consistently draw on such adverbs as *clearly, specifically, directly,* and *definitely* when describing an actor's exploration of such basic concepts as circumstances, intentions, obstacles, and actions. Generality in any of these matters will always yield inferior results.

Strategy is another term that turns up often in our discussion. The military definition of this term is "the art and science of employing armed strength to meet the enemy in combat." While conflict between the character and the obstacle is not always open warfare, the actor would do well to conceive his whole performance as a strategic plan to overcome the forces working against him. Far too often in answer to the question, "What are you doing in this scene?" the young actor says casually "Oh, I'm just talking to this banker about loaning me some money." Or "I'm just asking my husband what he did while I was away this afternoon."

"Just" marks a telltale flaw in these answers. The actor must have discovered, either from the script or in his own imagination, an urgent need to get the money or to find out what was happening during the afternoon, and a hardheaded banker or a secretive husband provides a genuine obstacle that must be overcome. Even when the circumstances demand a subtle strategy of which the opponent will be unaware, the inner urgency must be undiminished and may be all the greater.

Attempt always to simplify the conflict by finding the character's elemental need; do not try to complicate it. Satisfactory answers in these instances might be "I must get this money to pay the debts I have incurred before my father finds out about them" and "I must find out whether the gossip about my husband and the girl next door is true." If these answers sound melodramatic, remember such material is the stuff of which drama is made. The content of Shakespeare's plays in the hands of a hack writer produces soap operas, and the Greek tragedies become horror stories.

British critic Kenneth Tynan wrote:

> Good drama, of whatever kind, has but one mainspring—the human being reduced by ineluctable process to a state of desperation. Desperate are the cornered giants of Sophocles; desperate, too, as they huddle in their summerhouses, the becalmed gentry of Chekhov; and the husband of French farce, with a wife in one bedroom and a mistress in another, is he not, though we smile at his agony, definably desperate?...How, in this extremity, will they comport themselves? It is to find out that we go to theatres....[2]

The actor must conceive the carrying out of his intention as a "desperate quest" to overcome an obstacle.

EXERCISE

You were asked to use the problems at the end of Chapter 3 as exercises in making and carrying out a score of physical actions. Without being aware of it as a technique, chances are you performed the actions for some purpose, since it would be unnatural to do otherwise. Now that you have been introduced to the technique, choose again a problem from Chapter 3, and extend it consciously to include finding the intention—both physical and psychological—and playing the action to accomplish your objective. To make the procedure most helpful, be sure to:

(1) Find the intention in the given circumstances. It must allow you to satisfy the needs of your character and the demands of the play.
(2) Make it attractive to *you*. You personally must feel compelled to carry it out.
(3) Make it truthful. You must without reservation believe it is what you would do if you were the character in the circumstances.
(4) Provide an *obstacle* either derived from the circumstances or appropriate to them.
(5) Be sure your intention suggests a range of physical actions.
(6) Start the statement with "I must..." or "I want to..." followed by an active verb.

ADAPTING TO OTHER CHARACTERS

Although the problems, so far, have involved only one person, you must be vividly aware that dramatic art is a collective art. Richard Schechner once proposed the maxim that "the theatrical event is a set of related transactions."[3] Certainly one of the essential transactions is among performers. An individual actor's performance always must be conceived in relation to other characters who either help or hinder him in accomplishing his objectives, and he must consider these other characters in planning his actions. He must also be able to adapt and sometimes to abandon his plans as he is confronted with the unexpected. He must watch and listen and be alert and ready to adjust what he does and says to the needs of the moment. Adapting to other characters turns actions into *transactions*.

In life everybody must be able to adapt to changing circumstances. Those who cannot will never get across the street alive, much less manage the more subtle interpersonal challenges they face. We deal with people both logically and psychologically, and the kind of adaptation we make—whether it is bold, delicate, daring, cautious—is important to our success. Each day brings an infinite number of situations requiring a wide range of adjustments.

In contrast, stage action often seems dull and remembered because a lifelike sense of adjustment has disappeared in the actor's struggle to remember and repeat lines and movement. A technique that allows for adaptation to the needs of the moment is a necessity in the actor's training, and learning to think of acting as a transaction is the first step in mastering this important lesson. When performing a transaction, the actor concentrates on how he can affect the behavior of the other performers as well as on what they are doing to cause him to adjust his strategy. The focus, then, is on what happens among the performers, not on the individual or on the mechanics of acting.

EXERCISE

(1) For work in the technique of adaptation, try this "coach and actor" exercise. Work in pairs. One actor serves as "coach," telling his partner firmly and quietly (the class should be able to hear, too) what actions to perform. His instructions should constitute a logical sequence of physical actions having a beginning, a middle, and an end. The coach should prepare carefully in advance. He should be certain the sequence can be psychologically motivated, but he should not tell his partner what the motivation is. As he proceeds, the actor must discover a motivation and adapt accordingly. The coach should vary the tempo-rhythm of his instructions as the actions develop toward a climax and as he senses his partner's responses. Later discussions should compare the motivation the coach had in mind with what the actor discovered. The actor's job is to find a motivation, not to guess what the coach intended. There is no absolute right and wrong. Although some motivations might be illogical under the circumstances, two quite different motivations could be well-justified.

(2) In the following problem, the "coach" becomes an actor within the imaginary circumstances. The two characters are a window dresser and an assistant. The window dresser is on the sidewalk directing the assistant where and how to place the objects for display. They are separated by a plate-glass window, so all communication must be visual rather than oral. The physical intention clearly is to get the window dressed, and the physical separation provides a definite obstacle. From your imagination supply additional specific circumstances. Know exactly what objects are being arranged for display. Some other members of the group might be used as mannequins. The dresser should know exactly what effect he wants to achieve. Supply psychological intentions and obstacles as well as the obvious physical ones. Remember the necessary element of urgency. Structure the exercise, giving it a beginning, a development leading to a climax, and a conclusion. All exercises accomplish their purpose more fully when they are followed by a discussion regarding the clarity and urgency of the intention, the precision of the physical actions, the strategy for overcoming the obstacles, the adaptations, and the effectiveness of the structure. Both participants should discuss how the nature of the transaction affected their strategies for performing their actions.

IMPROVISING GROUP SCENES

The actor may obtain further practice in adaptation through exercises in group improvisation, a further extension of the exercises you have already been doing. Improvising with a group involves more complicated and interesting problems, bringing you closer to your ultimate aim of a shared performance. You will begin, as always, with given circumstances out of which you must create an active, attractive, and truthful intention. You will face an added complication because you cannot know what you will need to do until you know what the others are going to do. As they play their intentions, they will create obstacles for you. Since the final definition of the scene will depend on your transaction with the other performers, you will need to be ready to adjust moment by moment. And again, the actions you adjust must be truthful and logical; you must believe they are what you would really do if you were the character in the circumstances. As you begin to sense your effect on the actions of the other performers and as you adjust your actions to the obstacles they present, you will be on your way toward learning one of the most important lessons of the theatre: Acting is communal, and successful performance depends utterly on the stimulation you receive from, and give, your fellow actors.

EXERCISE

For a first effort in group improvisation, we will set circumstances that permit communication through psychologically motivated physical actions and expressive sounds—*without the use of dialogue.* The situation is suggested by the first scene of *Romeo and Juliet,* in which the servants of the rival houses of Capulet and Montague confront each other in the public square. Because the two families are ancient enemies, the servants feel compelled to challenge each other whenever they meet, although they may have forgotten (or perhaps never knew) the cause of the age-old hatred. The servants are uneducated, not dangerously armed, and not overly courageous. Their purpose is to insult and perpetrate minor physical assaults. In this exercise the objective is to be accomplished through physical actions (including gesture and facial expression) and vocalized sounds—no articulated words. The servants of one house should create obstacles for the others. Each actor should strive to play his intention as fully as possible. Remember, though, that the actions must always be logical and appropriate within the given circumstances. The scene should not become chaotic. Each action must be purposefully performed. The circumstances prescribe a number of obstacles to a realization of the intention: the natural timidity of the characters, the need for self-protection, and the need for a degree of furtiveness because these encounters in the public streets have been forbidden by law.

Let the beginning consist of the meeting in the street and some cautious advances by one or two of the servants, followed by hasty retreats. Let the middle develop the confrontation, as some of the servants, exhorted by others, become bolder in their actions and ultimately involve the whole group. Let the end consist of the arrival of someone of authority who breaks up the quarrel.

The group could decide to set the scene in circumstances other than those of Verona in the Italian Renaissance. In *West Side Story,* a modern musical based on *Romeo and Juliet,* the enemies were not "two houses both alike in dignity" but rival street gangs in New York. It would be valuable to work on the same situation in different sets of circumstances.

EXERCISE

George Washington Slept Here provides a situation for work in improvisation. The Fuller family—Newton, Annabelle, and daughter Madge—having restored an old colonial house in Pennsylvania, is entertaining weekend guests. Rain has kept them constantly indoors. On Sunday afternoon they sit around the living room in bathing suits hoping the weather will clear and permit a little pleasure in an otherwise dreary weekend.

Before starting actually to improvise, each member of the group needs to draw from his imagination a few additional circumstances. Remember an actor cannot work to any purpose, either in an improvisation or in a play, until he considers the "W's." *Who* is he? *Where* is he? *What* does he want? *Why* does he want it? For a group improvisation the answers do not need to be detailed, but they must be specific. For this problem from *George Washington Slept Here,* the group needs first to decide who will be Newton, Annabelle, and Madge. Other actors must know who they are in relation to the Fullers— Madge's boyfriend; her college roommate; her cousin, to whom all the boys are attracted; an athlete who does not mind the rain; a business associate of Newton's (decide specifically what business he and Newton are in); a hired girl; and so forth.

Do not seek to be melodramatic or bizarre. Supply yourself with a character who would readily be found at such a party and whose behavior you can easily understand. Many young actors seek to be interesting through being exotic. A domestic Annabelle really trying to make her guests comfortable and happy will be more engaging than, say, a phony maharani. Who knows what a maharani does at a house party on a rainy afternoon, anyway?

Now, set up the living room with the necessary chairs, tables, sofas, doors, windows—probably a fireplace and a bar. Technically, this is the process of making a *ground plan.* Although we should note that a good ground plan always provides actors with a range of positions in which they can be readily seen, at this juncture you should concern yourself primarily with an appropriate arrangement of the room. Each member of the group must clearly understand the essentials of the plan. Then his imagination will allow him to accept a placement of miscellaneous chairs and tables as in a finely restored colonial house, and he will be able to relate to them exactly as he would if they were real. An imaginative actor can be genuinely upset when some dolt treats a folding chair like the thing it is instead of like the rare antique it has been designated as being.

Having established the who and where, decide on the what and why. This means finding your intention and the reason for it. Everyone will want to pass the afternoon either as pleasantly or as profitably as possible, but to realize this general objective you need specific actions. Madge's roommate may want to sit by herself and read a book in preparation for an examination she has to pass the next day. The business associate may want to discuss business, while Newton wants to see that his guests are properly supplied with drinks and food; restoring the house was his idea, and it is essential to his ego that everyone has a good time. Madge's boyfriend may want to get the cousin into a corner, and Madge may want to keep him from doing it. Annabelle may want to organize a card game, keep Newton from drinking too much, see that Madge does not neglect the guests, and keep the harassed and inexperienced hired girl functioning as a proper maid.

Another important point to remember is that each intention ought to be selected with a clear idea in mind of what you want or need others in the scene to do. Madge may want to sit by herself and read, but this intention will be much stronger and clearly associated with those around her if she understands that in order to accomplish it, she must, in fact, keep the others away. By including other performers in her intention, she elevates her action to a transaction, because she is performing it at least partially to influence the behavior of those around her.

The value of group improvisation lies in your learning to make real contact with other actors, to heed what they do and say, to adapt the playing of your intention to the need of the moment, and to work freely and logically within the imaginary circumstances. What you learn should carry over into everything you do because all good acting is to some degree improvisational. Even a scene that has been "set" demands constant adjustment—a living connection with fellow players. The choices you make in the adjustments must be credible and appropriate. The social situation of a house party places restrictions on both hosts and guests. Behaving logically within the circumstances is the beginning of truthful acting. Avoid choices that are sensational, that are calculated solely for dramatic effect, or that mindlessly repeat what you have seen other actors do or even what you have done in the past. Group improvisation is best when your imagination leads you truthfully into *spontaneous* adjustments.

Do not talk more than necessary! Do not try to make what you say clever, dramatic, or literary. In fact, do not think about it. You are an actor, not a playwright. An actor's job is to use his lines to accomplish his intention.

Set a time limit—at the beginning, ten to fifteen minutes for a group exercise. After it is over, the work should be carefully analyzed (preferably by a competent observer) so each actor is aware of the points at which he has or has not behaved logically and truthfully and at which his adjustments have fallen short of what could have been expected. Each actor can help himself and sometimes help others by recalling when he was making real contact, when his actions seemed true and spontaneous, and when they did not. The analysis should not be concerned with whether the scene would be entertaining or exciting to an audience. Improvisation is a means, not an end, and you will defeat its purpose if you think about results other than truthful behavior.

Your first attempts may be frustratingly unfruitful, for group improvisation is a technique that takes time to learn. But it is time well spent, and it is essential to your training.

EXERCISE

The following situations provide opportunities for group improvisations. In each case additional circumstances must be supplied from either the play or the imaginations of the actors. Each character must clearly understand his intention and attempt to realize it through actions appropriate to the circumstances.

(1) In *Cyrano de Bergerac,* by Edmond Rostand, a crowd of men and women, originally assembled at the Hotel de Bourgogne to watch a play, are instead treated to a duel between Cyrano and Valvert. They take sides, enjoying the excitement. Cyrano dispatches Valvert while simultaneously composing a ballade. At the end of the duel, some applaud and throw flowers or handkerchiefs, others surround Cyrano to congratulate him, and others (Valvert's friends) hold the unfortunate loser up in order to lead him away.

(2) In *Gammer Gurton's Needle,* an early English farce—the author of which has never been determined—Gammer has lost her needle while sewing a patch on Hodges's breeches. In those days a needle was a rare and greatly prized possession, so the entire village becomes involved in a search. Plan an improvisation in which the group are sixteenth-century villagers hunting for the needle. Make it more real by having someone who is not taking part hide a needle somewhere on the stage. Read the play to find out where the needle was found.

(3) In *Big River,* by William Hauptman and Roger Miller, Huck and The Duke wander among the people of the Mississippi River town of Bricktown, Arkansas, passing out handbills announcing the imminent appearance of the "Royal Nonesuch." They encounter loafers, slaves loading goods on the wharf, tarts at the window of a brothel, and other run-of-the-mill townspeople going about their regular business. The Duke and Huck finally scare up an audience, but the "Nonesuch" is so ludicrous that the crowd roars with anger and pelts the stage with vegetables until one member leaps on the stage and settles them down.

(4) In *A Soldier's Play,* by Charles Fuller, a group of black soldiers return to their barracks after a baseball game. They are carrying their equipment, and they engage in the exuberant, loud, locker-room banter of young

men in the army. A sergeant unexpectedly enters, and the raucousness of their conversation abruptly abates.

(5) In *Bus Stop,* by William Inge, the passengers on a Greyhound bus are forced to wait out a snowstorm in a tiny bus-stop cafe in Kansas. They come in from the cold, order food or drink, and plan ways to pass the time during the delay.

(6) In *Geniuses,* by Jonathan Reynolds, a motion-picture crew is trapped during a typhoon in a house in the Philippine jungle. They are short of food, so their Filipino assistant, Winston, prepares a meal consisting of a local delicacy—dog. He brings it in a bowl on a tray with spoons and napkins and sets it on the table. The crew must decide whether or not to try it. The scene is written for three men and a woman, but for purposes of this exercise, any number can play.

(7) In *Playboy of the Western World,* by John Millington Synge, Irish villagers gather at the pub to watch a fight between Old Mahon and his son, Christy, who has become a local hero.

(8) In *The Visit,* by Friedrich Duerrenmatt, enormously wealthy Claire Zachanassian returns to the small town she left years ago as a disgraced and penniless girl. The townspeople give her a gala welcome at the railway station, hoping she will become their generous benefactor.

(9) In *Our Town,* by Thornton Wilder, the people of the town of Grover's Corners, New Hampshire, gather at the church for the wedding of George and Emily, two of their favorite young people.

(10) In *The Rainmaker,* by N. Richard Nash, H. C. Curry and his two sons go to town to try to get the deputy sheriff, File, to pay a call on Lizzie (H. C.'s daughter), who is nearing that time when she will be thought of as an "old maid." They try to work the invitation into their conversation without being obvious about it.

(11) In *The Birthday Party,* by Harold Pinter, the presence of two unidentified strangers at a birthday celebration mystifies the guests. The actors playing the strangers must find reasons to justify their presence and behavior.

(12) In *Rhinoceros,* by Eugene Ionesco, a group of French townspeople sit around tables at an outdoor cafe or go about their business on the street. Bellowing wildly, a rhinoceros runs full speed down the opposite sidewalk.

(13) In *Doonesbury,* by Gary Trudeau, the entire gang gathers for dinner at Walden. The meal is interrupted by a telephone call from their landlady, who tells Zonker she has sold the house.

(14) In *Inherit the Wind,* by Jerome Lawrence and Robert E. Lee, the townspeople of Hillsboro, Tennessee, prepare for the arrival of Matthew Harrison Brady, a renowned lawyer who will help prosecute a local man who has dared to discuss the theory of evolution in his high-school science class. Many carry banners, and the mood is that of a revival meeting, as they surge back and forth in a kind of parade. Finally, they break into a rousing rendition of "Gimme That Old-Time Religion," as Brady arrives.

(15) In *Prelude to a Kiss,* by Craig Lucas, family and friends have gathered for Peter and Rita's wedding. The minister has just completed the ceremony. Everybody is crowding around, shaking hands, and congratulating the young couple. An old man, who is a complete stranger to everybody, joins the party and unexpectedly kisses the bride.

(16) In *The Royal Hunt of the Sun,* by Peter Shaffer, Spanish soldiers led by Pizarro climb the Andes in search of gold. Motivated by greed and by loyalty to the Spanish crown, the soldiers face exhaustion as they make "a stumbling, tortuous climb into the clouds, over ledges and chasms."

NOTES

1. Robert Lewis, *Method—Or Madness?* (New York: Samuel French, 1958), p. 29.

2. Kenneth Tynan, *Curtains* (New York: Atheneum, 1961), p. 77.

3. Richard Schechner, *Public Domain* (Indianapolis and New York: Bobbs-Merrill, 1969), p. 157.

CHAPTER 5

TAKING IT EASY

The first time you performed an exercise in class, you probably became aware that muscular tension and the inability to relax can keep you from achieving anything near your potential. No actor is ever entirely liberated from these enemies because they cannot simply be outgrown as one gains experience. All actors, therefore, must develop more-or-less conscious techniques of relaxing. The actor's goal is to be able to eliminate all tension not absolutely needed to execute a movement, say a line, or maintain a position. Good movement and good speech are characterized by economy of effort.

The ability to relax is necessary to the internal as well as the external aspects of acting, for the tense actor finds it impossible to focus on the subtle process by which a character is brought to life. Excessive tension inhibits freedom of action and clarity of intention, a point Stanislavski made clear by demonstrating that it is impossible to multiply thirty-seven times nine while holding up the corner of a piano. The actor's unwanted tension is often just as great as that required to lift a heavy weight, and playing a clear intention certainly demands as much mental acuity as solving a problem of multiplication.

The inability to relax shatters the actor's ability to perform a believable character. Watching a tense actor, the audience inevitably focuses on the resulting nervous mannerisms rather than on the actions of the play. Instead of the character the actor wishes to create, the audience sees an externalization of the actor's need to relieve his tension. These mannerisms belong to the actor, not to the character, so they destroy the believability of the scene.

In addition to learning to relax, professionals all over the world recognize that physical exercise to develop coordination and muscular control is an essential part of the actor's training. Indeed, fencing and some form of dancing are required in most schools of drama to help the student develop poise and alertness. Most actors also value the regimen of some sort of athletic training such as swimming, tennis, or gymnastics. Many also undergo training in stage combat, mime, and circus techniques. Anyone seriously interested in acting understands the need to develop a coordinated and responsive body.

Currently, no universal agreement prevails as to just what program of body training the actor should employ, so the student is faced with a considerable range of choices. They include acrobatics; circus skills of juggling, tumbling, and trapeze; Asian disciplines such as yoga and t'ai chi ch'uan; various techniques in mime; and a number of programmed exercises.[1] Each approach has its exponents and its detractors, and each will yield some benefits if the actor commits himself consistently to practicing it; however, relaxation and physical readiness are only partly a matter of general conditioning. An athlete whose movement on the tennis court is a model of economy and coordination may be awkward and ill-at-ease when he attempts a simple assignment in acting.

In recent years intensive efforts have been made to discover a genuinely effective program in body training for the actor. These efforts have produced significant changes both in concept and practice, together with an increasing emphasis on carefully directed work in stage movement. Several influential

TRAINING THE BODY

Famed and revered American teacher Arthur Lessac leads a class. Mr. Lessac's method emphasizes freeing the body as a technique for freeing the voice. (Photo by Tim Hinz, courtesy of Central College.)

approaches to actor training were developed by such modern "pioneers" as Jerzy Grotowski, Peter Brook, Joseph Chaikin, and Arthur Lessac, great innovators who were oriented to physical training as a means of developing the actor's total instrument. Literally hundreds of teachers and "systems" have sprung from the work of one or another of these individuals, some of brief duration and others that have made genuine contributions to actor training throughout the world. All these people would agree with Grotowski that "the most elementary fault [of the actor], and that in most urgent need of correction, is the over-straining of the voice because one forgets to speak with the body."[2]

Practically, body training is designed to accomplish two basic, closely related objectives: (1) proper body alignment and (2) freedom from excess muscle tension. Accomplishment of these objectives enables the actor to move in any direction from a standing, sitting, or lying position with a minimum of effort and without a preparatory shifting of weight. Together they produce strong, efficient, unforced movement. Proper alignment, sometimes called *centering*, is the correct relationship among the principal weights of the body—head, chest, and pelvis. Centering exercises actually produce a normal posture, but one seldom achieved without conscious effort, because most of us suffer from bad physical habits and from adverse psychological and environmental influences. Certain primitives who have not been similarly affected move and repose naturally, with the kind of posture actors seek through exercise. Natural alignment is best achieved under the guidance of a competent teacher; however, a description of the ideal will help you understand how much work you have to do to attain it.

We unconsciously achieve proper body alignment when we are lying on our backs on a reasonably hard surface. We can then easily eliminate all tension, and, when we do so, the weights of the body come naturally into a correct relationship. Our goal is to transfer this relationship and this feeling of relaxation from a prone to an upright position.

When we do so, we will be *standing tall,* and the "tip at the back of the top of the head" will be the tallest point. Our head position will be such that the bottom line of the chin is parallel with the floor, and the front neck muscles will be relaxed—a condition essential to ridding ourselves of vocal tension. The shoulders will be rounded forward to obtain the widest possible space between the shoulder blades. We should think of the shoulder blades as a double gate that is always kept open. Square-shouldered, closed-gate military posture produces tensions and inhibits the natural expressiveness of the body. The abdominal muscles will be held in firmly and the buttocks "tucked under," so the spine is properly aligned from top to bottom. When we stand in this position against a wall, little or no space should remain between the wall and the small of our back. The arms swing freely from the shoulders, and the knees will be relaxed.[3]

You should seek to achieve proper alignment not only for use onstage, but also for an easy, natural posture for your normal life. It will improve your appearance, eliminate eccentricities in your movement, decrease fatigue, and increase your efficiency in physical and mental activities.

The second objective of body training—muscular relaxation—is a quality that characterizes all fine acting. The goal of relaxation is not dormancy. Instead, it should provide a state of alertness in which the actor can attain his utmost capacity for accomplishing any activity. It bolsters his courage and increases his self-confidence. This condition has been variously called "blissful relaxation" (Morris Carnovsky), the "potent state" (Moshe Feldenkrais), and the "creative state" (Stanislavski).

The actor who has not attained a state of muscular freedom will often be told, "Just relax; take it easy." These words can easily produce the opposite of the desired effect by causing the actor to become more aware of his tension and, consequently, to become more tense. Unfortunately, no program will eliminate tension and allow you to achieve relaxation in a few easy lessons. Such a regimen of exercise is a lifelong process, relentless in its demand on your time and energy.

Although it will not eliminate the need for training and exercise, the actor can help induce a state of relaxation by *justifying* his actions and *concentrating* on performing them. These aspects of the actor's technique are exceptionally pertinent to the thrust of this book, so we will take them up here and in the following chapter.

RELAXING THROUGH JUSTIFICATION

We have already mentioned that athletes are often unable to transfer their muscular coordination from the playing field to the stage. The gallery of spectators watching a proficient tennis player as she serves and returns does not unnerve her in the least. In fact, she is hardly aware of being watched. But the few observers at a rehearsal may make her painfully self-conscious, unable to function with any degree of ease.

The difference between the athlete's performance on the tennis court and that on the stage is that, as an athlete, her actions are justified. She knows why she is doing them, and she has developed a technique for doing them efficiently. All her attention is directed toward accomplishing a purpose she knows to be right and clear. She is relaxed mentally as well as physically. She forgets herself and concentrates on winning the game. In contrast, she is nervous as an actor because she is worried about herself rather than her task. She has not justified her actions to the extent that they consume her attention, nor does she command a technique capable of giving her confidence in her ability to do what the situation requires.

Phrases frequently heard in describing an actor's state of being are "He forgets himself on the stage" or "He loses himself in the part." To gain freedom from tension, the actor must "forget himself" and concentrate on the action of his character, but this phrase is misleading. It does not refer to a trancelike state in which the actor is unaware of his surroundings, surrenders himself to his emotions, and loses control of the situation. In fact, the actor, like the athlete, is in greatest control of his abilities when he can "forget himself." The phrase means that the actor has rid himself of anxieties over his shortcomings and is concentrating solely on performing his stage tasks.

Worrying over what audiences may think or over the responsibility of keeping them "entertained" produces instant tension. The athlete also cherishes the approval of the spectators, but during the game she forgets them and concentrates on winning. This is her purpose. She knows that if she accomplishes it by fair means, the spectators will be satisfied and overlook minor errors or shortcomings of form. The actor "wins" by creating a believable character. To accomplish this, he must free himself from worry over nonessentials; he must relax and perform the character's actions. He must overcome his consciousness of himself because only then can he command his energies to serve his stage purpose freely and fully. He knows that if he is totally absorbed in carrying out his character's action, his personal tension will disappear.

ABOUT INHIBITIONS

Social inhibitions can occasionally be another source of tension for an actor. In such cases, it may prove helpful to realize that social inhibitions take many forms and that they vary substantially from society to society, from era to era, and from individual to individual. In our society, for instance, men rarely touch one another except to shake hands. But in other societies, such as Mexico or Italy, it is perfectly acceptable for men to embrace and walk arm in arm in public. Even succeeding generations within the same culture have different sets of social inhibitions. Our great-grandparents would almost certainly have been inhibited had they been asked to wear bikinis or shorts. An important key to freeing inhibitions, then, is understanding them—knowing why your character's society has developed its customs and mores.

Still, the relationship between social inhibitions and the individual person is complex. Why is it that some actors are less hindered by social inhibitions on stage than others are? Can an actor from a conservative background learn not to wince (either internally or externally) at using suggestive behavior or foul language on stage? What are the actor's rights and responsibilities in these delicate areas?

These questions have no easy answers. You must develop your own sense of ethics and turn down roles in which you feel yourself exploited. On the other hand, once you have accepted a role, then it is your responsibility to carry out the actions appropriate for the characterization, even when those actions are not what you would do personally. If you believe in a play and in your role and concentrate on the reasons that characters behave the way they do, you soon will lose your inhibitions. They will slip away as you involve yourself in your task and will be replaced by the internal logic of the role and by an increased empathy with the character.

It is realistic to expect that today's actor may have to decide whether playing a character in the nude is artistically justified. David Storey's *The Changing Room,* for example, takes place in the locker room of an English rugby team. At one time, all the players appear nude while changing from street clothing into their uniforms. The nudity is not central to the meaning of the play, but it is a necessary and rational part of the play's locale. Obviously, too much self-consciousness would work against an actor's ability to create the easygoing, uninhibited locker-room banter. If an actor is not comfortable enough with his body to rehearse and perform the play in the nude, he obviously should not audition for the role.

The late Judith Lowry, who played roles well into her nineties, was often required to use foul and abusive language onstage because it created such a vivid comic effect. When questioned by her granddaughter, Lowry explained that it was not Judith Lowry saying those things, but a character whom she was creating, someone make-believe.

Let us now turn to a few exercises designed to help you remove tensions and lose your self-consciousness. Our primary instruction for all these exercises is, "Just relax. Take it easy." Remember that relaxation is a mental as well as a physical state.

"JUST RELAX"

Please realize that these exercises are a mere taste of the organized, rigorous physical-training regimen that serious acting students ought to undertake. We have also included a sample of vocal exercises, for training the voice and the body go hand in hand. Again, however, we assume that serious acting students are taking speech classes simultaneously with courses in acting. We cannot emphasize too strongly that we agree completely with Kristin Linklater, Arthur Lessac, and others who believe that the creative impulse emanates from a synthesis of a sound, tension-free voice and a healthy, relaxed body. Excellent exercises may be found in both of their writings, which are detailed in the Bibliography at the end of this book.

Incidentally, a combination of the following exercises can serve very well as a *warm-up routine* to be used at the start of your class or prior to rehearsals or performances. Just as the athlete warms up before practicing or playing the game and the pianist does finger-stretching and relaxation exercises before rehearsing or performing, the actor must always prepare his tools and his mind for the work at hand. You should *never* commence a sustained period of practice or performance without warming up.

EXERCISE

These exercises may be done either individually or in a group. You must have enough room so your movements will not be restricted, and you should not wear clothes that will hamper your freedom. These exercises involve consciously tensing and relaxing your muscles.

(1) Fill as much space as you can vertically. Make yourself as tall as possible, and stretch upward as far as you can. Justify this action by imagining you are removing a burned-out light bulb that you can barely reach.

(2) Fill as little space as you can vertically without bending or stooping. Make yourself as short as possible. Imagine you are walking through a low cave.

(3) Fill as much space as you can horizontally. Make yourself as wide as possible. Stretch as far as you can from side to side. Imagine you are holding back two boulders that may roll together and crush you.

(4) Fill as little space as you can horizontally. Make yourself as narrow as possible without decreasing your height. Justify this exercise by imagining you are walking through a narrow tunnel.

Practice these exercises while feeling the alternation of tension and relaxation. Check carefully to see that you are making full use of every muscle that will help you accomplish your purpose. When you are stretching upward, be sure your feet, legs, abdomen, chest, shoulders, arms, hands, and fingers are fully extended. When you are as tall as you can be, stretch a little more. Then relax as much as possible without losing any height. Make sure you are using tension only in the muscles you need to accomplish your task. For instance, when you are stretching upward, check your facial muscles. Relax them completely because they can't make you any taller.

(5) Again, stretch upward as far as possible. Check once more for excess tension; use no more tension than necessary to maintain the position. Now, beginning with your fingers, slowly relax. Continue downward with your arms, neck, shoulders, chest, and abdomen, letting yourself fall forward until the upper part of your body is hanging like a rag doll. Maintain tension only in your legs and thighs to keep you from collapsing into a heap on the floor. Alternate the upward stretch and the "rag doll" positions, getting the feeling of purposefully tensing and relaxing your muscles.

(6) Sit well back on a straight chair, feet flat on the floor about six inches apart, hands resting on your knees. Take a comfortable erect position, and eliminate any tension not necessary to maintain it. Now fall forward at the waist, letting your face rest upon your knees. Eliminate all tension not necessary to keep you in the chair. Alternate the two positions.

(7) Return to the sitting position, checking again for excess tension. Now concentrate on relaxing your facial muscles. Beginning with your forehead and temples, let the energy drain out of your face until your lower jaw hangs loose and you feel like a retarded child. Maintain good sitting posture. If you "salivate," don't worry. Use your handkerchief or a tissue.

(8) Make your body feel like an inflated balloon. Resist the temptation to puff out your cheeks. Deflate yourself. Alternate these two muscular states.

(9) Take a deep breath, inhaling to the very bottom of your lungs. Exhale slowly through lips shaped to say "ooo." Repeat.

(10) Take a deep breath and count silently to five, hold for a count of five, then exhale for a count of five. Repeat, increasing by two counts each time for as long as you can continue.

(11) Take a deep breath, and, without opening the mouth, hum for as long as you can sustain a strong sound. Hold your hands against your throat and diaphragm. Repeat with the mouth open. *Note:* Do not strain. No sound should be produced beyond the point where it comes easily. Holding your hands against your throat and diaphragm will help you to know when strain is about to occur.

(12) Repeat exercise 4 until you have achieved a completely relaxed state. Place your hands on your abdomen, take a deep breath, and exhale as you

shout in short bursts of breath "hah," "hay," "hee." Repeat with "bah," "bay," "bee." Assume the same position, take another deep breath, but this time sustain the vowels instead of cutting them short. See the note in exercise 11 concerning "strain."

Throughout these exercises you have been asked to check yourself against excess tension. Most of us have tensions of which we are not aware, and relieving them is an ever-present problem, in life as well as on the stage. We go about our daily activities—walking, sitting, driving, even lying down—using more than the required energy. We should develop a habit of frequently checking ourselves in whatever we are doing to discover what muscles are unnecessarily tense and then proceed to relax them. We may often find we are holding onto a pencil as if it would jump out of our fingers, or we are walking with tense shoulders or standing with our knees locked, talking with a tight jaw, or reading with a frown.

Routinely checking for tensions and relieving them yields several benefits. Although it may be impossible, onstage or off, to keep tensions from occurring, this habit will induce a state of more general relaxation. Our goal is to be able to eliminate tensions at will—a capacity of great value to the actor, who is always subject to nervous strain. Perhaps most important, finding tensions helps the actor discover his own nervous mannerisms. Different people reveal tensions in different ways—some by contracted muscles, others by random movements. Among the most common movements are shaking the head, pursing the lips, frowning, snapping the fingers, raising the shoulders. Make an inventory of your personal signs of tension, and get rid of them.

You will discover that eliminating tension demands repeated effort and diligent concentration. As you relax one muscle, another tenses in its place; perhaps the process could best be described as "chasing your tensions." Determination and relentless practice may be necessary to achieve success.

Your goal is to develop a "controller" inside yourself who will instantly find the spot of unnecessary tension and as instantly eliminate it. Being free of tension is as equally important when acting scenes of quiet contemplation as when performing climactic scenes of rigorous physical excitement. In the latter case, your natural tendency is to increase the tension; thus, the need for relaxed control is even greater.[4] Incidentally, developing an automatic habit of spotting and removing tension will help you in life as well as on the stage.

JUSTIFYING YOUR EXERCISES

The next group of exercises will provide further practice in physical training. For an actor, the value of exercises increases when they include circumstances to *justify* the action. Exercises that involve the actor's imagination and his internal resources are more profitable than the mere repetition of physical activity.

In performing any action, your gestures and movements should be free and unrestrained. Your "controller" should constantly check your shoulders, where tension most often occurs. François Delsarte, a nineteenth-century Frenchman whose theories for relating body positions and gestures to emotions, attitudes, and ideas were too systematized but not altogether unsound, believed that the shoulders were the most expressive part of the body and that all emotions were first registered there. Tense shoulders will not respond to inner impulses. Arm movements should come effortlessly from the shoulders. Many young actors tend to gesture with the forearms only, holding the elbows close to their body. Be sure the wrists are free from excess tension, but not limp. In a walk free of tension, the legs swing freely from the pelvis, and the knees are relaxed.

EXERCISE

(1) Believe you are picking apples from branches that can be reached only by standing on your toes and extending your arms to their utmost. To avoid bruising the apples, place each one carefully in a basket on the ground. Let your imagination bring this situation to life. Your objective is not to *pretend* you are picking apples. Let your imagination make the tree and the apples true, and let it compel you to purposeful action. Check frequently to discover and eliminate excess tension.

(2) Supply additional circumstances that will justify the action to an even greater extent. Pick the apples for a number of different purposes:

As if you were a horticultural student hoping to win a prize at the state fair.
As if you were stealing apples from a neighbor's backyard.
As if you were preparing a basket of fruit to take to a sick friend.
As if your father had forced you to pick a bushel of apples before he would let you take the car.
As if you were Eve picking apples in the Garden of Eden.

(3) Household tasks offer opportunities for exercises in relaxation through justification. Believe that you are

Hanging wallpaper
Painting the ceiling
Putting up window draperies
Scrubbing the floor
Waxing the floor
Shaking throw rugs
Pumping water
Chopping wood
Spading the garden

In every case, supply circumstances to justify the physical task. Wax the floors, and make them shine because your mother-in-law is coming to visit. Chop wood because the temperature is falling below zero, and your wife has pneumonia. Commit yourself completely to the action, using fully all the muscles needed to perform it. Continue frequently to check and eliminate excess tension.

In performing these exercises, and in all other physical activities, strive to make the movements precise and clear, *stripping away whatever is unessential*. Jacques Lecoq, whose work in mime provides actors with excellent body training, says, "Movement begins first with economy, that minimum of effort for a maximum of result...." One of his general principles is to break movement down to its essentials, which

> involves the ability to separate action into its components. In order to shovel, one: *stands* with the instrument poised, *thrusts* it into the earth, *presses* the blade deeper with one foot, ... *turns* in preparation to one side in order to *throw* the contents of the shovel to the other side. Such is one series of functional gestures. They are executed with precise economy, eliminating any unnecessary movements like shifting of weight, grimacing, wiping hands, hitching trousers, or whatever. Of course, these movements are often a part of real-life shoveling, but they are not needed in order to shovel; there are no slippery shafts or extra hard earth or loose trousers in the simple act.[5]

As a means of making your movements precise and economical, practice analyzing them and breaking them into their components. Then do only what is absolutely necessary. You may be surprised at the strength and clarity you can achieve. Much acting is cluttered with realistic but unessential details.

(4) Athletics offer additional opportunities. Believe that you are

Throwing a baseball
Serving a tennis ball
Kicking a football
Driving a golf ball
Hurling a javelin
Thrusting a foil
Putting a shot
Lifting weights
Punching a bag
Shadow boxing

Again, supply imaginary circumstances in each case. Put your whole body into the action. Check yourself constantly to see that all muscles except those needed to perform the action are relaxed. Concentrate on keeping your face free of tension.

(5) These exercises call for walking (or moving) in various circumstances. Each will require some modification of your natural walk. Again, commit yourself fully, but do not permit excess tension. Supply additional circumstances as needed. Move as if you are

A hunter stalking a deer
A soldier marching in parade
A goose-stepping soldier marching in a parade

A high-fashion model at a showing

A candidate for the title of Miss America parading on the runway

A burglar hugging the sides of the buildings in a dark alley

A trapper on snowshoes

A boy crawling through a low tunnel

A soldier crawling on his stomach under gunfire

A drum major or majorette

A thief forcing a victim to march by holding a revolver against his back

The victim being forced to march

A native balancing a can of water on her head (no fair using your hands)

A guerrilla fighter creeping up on an enemy

(6) In this group of exercises, you will make fuller use of your body by combining movement with inarticulate sounds. Use the widest pitch range and the most varied intonations of which you are capable. Do not constrict the larynx. Your "controller" should continually check for tension in your throat. Your purpose here is not to imitate the sounds and movements of animals but, rather, to realize their quality. Either individuals or groups of two or three may work on these problems. Each participant in every exercise must have clear intentions and adjust to obstacles.

A dog barking

A lion attacking his prey

A crowing rooster (Be sure to play an intention.)

A hissing snake

A meowing cat

A howling wolf

A soldier at bayonet drill (In training for a bayonet charge, recruits are required to make frightening sounds and use fearful facial expressions to intimidate the enemy. This follows a primitive practice, in which warriors going into battle painted their faces in grotesque patterns and made terrifying noises. These trainees are acting, for they are attempting to convince themselves and their "audience" that they are capable of winning the battle. Their intention justifies both their speech and their action.)

NOTES   1. For a description of some of the possible choices in physical training, see "The Acting Issue," *The Drama Review* 16 (March 1972).

2. Jerzy Grotowski, *Towards a Poor Theatre* (New York: Simon & Schuster, 1968), p. 185.

3. For a more detailed description of correct posture, see Arthur Lessac, *The Use and Training of the Human Voice* (New York: Drama Book Specialists, 1967).

4. See David Magarshack, "Introduction," *Stanislavsky on the Art of the Stage* (New York: Hill and Wang, 1961), pp. 44–45.

5. Bari Rolfe, "The Mime of Jacques Lecoq," *The Drama Review* 16 (March 1972):37.

CHAPTER 6

DIRECTING YOUR ATTENTION

We have now learned that concentration helps the actor to relax by properly channeling his energies toward the accomplishment of his purpose. It is also the principal means of commanding the attention of the audience, which is one of the actor's primary responsibilities. If the audience hears what the actor wants it to hear and sees what he wants it to see during every moment of performance, he has laid the foundation for a job well done. On the other hand, if the audience's attention wanders casually around the stage or strays to other points in the auditorium, the actor will have little chance of success, no matter what the other virtues of his performance may be. And his chances will be even slimmer if the attention of the spectators drifts to personal matters that have no connection with the production.

Fortunately, the audience is likely to be interested in whatever interests the actor. *Attention demands attention.* When you are walking down the street and see a number of people looking up at a high building, you are either greatly preoccupied or surpassingly self-satisfied if you do not try to find out what is attracting their attention.

But concentrating, like "just relaxing," is easier to talk about than to do. Too many young actors are like the fellow described by Stephen Leacock who jumped on his horse and rode off in all directions. Their attention is scattered to all points of the compass. Their minds wander from their particular action to what they think the audience is thinking about them, to what is going on offstage, to what their next lines are, to where they cross next, to the difficult scene that looms in the next act, to whether someone else is going to break up, and so on. They do well to focus 10 percent of their attention on anything related to the action they are trying to play or the character they are trying to create. Thus 90 percent of their mental energy is dissipated.

An actor can make full use of his talent only by learning to concentrate his energies. *"Creativeness on the stage, whether during the preparation of a part or during its repeated performance, demands complete concentration of all his physical and inner nature, the participation of all his physical and inner faculties.*"[1] Successful actors achieve maximum concentration. They find ways to control their attention in spite of the pressure of the audience, the distraction of backstage activities, and the mechanical demands of the role. The ability to concentrate, then, is an additional specific skill that an actor must possess. Like most other acting skills, the technique for marshaling the forces of concentration and knowing where to direct one's attention can be attained only through hard work.

EXERCISE

Any activity that requires concentration, especially in the presence of distracting influences, is excellent discipline for the actor. A person training for the stage needs to develop his power of attention through increasingly complicated exercises. Their value is derived only when they are practiced regularly over a period of time. No exercise has served its purpose until it can be done satisfactorily with a minimum of effort. Students of Stanislavski suggest the following kinds of activity for developing an ability to concentrate:

(1) Read expository material in the presence of a group that constantly tries to interrupt and distract. Hold yourself responsible for remembering each detail you have read.

(2) Solve mathematical problems under the same conditions.

(3) Memorize a passage of prose or poetry under the same conditions.

(4) With a group sitting in a circle, one person says any word that comes into his head. The second repeats the word and adds another that has no logical relation. The next person repeats the two words and adds a third. The process continues around and around the circle until no one is able to repeat the entire series. Anyone who fails is eliminated. The exercise provides training in both concentration and memory.

(5) Under similar circumstances, play a game of numbers. The numbers may be unrelated, or you may progress by having each person add four or seven, eleven or nineteen. The game can become quite challenging.

(6) Do Rapoport's "Mirror Exercise," in which "two people ... stand opposite each other; one makes a movement, the other copies him exactly as in a mirror. The director of the group looks on and points out any errors."[2] Do the exercise first with abstract, nonrepresentational movements. Then do it performing realistic physical tasks such as sewing on a button, manicuring your nails, and applying makeup. By using a prearranged signal, the "director" indicates that the initiator and the mirror image should change roles. The participants should not break the movement when the change occurs. After some practice, the two actors will develop a rapport in which neither seems to initiate the movement. They will feel they are moving simultaneously under the direction of some inner impulse.

(7) Extend the above exercise into a "Sound Mirror," in which, along with the movements, the first person utters gibberish, which the other repeats accurately.

(8) Concentrate on coordination of arm movements. With the left arm fully extended, continue making a large circle in the air; with the right arm, continue making a square by extending it straight out from the shoulder, then up, and then to the side. Once coordination is established, reverse the arms, making the circle with the right arm and the square with the left. You may find this exercise surprisingly difficult.

A scene from the New York Shakespeare Festival production of "Sweat," one of the plays and skits that were a part of *Spunk*. Study the picture as an example of concentration of attention and the physical representation of emotional involvement. (Photo by Martha Swope.)

(9) Do a "Copy Exercise," in which one of the group performs a sequence of simple actions such as entering a room, removing a coat, getting something to eat from the refrigerator, and sitting down to read. Others concentrate on watching, and then repeat the movements in exact detail and with the same tempo-rhythms. If available, use video equipment, so each actor can see for himself how accurately he has observed and repeated the movements.

CONCENTRATING ON ACTION

Much of this book has been devoted to the importance of action. In earlier exercises, you have been asked to write down—make a score of—the physical actions you would undertake if you were in the situation of an imaginary character. Actions are tangible and specific for both the actor and the audience, bringing a character to life and revealing the dramatic events of the play. Since they are never divorced from some desire, their advantage lies not just in the actions themselves but also in the meaning and feelings they have the power to evoke. Carrying out physical or psychophysical actions also gives the actor something on which to focus his concentration. A student will make scant progress toward refining his skills as an actor if he cannot focus his attention totally on completing a simple stage task.

Good plays are filled with opportunities for concentrating attention on such actions. In *The Crucible,* by Arthur Miller, Sarah Good and Tituba huddle in a cold cell in the Salem jail trying to sleep. The actions that satisfy our desire to keep warm in winter are so common that every actor should be able to commit "all of his physical and inner faculties" to performing them. From such commitment comes intense concentration that will help secure the attention, deepen the understanding, and trigger the emotional response of the audience.

Other examples abound. In the opening scene of *Romeo and Juliet,* the Capulet servants make faces and "bite their thumbs" at the servants of the Montagues for the purpose of insulting them and inciting them to a quarrel. In *Ceremonies in Dark Old Men,* by Lonne Elder III, Mr. Parker spends his time loafing in his barber shop (he never has a customer) and playing checkers with a neighbor, while his daughter Adele supports him and her grown-up brothers. Late in the afternoon, he gets out the checkers for another quick game before Adele comes home from work. He concentrates on setting up the game, beating Mr. Jenkins, and watching the door for his daughter's return. In *A Doll's House,* by Henrik Ibsen, Nora wants to keep her husband from going to the mailbox, knowing he will find a letter that may ruin their marriage. She dances a tarantella to keep his mind from the mail as long as possible. Lady Macbeth, in her great sleepwalking scene, concentrates on removing the bloody signs of guilt from her hands. It is said the French actress Rachel attempted to lick off the blood with her tongue instead of rubbing it away, proving again that personal choices within the given circumstances of the script individualize the interpretation of a role.

Yes, good dramatists provide ample chances for actors to concentrate their attention on performing physical action. Sometimes the action is to satisfy a simple desire, such as Sarah Good's wish to keep warm, and sometimes it is to satisfy a wish, such as Nora's, complicated by emotional frustration and deep psychological need. Even when the dramatist has not directly provided it, however, the actor's task is to find a logical pattern of action to satisfy the pressing needs of his character. Good actors and directors display great imagination in inventing physical action organic to the character and the situation.

EXERCISE

Learning to act is an accumulative process. Return to any of the earlier exercises for actions and intentions. Work until you can repeat the exercise without any feeling of distraction from outside influences and until you are satisfied that every bit of your energy—all of your physical and inner faculties—is concentrated on carrying out the action. More problems to help you work on concentrating your attention on physical action follow. Plan and rehearse a sequence of actions for these situations. Supply additional circumstances, giving yourself specific details that will lead you to believe what you are doing.

Write out a score. Be sure each series of actions is structured with a beginning, a middle, and an end. State an intention that you must accomplish. Perform with the greatest possible economy, discarding any details that do not help in achieving your purpose. Remember that you must complete each action and intention before you move on to the next one.

(1) You are visiting a museum, and you accidentally break a valuable antique vase.
(2) You are sitting on a park bench in a strange city feeding crumbs to the pigeons.
(3) You are searching for a lost article that is very important to you.
(4) Late on a cold winter night, you are standing on a street corner waiting for a bus.
(5) You are packing your suitcase in preparation for running away from home.
(6) You are soaking and bandaging a painfully swollen ankle.
(7) You are bailing water from a leaking boat.
(8) You are administering first aid to someone who has been injured in an accident. Seek the help of another actor to serve as the victim.
(9) You are taking your first steps after a serious illness.
(10) You are searching for interesting shells along the seashore.
(11) You are stranded alone on a deserted island and are trying to attract the attention of a plane flying overhead.

CONCENTRATING ON OTHER ACTORS

The actor must be able to concentrate on his character's physical actions while simultaneously listening to other actors in the scene and observing their actions. We have learned that he should engage in a transaction with the other players and attempt to influence them, yielding to or resisting their influence in turn. The "connection" established by this process is one of the actor's surest sources of stimulation and leads to a rewarding theatre experience for the audience.

Drama is fundamentally about conflict, about one character's attempt to force his will on another. The audience becomes interested in the ups and downs of the struggle, the suspense of which is resolved when finally the protagonist either succeeds or fails. Shakespeare's plays, as complex as they are, still center around elemental conflicts of will. *King Lear* begins with Lear's attempt to force his will on his daughters by requiring extravagant declarations of love from them. Othello's tragedy comes from Iago's determination to ruin his contentment, and *The Taming of the Shrew* is a straightforward clash between the robust wills of Katharina and Petruchio. In *The Winter's Tale,* Hermione's honor and her life depend on her ability to convince her husband he is wrong in suspecting her of being unfaithful.

The example mentioned earlier from *A Doll House,* in which Nora dances to keep Helmer from going to the mailbox, will serve as a vivid description of a transaction. The actress playing Nora concentrates on the action of the dance, but at the same time she must be concerned with how she is influencing her husband. The moment she perceives that he may be thinking of checking on his mail, her tarantella becomes more animated. Especially in rehearsal, a director might improve Nora's performance by telling the actor playing Helmer to go to the mailbox as soon as Nora's dance fails to hold his attention. Nora's intentions are inextricably linked with Helmer's actions, and the audience's perception of this connection will greatly enhance its appreciation of the scene.

"Character connection" is accomplished through concentration. The actor concentrates on using actions and lines to get what his character wants from the other actors in the play. He seeks to arouse honest feelings and stimulate genuine responses in the other actors. In this exciting way, the imaginary world of the play merges with the real life of the actor. An actor must constantly strive to influence the behavior of his fellow actors, for he needs their real responses in order to build a believable characterization of his own.

The life of a performed play is the sum of the transactions among its actors, and the example from *A Doll House,* though striking, can be extrapolated to the other plays just mentioned. For example, in the opening of *Romeo and Juliet,* the Capulet servants concentrate on making the Montagues angry. They actually make every effort appropriate to the characters and the situation (we must always accept the given circumstances!) to provoke to anger the actors playing opposite them. In *The Winter's Tale,* the actress playing Hermione must strive to win real sympathy from the actor playing Leontes. The circumstances demand that Leontes refuse her. If the actor's own feelings incline him to take her back, it will make his decision as the character more difficult, provoking an inner conflict that heightens the impact of the scene.

To excite an audience, actors must excite one another. Stanislavski wrote: "Infect your partner! Infect the person you are concentrating on! Insinuate yourself into his very soul, and you will find yourself the more infected for doing so. And if you are infected everyone else will be even more infected."[3]

MAKING AN ACTION OF SPEECH

Speaking is of great importance in the actor's transaction. Both in life and onstage, we use words as a means of getting what we want, as a way of realizing our intentions. We use words to ask, beg, demand, plead, explain, persuade, woo, threaten—for countless purposes. Consideration of the particular problems of interpreting lines (an important part of the actor's job) comes later, but, at this point in your training, you need to understand how to incorporate speech in the overall task of performing. A mere reading of the lines, no matter how intelligent or how beautiful, is only a part of the actor's responsibility. No matter how glibly and mellifluously delivered, all dialogue will appear superfluous, unless it is demanded by the action of the play.

The basic function of stage speech is to help the actor accomplish his purpose. The actor has already been admonished to know what that purpose is at all times. When he is called on to speak, he must also know how each word he utters relates to it. He must have this relationship clear in his mind for every moment of the play, both during rehearsal and in performance. Acting is not only believing, it is also thinking! Concentrating on speaking smoothly or beautifully will interfere with thinking about the action of the play. The actor must discover a genuine need to use the playwright's words and train himself to keep his thoughts alive as he speaks them. He must particularly guard against the abandonment of live thinking during repetitious rehearsals.

It should be clear by now that, in terms of this book's methodology, *speech is an action*. Speaking is doing. In some primitive languages, the word for acting and speaking is the same. The actors words are important tools for engaging in the transaction of the moment. Simply saying "good morning" has no justification on the stage (or in real life, for that matter) unless the speaker says these words to influence the listener in some way or other. The greeting may "infect" the listener with casual indifference, deep love, or intense hate. It may say any one of a dozen things, each intended to evoke a different response. It may say, for example:

I am in a friendly, leisurely mood. Let's have a chat.
I am perfectly friendly but in a hurry. Please be brief in what you have to say.
I got up on the wrong side of the bed. Don't say a word.
The occasion demands a civil greeting. Don't presume it means anything more.

In each case, the actor concentrates his attention on influencing the behavior of the listener.

A transaction, of course, demands a two-way influence. The actor concentrates not only on *affecting* others but also on *listening* to what is said to him, and he resists or yields to the desires of the speaker. A special ability to *listen* is often mentioned as one of the specific skills required of the actor. The actor must be able to hear and respond to everything said at each rehearsal and performance as if it had never been heard before. He creates what William Gillette aptly called "the illusion of the first time." It is the illusion, necessary both to him and to the audience, that no matter how long he has worked on a part—no matter how often he has rehearsed or performed it—each time is a new and fresh transaction. A close connection between and among actors is necessary for creating this illusion. In this way, live feelings are aroused each time, and, in a sense, the experience really is new.

EXERCISE

Do a "greeting exercise," the object of which is to infect another actor, so he will respond as you would like him to. You are limited to one phrase of greeting and one physical action. You should carefully choose your intention to evoke the desired response, and your partner should not know what your intention is, nor the imagined circumstances in which you are playing it. Possible situations might be:

Intimate friends who have not seen each other for a long time
A former husband and wife meeting socially for the first time after an unpleasant divorce
A peasant meeting a king
Two prima donnas who habitually try to avoid speaking to each other

When your partner has adapted to your greeting, you should adapt to his response and continue to improvise a short scene. Discuss later whether your partner responded as you desired.

A short dialogue from a scene we discussed earlier from the beginning of *When You Comin Back, Red Ryder?* gives both actors an excellent opportunity to speak for a purpose. The scene, recall, is a diner on the desert in southern New Mexico in the late sixties. Stephen/Red has worked the night shift and is waiting for Angel to relieve him. She is five minutes late.

ANGEL: Good mornin, Stephen. (*Stephen does not look at her, but glances at the clock and makes a strained sucking sound through his teeth—a habit he has throughout—and flips the newspaper back up to his face. Unperturbed, Angel proceeds behind the counter.*) I'm sorry I'm late. My mom and me, our daily fight was a little off schedule today. (*Stephen loudly shuffles the paper, sucks his teeth.*) I said I'm sorry, Stephen. God. I'm only six minutes late.

STEPHEN: Only six minutes, huh? I got six minutes to just hang around this joint when my shift's up, right? This is really the kinda dump I'm gonna hang around in my spare time, ain't it?

ANGEL: Stephen, that's a paper cup you got your coffee in. *(Stephen is entrenched behind his newspaper.)*

STEPHEN: Clark can afford it, believe me.

ANGEL: That's not the point, Stephen.

STEPHEN: Oh no? You're gonna tell me the point though, right? Hold it—lemme get a pencil.

ANGEL: The point is that if you're drinking your coffee here, you're supposed to use a glass cup, and if it's to go, you're supposed to get charged fifteen instead of ten and ya get one of those five cent paper cups to take it with you with. That's the point, Stephen.

STEPHEN: Yeah, well I'm takin it with me, so where's the problem?

The intention of each of the characters is clear. Angel wants to gloss over her lateness. Stephen/Red wants to make her as miserable as possible. The playwright, Mark Medoff, is exceptionally aware of the importance of physical actions, and he supplies an excellent set of them for Stephen/Red. Angel, on the other hand, must devise her own from the given circumstances of arriving at work and settling in behind the counter.

Even though the intention of each character emerges clearly from this scene, the actor will want to state the intention in each line in his own words. They might be stated as

ANGEL: I must evoke a normal, friendly response from Stephen.

STEPHEN: I must make her admit that she's late.

ANGEL: I must gain his sympathy.

STEPHEN: I must punish her.

ANGEL: I must turn the tables on him.

STEPHEN: I must belittle her accusation.

ANGEL: I must not let him off the hook.

STEPHEN: I want to shut her up.

A few moments later, a dialogue between Stephen/Red and Angel does not provide so clear a reason for the lines:

ANGEL: I saw ya circle somethin in the gift book the other mornin.

STEPHEN: What *gift* book?

ANGEL: The Raleigh *coupon* gift book.

STEPHEN: Hey—com'ere. *(Angel advances close to him. He snatches the pencil from behind her ear and draws a circle on the newspaper.)* There. Now I just drew a circle on the newspaper. That mean I'm gonna get me that car?

ANGEL: Come on, Stephen, tell me. What're ya gonna get?

STEPHEN: Christ, whudduyou care what I'm gonna get?

ANGEL: God, Stephen, I'm not the FBI or somebody. What are you so upset about? Just tell me what you're gonna get.

STEPHEN: *(Mumbling irascibly.)* Back pack.

How does Stephen want this information to affect Angel? What is Angel's purpose in asking him in the first place? Does she suspect that he wants to leave and fear that she will be left completely alone with no prospect of anybody her age to share her life? Does Stephen understand her fear and lead her on to make her suffer? Note that the playwright has provided fewer physical actions in the given circumstances. The actors must develop their own intentions, create imaginative physical actions to support them, and concentrate their attention on influencing the behavior of the other in order to complete the transaction demanded by the scene.

Of course, in developing a role completely, an actor may be certain of the action of each line only after he understands the desires that motivate the character's total behavior. Understanding this motivating desire is a problem we will engage in with Part III, which considers the actor in relation to the play. At this time, you should continue to work on small scenes without assuming the responsibility of finding their total meaning in relationship to the rest of the play.

EXERCISE

Using the example given from *When You Comin Back, Red Ryder?* as a model, work improvisationally in the following situations. Your intention here is to influence your partner—to elicit specific responses from him—and his intention is to influence you. This means a transaction, a give-and-take that is the essence of a lively stage performance. It means that you are sensitive to every detail of your partner's presence, that you hear and understand what he is saying, and that he, in turn, is equally aware of you.

Remember that these improvisations are free only within certain limitations. They require thoughtful preparation. Your intention—the response you want to provoke—should be determined and recorded in advance. You and your partner in the exercise should offer additional circumstances to supplement those briefly given here, and your behavior should be appropriate within those circumstances. The exercise should be structured into its three parts, and the "key lines" should be used in the beginning unit. You might do well to determine in advance other key lines to be made part of the other units.

This kind of preparation gives you direction and purpose, and it does not eliminate spontaneity and immediate adaptations. It is like playing any game. You know the rules and the objectives, but you do not know what offensive actions your partner will attempt or what defenses he will use against your attacks.

(1) In *The Voice of the Prairie,* by John Olive, a young man, Davey, is hiding in a barn that belongs to Frankie and her boorish, drunken father. Frankie discovers Davey in the barn and tackles him. After a struggle and a few tests he devises, Davey determines that Frankie is blind. Their key lines are

FRANKIE: You scared? Scared of a blind girl? Come on!

DAVEY: I can't.

(2) In *In the Wine Time,* by Ed Bullins, Lou and Cliff are a young married couple sitting on the street in front of their house on a hot summer night. They are drinking wine, and their conversation alternates between bantering and wrangling. Their key lines are

LOU: What should I do when I find lipstick on your shirt ... shades I don't use? *(Silence.)* What should I say when I see you flirtin' with the young girls on the street and with my friends? *(Silence.)*

CLIFF: *(Tired.)* Light me a cigarette, will ya?

(3) *The Shadow Box,* by Michael Cristofer, takes place in a group of cottages where terminal cancer patients can spend some time with their families while they are being kept comfortable until they die. Maggie cannot accept that her husband, Joe, is dying, and she insists that they should resume a normal life. Their key lines are

MAGGIE: We'll go home tomorrow. I got another ticket. We can get a plane tomorrow.

JOE: No. This is all. This is all we got.

(4) In *Who's Afraid of Virginia Woolf?,* by Edward Albee, a married couple has just returned home after a party. Martha wants to continue drinking and having a good time, but George is tired and wants to go to bed. Their key lines are

MARTHA: Come on, make me another drink.

GEORGE: It's two o'clock in the morning.

(5) In *The Woolgatherer,* by William Mastrosimone, Cliff, a truck driver, meets the shy Rose in a department store where she is a clerk. He goes home with her to discover that she lives in an extremely dark apartment with boards covering the one window that could let in some light. He wants to remove the boards, but she prefers the dark. Their key lines are

CLIFF: You're missing out on all that wonderful scenery out there.

ROSE: I go for a lot of walks.

(6) In *Plaza Suite,* by Neil Simon, Jesse, a forty-year-old, self-assured, "Hollywood-mod" bounder calls Muriel, a former high school friend and now a plain, suburban housewife, to meet him at his suite in the Plaza. He wants to seduce her. She is tempted but marshals considerable power to resist. Their key lines are

JESSE: ... Sit down and have a drink.

MURIEL: No, no, I just dropped by to say hello.

(7) In *The Boys Next Door,* by Tom Griffin, the good-natured but mentally marginal Sheila has been "dating" the retarded Norman and has greatly admired a large ring of keys Norman wears attached to his belt. For her birthday, Norman presents her with a box covered with stuck-on bows. She opens it, and inside is her very own ring of keys. Their key lines are

SHEILA: Oh, Norman, keys.

NORMAN: Try them on.

(8) In *Steel Magnolias,* by Robert Harling, the diabetic Shelby begins to slip into insulin shock while having her hair fixed at the beauty shop for her wedding. Her mother, M'Lynn, tries to give her a peppermint candy, then orange juice, which she resists firmly at first before sipping from the glass and slowly returning to normal. Their key lines are

M'LYNN: You need some juice.

SHELBY: Leave me alone.

(9) In *Waiting for Lefty,* by Clifford Odets, Edna tries to get her husband, Joe, to join a strike for higher wages. The time is early post-Depression America, when the labor movement was just getting up steam and when strikes often meant violence, hunger, and retribution. Their key lines are

EDNA: My God, Joe—the world is supposed to be for all of us.

JOE: Don't insult me. One man can't make a strike.

(10) In *Fences,* by August Wilson, Troy gathers enough courage to tell his wife, Rose, that he has fathered a child by another woman. It is difficult. He tries to get her to understand what he is saying without actually saying the words. Finally he tells her, straightforwardly, what the situation is. Their key lines are

TROY: I'm gonna be a daddy. I'm gonna be somebody's daddy.

ROSE: Ain't nothing you can say, Troy. Ain't no way of explaining that.

(11) In *The Zoo Story,* by Edward Albee, two men quarrel violently over which one has the right to occupy a particular park bench. Their key lines are

PETER: This is my bench, and you have no right to take it away from me.

JERRY: Fight for it, then. Defend yourself; defend your bench.

(12) In *A Coupla White Chicks Sitting Around Talking,* by John Ford Noonan, Maude comes in with great dismay to tell Hannah Mae that she has consummated an adulterous affair with Hannah Mae's husband. Much to her surprise, Hannah Mae takes the news very calmly. Their key lines are

HANNAH MAE: The only thing I feel, Honey, is closer to you.

MAUDE: Get those hands off me! I already had his on me, I don't need yours.

(13) In *Album,* by David Rimmer, Trish and Peggy are sixteen and best friends. Trish thinks Peggy has had her first sexual experience, and she wants her to tell her about it. In fact, Peggy is also a virgin. Their key lines are

TRISH: You look the same to me. Didya feel different after you did it?

PEGGY: Will you leave me alone?

(14) In *Dutchman,* by LeRoi Jones, the scene is a subway car. A white woman, a stranger sitting beside a young black man, tries to tempt him erotically. Their key lines are

LULA: *(Grabbing for his hands, which he draws away.)* Come on, Clay. Let's rub bellies on the train.... Get up, Clay. Dance with me, Clay.

CLAY: Lula! Sit down, now. Be cool.

EXERCISE

(1) In *Kataki,* by Shimon Wincelberg, an American soldier during World War II parachutes to a lonely island inhabited by a single Japanese soldier. They are enemies, their only weapon is a knife, and they have no common language for communication. Gradually they learn that they must become friends or die. Improvise scenes from this situation with both actors speaking only gibberish, so neither will understand the words of the other.

(2) Act II of *The Kingdom of God,* by G. Martinez Sierra, takes place in a "maternity home (for women who have 'come to grief') which has been established in some old noble mansion in the north of Castile." Among the inmates is the Dumb Girl, strongly possessive of her baby, who utters only strange unintelligible sounds. The Mother Superior attempts in several languages and through gestures to find out who the girl is and where she came from. Improvise the scene with the Mother Superior using gibberish, so the Dumb Girl actually will not understand what is said to her.

(3) Return to any of the situations in the previous group of exercises, and improvise them in gibberish. This kind of improvisation can be made a valuable part of your work, creating an increased awareness of the function of lines in accomplishing intentions. Too often actors speak their lines while concentrating too much on the words and not enough on their purpose. Overcome immediately any feeling of ridiculousness that may occur in speaking gibberish. Remember when an actor is working with a purpose, he is ridiculous only when he is afraid of being ridiculous.

NOTES

1. Constantin Stanislavski, *Stanislavski's Legacy,* ed. Elizabeth Reynolds Hapgood (New York: Theatre Arts Books, 1958), p. 174.

2. I. Rapoport, "The Work of the Actor," in Toby Cole, ed., *Acting: A Handbook of the Stanislavski Method* (New York: Lear Publishers, 1947), p. 38.

3. Constantin Stanislavski, *Building a Character* (New York: Theatre Arts Books, 1949), p. 118.

CHAPTER 7

SEEING THINGS

The study of human nature is a major lifelong concern of the actor. The great actors of France have long been famous for their ability to dazzle an audience by means of their technical perfection and the incisiveness of their character portrayal. One of the greatest was Constant Coquelin, creator of the role of Cyrano de Bergerac. Coquelin wrote, "It is one of the necessary qualities of an actor to be able to seize and note at once anything that is capable of reproduction on the stage."[1]

"Seizing and noting," which we call *observation,* is another necessary skill. We have already noted that an actor may well not have experienced everything necessary to play a broad range of characters. He must constantly augment this experience by observing the world around him. He must perpetually enlarge his impressions of life, for these are the materials from which he creates. He must make it a practice to seize and note, as Coquelin suggests, not only anything that can be reproduced onstage but also anything that reveals truth or provides understanding about what may be produced there.

The technique of observation begins with a conscious effort to develop fuller awareness of happenings around us, a fine-tuned sensitivity to what we see, hear, taste, feel, and smell. Jean Louis Barrault is fond of telling a story about Charles Dullin, a noted French director whose productions were always vital and vibrant. Dullin himself was marvelously childlike in his appreciation of everything in his environment.

Once Dullin was asked, "How can you stare at the same scenery every day? You stare out of the train window as if seeing the scenery for the first time, even though you travel on this same train practically every day."

"Because," he responded, "every night, before I go to sleep, I 'kill' the old Charles Dullin. Each morning, I am reborn." This was Dullin's method for maintaining his powers of observation: Each day he saw the world anew through the eyes of a child.

Our senses are so intensely bombarded by our comprehensive surroundings in the modern world that we tend to take most things for granted. We do not really look at people's faces, hear their voices, listen to sounds, nor even taste the food for which we have paid dearly in an expensive restaurant. This indifference is movingly expressed by Emily in *Our Town,* by Thornton Wilder. Returning from the dead to relive a childhood experience, she sees people going insensitively about their everyday tasks. She says of her family at breakfast: "They don't even take time to look at one another." The actor must learn to observe familiar things as if he had never seen them before, and he must remember the experience. Through remembered observation, he will build a stockpile of materials from which he can construct performances. But, more importantly, he will enrich his life, and an enriched life will increase his chances of being an insightful actor.

Observation is both intellectual and sensory. The mind tells us the uses of things, classifies them, analyzes them in any one of a number of ways, and permits us to retain them in memory. Recognizing that a flower is a carnation and not a buttercup, is red and not yellow, and is a variety of the clove, pink, spicy-scented, double-blossomed carnation used for bouquets and buttonholes is an intellectual response. We perceive the flower, however, through the senses. Experiencing a carnation is not just knowing about it. It is seeing its color, smelling its fragrance, holding it, touching it. Fortunately our memory can retain sensory as well as intellectual experience, and sensory perception is the bedrock of the technique of observation. The actor must be able to recall not only his knowledge of the carnation but also the way it affected his senses.

EXERCISE

(1) A first step in developing a technique of observation is to train yourself to experience the regular events of everyday life. To get into the habit, take time to perceive fully these common activities. Remember that observation involves all the senses—sight, hearing, taste, touch, and smell. Pretend you are

Peeling and eating an orange, apple, peach, or pear
Shaving
Brushing your teeth
Manicuring your nails
Putting on your shoes
Putting on and taking off a coat
Hearing a bird call, a siren, a clock ticking
Arranging a bouquet of flowers
Tasting a strong cheese
Eating celery, artichokes, corn on the cob
Eating marshmallows, caramels
Cleaning a fish
Cleaning a pan with a scouring pad
Sandpapering a piece of furniture

Walking barefoot on wet grass, hot sand, cold tile
Pouring and drinking a cup of hot coffee
Drinking cold lemonade
Smelling and tasting vinegar, lemon juice
Warming yourself by an open fire
Cracking and eating pecans, walnuts, peanuts

(2) Concentrate on these observations until you can repeat them without the object. One caution: Thinking of this as an exercise in pantomime may lead you to concentrate on only the visual aspect, but your objective is to re-create the entire sensory experience. You should not only see the orange and manipulate it accurately but also should handle it (texture, weight, form), smell it, taste it, and feel it in your mouth. See whether you can elicit genuine sensory responses to imaginary objects. This part of the exercise has two important purposes: It trains you to observe more closely, and it develops your *sensory memory*.

(3) Spend a period of time each day making a careful observation. Sharpen all your senses. Concentrate for one week on taste experiences, another week on touch. After five weeks, begin again.

(4) Set a time limit. Observe an object for sixty seconds. Put it away and see how much you can recall. Check for accuracy. Do it again.

(5) Observe a classmate for sixty seconds. Without looking, describe the person as accurately and with as much detail as you can.

(6) Select a classmate to observe, then re-create the entire sensory experience of that person's

Walking into class
Sitting down
Taking off a hat and coat
Leaving class when the period is over

(7) Write a five-hundred-word "biography" of a perfect stranger, beginning your narrative by observing the person's hands and drawing inferences about his or her character from the type of shoes, watch, or glasses he or she wears.

(8) Close your eyes. Can you remember the following details about the room you are in?

What color are the walls?
How many windows are in the room?
What color is the rug?
How high is the ceiling?

(9) Sharpen your sensitivity to different times of day and night and weather conditions. With all your senses, observe:

A rainy day
Summer noon
Autumn evening
Midnight
Winter morning before daylight
Late summer afternoon
Winter sunlight
Spring morning

Combine these conditions with the following locales:

Home
A city park
A busy street corner in a big city
The country
A lake
The seashore
A strange town

Use your sensory memory to re-create the feelings that these various combinations arouse in you under conditions different from those that evoked them. Find a short scene or invent a sequence of actions appropriate to these feelings. Perform the actions using your sensory memory to create the atmosphere. Move and speak in harmony with the atmosphere you create; imagine the air is filled with it and you are moving and speaking through it.

(10) The following problem consists of picking up the listed object, carrying it, and disposing of it. Your work should be based on direct observation and sensory memory. Be sure your whole body is involved in performing the action; do not act with just your hands and your arms. Remember the standing instruction to plan your action in three parts. Each exercise should have a definite beginning that makes the situation clear, a development into a conflict with an obstacle, and an ending with some form of resolution. Find the correct tempo-rhythms for each part.

A piece of ice
A very hot dish
A piece of sticky candy
A live snake
A dog that has been struck by a car
A live fish
A worm
A crown on a cushion
A bloody knife
A lighted candle
A bucket full of water
A cross

Three heavy suitcases
Two overfilled bags of groceries
A person who has fainted

Increasing your awareness of what goes on around you and developing your sensory memory are your first steps toward sharpening the technique of observation. Once you have command of the technique, you will find that it

Students performing *Big River.* Directed by James Miller, scene design by Pat Atkinson, costumes designed by James Miller, lighting by Dan Warrick. Notice the relaxation of the two actors in the foreground despite their obvious physical involvement in the moment. (Photo courtesy of University of Missouri-Columbia Summer Repertory Theatre.)

provides you with three essential kinds of information that can be used as raw material for building a character. They are

1. Characteristics of human behavior (manners of walking, talking, gesturing, and so forth) that may be precisely reproduced on the stage

2. Other human characteristics, incidents, and situations that, when filtered through your imagination, may be adapted for use on the stage

3. Abstract qualities of animals, plants, and inanimate objects that can help stimulate your imagination about how characters *might* look or behave on the stage

In a description of her working methods, Helen Hayes gave examples of these uses of observation. After defining acting talent as "a peculiarly alert awareness of other people," she continued:

> When I was preparing for my role of the duchess in Anouilh's *Time Remembered,* I had some difficulty capturing the spirit of the role, until . . . I heard some music written by Giles Farnaby for the virginal—you know, one of those sixteenth-century instruments. . . . That old duchess, I told myself, is like the music, light, dainty, period, pompous, tinkling. And, poor me, I'd been playing her like a bass drum. I had one scene in Victoria Regina that I played like one of my poodles. . . . I had a poodle that used to just sit, and he'd look almost intoxicated when I'd say, "Oh, Turvey, you are the most beautiful dog," . . . and believe me every night for a thousand and some performances of that play, I saw that poodle. . . . There was a famous moment in *Coquette*—I didn't know what really true way to accept the news that my lover had been shot and was dead. . . . I remembered a picture on the front of one of the tabloids—the *News* or the *Mirror*—of a mother standing over her son's grave. He was a gangster, in Chicago, and this coffin was being lowered, and this woman was standing there and she was holding herself as if she'd had a terrible, terrible pain in her insides. And I knew that this was the complete, complete reaction to something like this.[2]

Explore these outcomes of observing through the following illustrations, explanations, and exercises.

Let's return to the hypothetical production of *Romeo and Juliet* for which we were rehearsing a few chapters ago. Suppose you are now cast not as Juliet or as Romeo but as Juliet's old nurse. Let's see how *observation* can help in understanding, and ultimately in believing, this character.

OBSERVING PEOPLE

What kind of person is Juliet's nurse?
She is old.
She is large.
She is short of breath.
She is good-natured.

She likes to tease.
She loves Juliet.
She is talkative.
She likes to put on airs.
She is bawdy.
She is an opportunist.
She is without real moral fiber.

Obviously this role is a considerable stretch for the young actor. Although the process of self-exploration will reveal at least the germ of these characteristics within your own experience (indeed, you will never come to believe the character otherwise), here is an acting problem for which your own resources will need to be reinforced. How can you create a picture of this vulgar, jovial old soul?

One relatively simple answer would be to find some person like this nurse. Observe her carefully. "Seize and note" the way she rolls from side to side when she walks, the way she pants after any physical exertion, and the way she rolls her head and holds in her stomach when she laughs. Copy these mannerisms, and practice them until you can reproduce them accurately. If you keep practicing until you know these external manifestations are true, you may be surprised to learn that you have also grasped many internal aspects of the character.

Unfortunately, you probably do not have among your friends even a reasonable facsimile of Juliet's nurse. You will rarely play a character for whom you can find a counterpart living in the next block. Developing a character through observation usually consists of piecing together details supplied by a number of different persons and, very possibly, noted at widely different times. Observing the people you come in contact with must be a continual process. The way your geology professor smacks his lips to express approval may be a mannerism exactly suited to the next role you will play. Using your newly heightened powers of observation, you may have noted that the way a casual acquaintance sips a soda reveals a great deal of his character. File this observation in your memory, for it may later provide the key to understanding a character you portray.

The material for bringing to life such a character as Juliet's nurse will spring not only from observing people while you prepare the role but also from the reservoir of details you have retained from past observations. The mannerisms of a talkative landlady at whose house you roomed three years ago might help you to believe this same quality in the Nurse. Remembering the way a neighbor used to put on airs when she dressed up to go downtown might help you to create the behavior of the Nurse when Juliet sends her forth to find Romeo. And your memory of the way an uncle used to tease you when you were a child might help you to appreciate the pleasure the Nurse derives from nettling Juliet when she returns with Romeo's message.

(1) Each day during the next week, make a special effort to use your powers of observation. Start an observation notebook. Carefully note mannerisms, gestures, and ways of talking, walking, and eating that reveal character traits. Visit a busy railway station, hotel lobby, or some other place where you will have the opportunity to observe people of all ages. Practice reproducing details until you can do them accurately and until you feel you have captured some of the inner quality of the person. Attempt to discover their intentions by observing their physical actions. Prepare a short scene with circumstances leading to action that you believe would be truthful for the character you create from the raw material of your observations.

(2) Observe someone doing a specific job expertly. Study him, and practice until you can perform the job with skill and authority. Observe:

A short-order cook
A barber
A shoeshine boy
A mother bathing a baby
A mother changing a baby's diaper
A golfer driving a golf ball
A tennis player serving a tennis ball
Someone knitting
A potter throwing a vase
Someone shuffling and dealing cards
A juggler

(3) Observe a painting—an original, if you have access to a museum—that reveals character. Re-create with your own body the posture and the facial expression. Make the character move; imagine how he would walk, sit, use his hands. If it is a period picture, read about the manners and customs of the period. Make him speak. Invent a scene in which you can bring him to life in a sequence of actions. Observing paintings of people in earlier times is a particularly helpful source for developing characters in period plays.

(4) Observe a room belonging to an acquaintance or, better yet, to someone you are meeting for the first time. Study the furniture. Speculate on the reasons for its choice and its arrangement. Observe the manner of the decoration. Are the colors carefully planned or haphazard? Is the room neat or disorderly? What feelings does the room evoke in you? What does it tell you about the person who occupies it?

Observe these paintings carefully, noting all external details and what they tell you about characterization. Improvise a scene in which you place one of these characters in imagined circumstances. *El Mocho* (1936) by Peter Hurd. Courtesy of The Art Institute of Chicago (Watson F. Blair Purchase Prize, 1937). *Mary and Elizabeth Royall* (c. 1758) by John Singleton Copley. Courtesy of Museum of Fine Arts, Boston (Julia Knight Fox Fund, 1925).

ADAPTING OBSERVATIONS THROUGH THE IMAGINATION

In the preceding exercises, you were asked to remember or observe, and then repeat, actions you knew to be true of some person. In order to understand these actions fully, you no doubt had to supply circumstances that could account for why the people behaved as they did. Supplying such circumstances involves imagination, and a facile imagination is an invaluable acting tool. For every time you are able to observe human behavior and transfer it directly to the character you are playing, you will encounter a hundred times when your observation will serve only to stimulate your imagination. The actor, therefore, should seize every opportunity to exercise and expand his power of imagination, and one of the best ways to do so is by observing human behavior, then creating circumstances to justify it.

Stanislavski provided a striking illustration. Walking down the street one day, he observed a forlorn-looking woman wheeling a caged bird in a baby carriage. He knew, of course, nothing of the circumstances. Very probably the woman was moving into a new apartment. The carriage was a practical means of transporting her pet bird, and the exhausting job of moving probably accounted for her forlornness. Stanislavski's imagination, however, created circumstances that provided him with a richer understanding of human experience, and his memory recorded the incident to use sometime in developing a character.

He adapted the observed fact in this way: The woman was a widowed mother who a short time before had lost her two children. To dispel her grief, she had directed her affection to the bird, caring for it as if it were a child. Each afternoon she took it for an airing in the carriage exactly as she used to take the children.

Such a combination of observed fact and imaginary circumstances is one of the actor's primary sources of stimulation, and physical objectives in which he can believe spring from it. Think of the number of short scenes based on the incident of the woman and the bird cage you might improvise. Can you see her bathing the bird, feeding the bird, caressing it, talking to it, getting it ready to go for the ride? Many questions will immediately arise, for which your imagination must supply the answers:

How old is the woman?
What does she look like?
What kind of place does she live in?
Is she rich or poor?
What kind of bird does she have?
How long have the children been dead?
How did they die?
What is the bird's name?
Is the substitution of the bird only a temporary outlet, or does it indicate some
    permanent mental derangement?

What attitude does the woman have toward friends who see her behavior with
the bird?

Having answered these and other questions, you can visualize a series of
actions designed to bring this character and this situation to life. In performing
them, you would concentrate on accomplishing these physical objectives so the
action would lead you to believe in the situation and the character. The belief in
turn would produce the desired emotional state. Remember, feeling comes not
directly but through association.

OBSERVATION + IMAGINARY CIRCUMSTANCES

↓

ACTION

↓

BELIEF

↓

FEELING

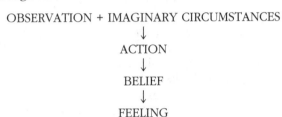

EXERCISE

Make careful observations of human behavior. When you see a situation that
stimulates your imagination, supply circumstances you can use as the basis
for an improvisation. Why, for example, might a sailor in a night club be
dancing with a child's doll? Why might an old woman selling pencils on the
street be reading a report of the New York Stock Exchange? Remember that
the purpose of these imaginary circumstances is to provide a reason for
action. Action means specific physical objectives that show behavior you can
believe of the person observed. Work out the details carefully.

Rehearse the scene until each part seems right and logical. *Warning:* Do
not attempt to substitute a "made-up" situation for the original observation.
Without the observed fact, you have no way of knowing whether your imaginary circumstances are true. *Imagination must have a basis in reality.*

OBSERVING ANIMALS AND OBJECTS

The study of plants, animals, and inanimate objects as a means of understanding a character is a third way an actor may use the technique of observation.
The process involves *abstraction,* a principle in art generally misunderstood by
the lay person but one that for our purpose may be simply explained and
illustrated. *To abstract* means, literally, "to separate, to take away." The actor
applies the principle of abstraction by observing an object for the purpose of
taking away from it ("seizing and noting") qualities that will be useful in
developing a character.

The qualities of elegance, glitter, and aloofness abstracted from the observation of a crystal chandelier might be important elements in coming to
understand some of the characters in Restoration drama. Observing, then

abstracting, the comfortableness, the homeliness, and the unpretentiousness of an old leather chair might provide insight into a character of a completely different kind. The qualities to be abstracted from a gnarled and weather-beaten tree could be an observed fact for developing yet another type of person.

Close observation of an eggplant might help in preparing to play Juliet's nurse. Looking at this vegetable, one is impressed by its bulky form, its grossness, its unvaried purple surface—a growth that has matured in size without acquiring character. On feeling it, one becomes aware of its bland smoothness, and, on cutting it open, one finds the inside to be a yellow-white mass—pliant and spongy—with no core at all.

If an eggplant could walk, it would waddle from side to side; it would have difficulty carrying its bulk; it would perspire, fan itself, and gasp for breath. Its bright purple color, symbolic of royalty and dignity, seems pretentious when everything else belies those qualities (the Nurse putting on airs before Romeo and his friends). Its smoothness suggests a good nature stemming from a lack of principles and its "corelessness" gives insight into the Nurse's lack of moral fiber, both amply suggested by her lines and actions.

People are often compared to animals. We say that a certain young girl is kittenish, that a certain person is as clumsy as a bear, that one man is foxy, another is wolfish, and that still another is a snake in the grass. These comparisons are examples of abstracting an animal's essential qualities and applying them to aspects of human behavior. An actor will find that creating such abstractions from animals is another worthwhile exercise in observation that can provide outstanding raw material for characterizations.

In the motion picture of *The Women,* adapted from the popular play by Clare Boothe, each character was introduced as a different kind of animal. The gossiping, sharp-tongued Sylvia Fowler was a cat. The spreading, complacent Edith Potter was a cow. The vicious, husband-snatching Crystal Allen was presented as a panther.

A more famous example of observing the qualities of animals and applying them to dramatic characters is found in Ben Jonson's *Volpone,* a vicious satire on greed. Each character is appropriately named after some beast of prey. Volpone, or the Fox, is a rich merchant whose ruling passion is greed. Like his namesake, he is also sly and has hit on a scheme of pretending he is dying so his equally rapacious friends will court his favor with extravagant gifts in the hope of being made his heirs. His friends include Corvino, or Little Crow, who offers Volpone his young wife; Corbaccio, or Old Crow, who sniffs at Volpone's body to make sure he is dead; and Voltore, or the Vulture, who is exactly what his name implies. Slyest of all is Mosca, or the Fly, who turns the tables on Volpone by trying to prove him legally dead. Actors performing these roles would certainly want to find true human behavior that could be imaginatively abstracted from observing the behavior of the animal associated with each character.

Returning once again to *Romeo and Juliet,* let's suppose this time you are cast as Juliet's cousin Tybalt. You need look no further than your script for inspiration, for Shakespeare himself has Tybalt compared to an animal three times! Mercutio first refers to him as "more than prince of cats." Later, in challenging him to a duel, Mercutio addresses him as "good king of cats," declaring that he means to take one of Tybalt's nine lives. And after Tybalt has mortally wounded him, Mercutio says he is a "dog, a rat, a mouse, a cat, to scratch a man to death." With this suggestion in the lines, it would be a poor actor who did not search for and exploit the catlike qualities that have motivated Mercutio's comparison.

How might you develop this approach to playing Tybalt? First of all, what is a cat like? The word *kitten* may connote playfulness and cuteness, but isn't the word *cat* generally associated with spitefulness, slyness, and malice? A quick trip to the dictionary will confirm this distinction: "The cat family (Felidae) includes besides the domestic cat the lion, tiger, leopard, puma, etc." When Mercutio calls Tybalt "king of cats," the context clearly shows he is not thinking of a household pet. More likely he is seeing a sleek black panther. Turning back to the script, an imaginative actor can now find several additional instances in which abstractions of the behavior of this species of cat might inform Tybalt's actions:

1. From his first entrance, when he *creeps up behind* Benvolio with the line, "Turn thee, Benvolio, look upon thy death," Tybalt is a *threatening, menacing figure*. Later, at the Capulet ball, he is *lurking* among the other guests threatening harm to Romeo. Still later, it is his determination to inflict harm that causes his own death and Romeo's consequent banishment.

2. Mercutio's description of Tybalt's manner of dueling indicates that he is an *expert* but *unsportsmanlike fighter*. He fights *viciously* and *inhumanly* by the "book of arithmetic," unwilling to give his opponent any advantage. He is willing to kill Mercutio "under Romeo's arm" as Romeo attempts to come between them.

3. His expertness in dueling would require *grace of movement* and *unusual muscular coordination*.

4. Mercutio's description indicates that Tybalt is an *extremely elegant creature* possessing a kind of haughtiness that does not sit comfortably among the others' old customs and manners.

An actor assigned to play Tybalt might well spend some of his time studying pictures or visiting a zoo to observe the characteristics and behavior of a panther. He could watch the panther's lurking stealth, its leanness, its elegant sleekness, its easy graceful movement, its latent strength and energy, and its inhuman green-yellow eyes. Through his imagination, he could visualize a person possessing these same qualities. That person, with these determinate internal and external characteristics, might be the starting point for creating a believable Tybalt.

An actress preparing for the role of Maggie in *Cat on a Hot Tin Roof,* by Tennessee Williams, might do well to study not the panther but the alley cat. Since Maggie is the "cat" of the title, once again the script provides the starting place for this exploration. Maggie struggles to wrench life out of her alcoholic husband with the cunning, persistence, and sensuality of a feline. She has scratched and clawed her way out of poverty, and she is determined to hang on to her marriage, with the tenacity of an alley cat struggling to stay alive in the streets. Hear Maggie purr when it becomes necessary. Her attempts to seduce her husband Brick and flatter Big Daddy are catlike. When Maggie walks, imagine her whole body in motion with feline grace. When she is spiteful, see her claws emerge from their sheath. The actress working on the part will note the human qualities in cats as well as the feline qualities in humans.

Equus, by Peter Shaffer, provides a more subtle example. This play deals with the psychiatric case history of Alan Strang, a seventeen-year-old who has blinded six horses with a metal spike. In the course of the play, the trauma peels away as he relives the experience. Because Alan has a love-hate relationship with horses, the actor might want to observe and catalog the characteristic behavior of these animals as he prepares to play the role. Some potentially usable abstractions might be nervousness; skittishness; restlessness (especially true of a young colt); gracefulness of motion; head carried high, moving from side to side to observe the world; wariness of trust; and rollicking playfulness. Experimenting with these qualities could be a useful springboard to the character.

The observation of animals and objects will become an important part of your arsenal of rehearsal techniques. After penetratingly observing an animal, bringing as many of the senses as you can into play, you should attempt to create, in so far as it is humanly possible, the physical and emotional attributes of the animal. If you enter into animal study freely and with an open mind, such stretching of the imagination should then allow you to create a human character who possesses many traits you observed in the animal.

Animal exercises can often put you in touch with feelings and emotions that have heretofore been strange to you. Of course, if animal study is to be useful in developing a specific character in a play, you will need to make certain that the animal traits can be justified by the script. No external characterization tool can substitute for careful study of the given circumstances of the text; therefore, animal improvisations should never be used until after you have selected images and actions for the basic makeup of your character. Once this step has been accomplished, applying the sensations that grow out of the study of pertinent animals and objects can help you discover the unique manner in which your character performs its actions.

EXERCISE

(1) Choose an animal or inanimate object for observation. Study it carefully. Remember that you can observe through all of your senses, not just through sight. In addition to how the object or animal looks, consider how it feels, how it smells, how heavy it is, and possibly how it tastes. List all of its characteristic qualities.

Plan a short individual scene, either with or without lines, in which you impersonate a character with these qualities. Remember you will not be trying to make yourself believe you are a radish or an old shoe or a Shetland pony. You will have abstracted the essential qualities, and, through your imagination, you will visualize a person with the same characteristics. You will use your imagination to "supply circumstances" that would require the person to act in a true and revealing manner. Carrying out these actions will help you to believe you are a person with the same characteristics as your chosen animal or inanimate object.

Suppose, for instance, you have chosen for observation a Scottish terrier puppy. Your list of its essential qualities might include the following:

He is shaggy.
He is cute.
He is playful.
He is friendly.
He is lively.
He is clumsy.
He likes attention.
He likes sympathy.

You might decide a child of ten or twelve years would have these qualities. Plan a series of actions that will lead you to believe you are a playful, friendly, clumsy child. Place your character in various imaginary circumstances, such as

Receiving a present unexpectedly
Being left alone and told not to go out of the house
Falling from a tree and hurting his leg

Determine your behavior in each of these circumstances by observing the Scottish terrier.

(2) Create characters based on observations through each of the senses:

On hearing music of different periods, music played on different instruments, music of different types; on hearing whistles, clocks, bells, nature sounds, city sounds, and so forth
On tasting lemon juice, whipped cream, vanilla, different spices, herbs, and so forth
On touching furs, fabrics, surfaces, shapes of objects, and so forth
On smelling flowers, perfumes, soaps, foods, and so forth

---

1. Benoit Constant Coquelin, "Acting and Actors," *Harper's New Monthly Magazine,* May 1887, pp. 891–909.

2. Lewis Funke and John E. Booth, *Actors Talk about Acting* (New York: Avon Books, 1961), vol. I, pp. 57–58. Reprinted by permission of Random House.

NOTES

CHAPTER 8

RELATING TO THINGS— EXTERNAL STIMULI

The foundation of effective acting is the ability to accomplish a specific objective by carrying out a sequence of actions (remember, speaking is an action) that is logical and believable within the given circumstances. The actor's ultimate purpose, however, is not to perform the action itself but to reveal its significance. The final interest of the audience is not in the events of the play—important as they are—but in what they mean to the characters involved.

Think of the opening scene of Shakespeare's great tragedy, *King Lear.* When the aging monarch gives away his realm, his physical action and his reasons for doing it must be clearly played, but the real import lies in how what he does affects him and the people around him. Or consider *Faust,* Goethe's most famous drama, in which Faust, an old scholar, has sold his soul to the devil in return for a year of restored youth. One of the youthful pleasures he seeks is the seduction of the innocent Marguerite, and, to help achieve this aim, he leaves a casket of jewels where Marguerite is certain to find them. She does so in the company of Martha, her older and more experienced neighbor. Here is the stuff for a stunning scene, but it will be meaningful to the audience only if they understand the effect of the action on Marguerite and her neighbor.

The actor uses both external and internal sources as a basis for suffusing action with meaning. In this chapter, we learn about external sources and the technique of *relating to objects and to other actors.*

Stanislavski wrote:

> You must have something which will interest you in the object of your attention, and serve to set in motion your whole creative apparatus.... Imagined circumstances can transform the object itself and heighten the reaction of your emotions to it.... You must learn to transfigure an object from something which is coldly reasoned or intellectual in quality into something which is warmly *felt.*[1]

Return for a moment to the scene from *Faust*. It offers the actresses playing Marguerite and Martha a wonderful opportunity to engage in an intellectual and sensory observation of the jewels. They must experience the color, shape, and brilliance, the feel of them dripping through their hands, and the way they look hung about their throats and from their ears. Since the "prop" jewels will not be real, the actresses can use remembered observation or sensory recall to believe and project the beauty and fire of precious stones. If this memory is not among their resources, they may need to visit a jewel collection in a museum or a jeweler's shop.

But they must not stop there. The next step for the actresses is to "transfigure" the jewels "into something that is warmly felt," to make emotional connections among themselves, their character, and the objects. They (especially Martha) are overcome with the beauty of the stones. They desire them; they covet them. The jewels become a burning temptation, a successful lure in Faust's seduction. In the hands of good actresses, this important prop performs a key dramatic function in the total action of the scene. In both rehearsal and performance, they will use their relationship with it to trigger their imaginations and to induce believable feelings.

The same object, of course, can evoke a variety of responses, depending on the character and the circumstances. Consider the differing relationships to a casket of jewels to a hungry beggar, a wealthy dowager contemplating a purchase, a customs inspector, and a jewel thief.

Good playwrights and directors are skillful and imaginative in supplying props that will help the actor find the truth of a scene. Such objects achieve their fullest meaning when, like the jewels in *Faust,* they are both logical and dramatically symbolic. Let us return to the scene in which King Lear carves up his realm for another example. Lear's throne, his crown, and the sword of state carried before him all symbolize the kingdom, which is his source of power and which he is now about to give away. The map depicting the newly divided kingdom visually represents the freedom from the cares of state Lear seeks in his old age; it is also a lure that entices his daughters to flatter his vanity by making boundless declarations of love before the assembled court. Shattered by Cordelia's refusal, Lear rashly changes his plan and violently tears the map. The actor who can personalize Lear's relation to these objects—"transfigure them into something that is warmly felt"—will find them to be a dependable source of believable feelings. They will also help him concentrate his energies on what he is doing and communicate the meaning of the play to the audience.

Relationships with characters are as important to the actor as relationships with properties. The first scene from *King Lear* requires the actor playing the title role to respond differently to each of the three daughters. Moreover, Lear's relation to Albany differs from his relation to Cornwall; his treatment of Burgundy differs from his treatment of the king of France. Each of these characters (and several others, as it is a large and complex scene) is at some time the object of the king's attention, and the actor who would perform him must make a specific and *personal connection* with them. He should use his experience and imagination to discover how Lear feels about each of these people. He should also carefully observe the behavior of the other actors performing each role and use their deportment to engender spontaneous responses.

The actor must also learn to relate to his costume and to the scenic environment. The costume must take on the nature of the character, must be a part of his very existence. It must not be treated as if it were recently hanging in the dressing room but rather as if it were personally selected by the character being performed. The actor's work with the costume may, in fact, tell the audience much about who the character is and how he feels about himself and his surroundings. In the same manner, the actor must find ways to relate to various aspects of the scenery. Like props, the best scenery is both logical and symbolic. In any case, no scenery will be meaningful to an audience until it is defined by the way actors relate to it. A door, for example, is merely a decoration until an actor uses it. Only then will it be given definition in relationship to the character, the play, and the particular scene. All the techniques by which an actor can imbue a prop with rich meanings can apply equally to scenery and costumes.

Many of the greatest moments in drama supply the actor with an opportunity to use the technique of relating to objects. From Shakespeare alone, think of Othello and the candle just before he murders Desdemona: "Put out the light, and then put out the light"; Hamlet and the skull, as he talks about the transitoriness of life: "Alas! poor Yorick. I knew him, Horatio . . . "; Lady Macbeth and her hands, which, in her deranged mind, she believes are covered with the blood of the murdered Duncan: "Out, damned spot! Out, I say!"; and Shylock and the knife he is sharpening on the sole of his shoe to cut out a pound of Antonio's flesh. Shylock's action motivates Bassanio's "Why dost thou whet thy knife so earnestly?"—a gentle reminder from Shakespeare that the actor playing Shylock should be concentrating on his physical action.

EXERCISE

For the beginning exercises in relating to objects, you will need a solid nondescript article about eighteen inches long and about nine inches in breadth and thickness. A rolled-up coat secured with a string, a small pillow, or a block of wood will do nicely.

(1) Handle the article as if it were a baby. Your task is not only to use sensory memory so you will handle it accurately but also to establish a specific relationship. Handle it as if you were

A new mother
A doting grandfather
An annoyed father
An inexperienced baby-sitter
A bachelor uncle

Supply various circumstances for the baby's condition. Handle it as if the baby were

Sick
Asleep
Soiled
Crying
Dead

(2) Handle the article as if it were

A cat
A puppy
A skunk
A pumpkin
A watermelon
A time bomb
A valuable antique vase
A bouquet of roses
A fish you have just caught
A tureen of hot soup

In every instance, supply circumstances that will provide you with a specific relationship and a logical sequence of actions.

(3) Working in pairs or in groups, you may make further use of these problems as exercises in relation, recall, observation, and concentration. Without saying what it is, one actor should decide on an identity for the nondescript article and establish a relation to it. Another actor should observe him carefully so, when the object is passed to him, he can establish the same identity and relation. He then should *change* the identity and relation and pass the object on.

(4) Return to the exercise in Chapter 7 that involved picking up, carrying, and disposing of a number of objects. Extend the problem by establishing definite and different relationships toward each object. For example, pick up the dead dog *as if*

It were your favorite pet
You were a passing motorist who loves and cares for animals
You were a road worker getting the animal off the pavement
You were a child "investigating" the mangled dog out of curiosity

Pick up the snake *as if*

You were afraid but had to remove it from your porch
It were a pet snake
You were a caretaker in a zoo or a circus
You were a snake charmer

Pick up the unconscious person *as if*

She were a dearly loved friend
You were a hospital orderly handling a patient
You had drugged him in order to carry out some "dark" purpose

---

At this time, we need to discuss briefly the actor's responsibility to the audience, a matter that we will take up in more detail later. Put simply, his job is to make clear everything he does and why he is doing it.

To begin with, an actor can make something clear to the audience only if he has made it clear to himself. Far too many student actors attempt an assignment with vague, general answers to the important "W" questions. Furthermore, to be clear to the audience, everything the actor does must be

Four actors perform a routine in *A Funny Thing Happened on the Way to the Forum*. In musical comedy, performers find ways to invite the audience to have fun with the material without compromising the reality of the character. Directed and choreographed by James Miller, Scenery by Patrick Atkinson, Lighting by David Feind, Costumes by James Miller. (Photo courtesy of University of Missouri-Columbia Summer Repertory Theatre.)

seen and heard. Many young actors get so lost in what they are doing that they forget to share it with the audience. Inaudible speech and actions that are either too small or too elusive to be visible are meaningless. The notion that an actor in training should begin by making his actions small and believable before later enlarging them for the benefit of an audience conditions him to a habit that is difficult to change. Early in your training, performing at an energy level sufficient to communicate with the spectators should become second nature to you.

Incidentally, everything the actor does should also be interesting, but attempts to accomplish this requirement can lead the actor into the trap of producing incongruous and illogical comedy, novelty, or sensationalism for its own sake rather than for the sake of illuminating the given circumstances. The actor must recognize that human behavior is inherently interesting and is the heart and soul of the theatre. An audience likes to see believable people dealing with real problems. The way to generate interest in your exercises, as well as when performing a role, is to make the circumstances specific, to provide conflict by having an explicit intention that can be realized only by overcoming a definite obstacle, and to let the audience follow the development of the conflict to a climax and a resolution. If you plan carefully and concentrate on each step necessary to carry out your plans, you have a solid foundation for a performance that will interest an audience.

Plan a sequence of actions that will make it necessary for you to relate to the objects you would find in these situations:

EXERCISE

(1) You are an archaeologist entering the tomb of an Egyptian king. You are the first person to enter there in more than three thousand years.

(2) You are setting the table for a special dinner. You are using heirloom silver, china, and crystal.

(3) You are a child holding a funeral for a pet of whom you were very fond.

(4) You are unwrapping a present you have long anticipated receiving. Its beauty even surpasses your expectations; or, you cannot restrain your disappointment.

(5) You are a young ruler performing a ceremony like the one required of the young Catherine of Russia. Before the court, she had to open the coffin of her predecessor, the Empress Elizabeth, who had been dead for six months. She had to remove the imperial crown from the dead woman's head and place it on her own.

(6) You are hungry and penniless in a strange town. (Provide your own circumstances as to why this is so.) You are in the street looking into the window of a bakery filled with delicious foods.

(7) You are putting together a homemade bomb (supply circumstances as to why). The handling of the materials is dangerous, and your relation to them will be further colored by your purpose in making the bomb.

(8) You are a professional wine taster (tea taster, coffee taster, whatever). You decide to which of five wines you will award the Grand Prize.

(9) You are counting a large sum of money.

(10) You are eating a meal.

(11) You are looking at an album of family photographs.

(12) You are on a long expedition in which "water discipline" is essential. You have one canteen that must be your entire water supply for another twenty-four hours. Relate to the canteen during a rest break.

EXERCISE

In almost all plays, the actor is confronted with the task of relating to objects and thus is provided with a means of "setting in motion his creative apparatus." The following situations require this technique. Using the given circumstances as a basis, plan and carry out a sequence of actions in which you relate specifically to the object.

(1) In *On the Verge,* by Eric Overmyer, two women and a man are exploring some unnamed country at some undetermined time. One of them (Fanny) happens on an old-fashioned egg beater, slightly rusty but in working order. She has no idea what it is. (*Note:* Three students can work together on this exercise. It is interesting to see how many potential uses or functions they can invent for this simple mechanical object, obviously created for a particular purpose.)

(2) In *Isn't It Romantic,* by Wendy Wasserstein, Janie rashly tells her new male friend Marty that she knows how to cook a chicken. He brings one for their dinner. While Marty is out of the room, she unwraps the chicken, holds it up by its wings, and examines it carefully without the slightest idea of what to do next. But, as she contemplates a relationship with Marty, she slowly cradles the chicken like a baby.

(3) In *No Place to Be Somebody,* by Charles Gordone, Johnny Williams has been given a copy of Sweets Crane's will. Sweets is an old man who befriended Johnny when he was a boy but with whom Johnny no longer wants to have association. Johnny does not read well and has difficulty figuring out that Sweets intends to leave him a good deal of property. In defiance, he throws the will on the floor.

(4) In *And Miss Reardon Drinks a Little,* by Paul Zindel, Anna is a schoolteacher who befriends animals. She is a strict vegetarian and refuses to have about her anything made of fur. When she receives a present of a pair of fur-lined gloves, she vehemently rejects them.

(5) In *Bedroom Farce,* by Alan Ayckbourn, Nick is alone, confined to his bed by a bad back that barely allows him to move. He reaches for his book and knocks it onto the floor.

(6) In *Buried Child,* by Sam Shepard, Vince realizes that his grandfather, Dodge, has quietly died. He covers his body with a blanket, smells some roses he is carrying, then places the roses on his grandfather's chest.

(7) In *Eleven-Zulu,* by Sean Clark, Jonsson is one of a group of six soldiers guarding a broken-down armored carrier in Vietnam. After being on a late-night watch for several hours, he looks through their dwindling case of C-rations for something with fruit cocktail.

(8) In *My Heart's in the Highlands,* by William Saroyan, young Johnny Alexander lives a happy life with his improvident father. Often they have little to eat, and he swipes grapes from a nearby vineyard. He eats slowly and appreciatively.

(9) In *Our Town,* by Thornton Wilder, the middle-aged Mrs. Gibbs helps her neighbor Mrs. Webb string beans, as she talks about her secret dream to sell an antique and travel to Paris.

(10) In *True West,* by Sam Shepard, two brothers clash while house-sitting for their mother. The slobbish petty thief, Lee, tries to write a screenplay on his brother Austin's typewriter. He pecks with one finger, makes many errors, tries to erase, rubs holes in the paper, gets the ribbon tangled up, and yanks it out of the machine in frustration.

(11) In *Arms and the Man,* by George Bernard Shaw, the romantic Raina is in love with a soldier who is reported to have performed great deeds of heroism for his country. Alone at night and thinking of "her hero," she takes up his portrait, caresses it, and returns it reverently to its place.

(12) In *84 Charing Cross Road,* by Helene Hanff and adapted for the stage by James Roose-Evans, Helene is spring-cleaning her books. She loves them—they are her dearest friends. She pauses to touch a special favorite, sorts and rearranges volumes, and occasionally decides to throw one out, dropping it in a box. When she is through, she dumps the box of books in the hallway leading to her apartment.

(13) In *That Championship Season,* by Jason Miller, the coach cherishes a huge silver trophy that was won by his basketball team some years before. It is a symbol of a glorious achievement. Improvise a situation dramatizing his relationship to the trophy.

(14) In *Mother Courage,* by Bertolt Brecht, Katrin is a young mute. Although she follows the army with her mother, she has been kept from any knowledge of men. Having observed the ways of the prostitute Yvette, she steals Yvette's plumed hat and red boots and practices walking about seductively. When an alarm sounds for an approaching enemy attack, she hides the articles of finery, contemplating further use of them.

(15) In *Man of La Mancha,* by Dale Wasserman, and with music and lyrics by Mitch Leigh and Joe Darion, the deranged "knight," Don Quixote, insists that a frightened barber's brass shaving basin is the stolen "Golden Helmet of Mambrino." Improvise a scene in which Don Quixote picks up the basin, adores it, tosses away his old casque, and dons his new "helmet."

(16) In *Day of Absence,* by Douglas Turner Ward, Mary is an incompetent mother who is wakened in the morning by the crying of her baby. The baby needs attention because the black servant on whom the family is

completely dependent has not appeared for work. Mary is sickened in her attempt to change the baby's "didee," a task she cannot perform.

(17) In *Androcles and the Lion,* by George Bernard Shaw, Androcles is a meek little man who befriends all stray animals. Walking near the jungle, he is confronted by a lion that is limping and roaring because it has a thorn in its paw. After an initial fright, he extracts the thorn and earns the great beast's gratitude. Enlist the aid of a partner and improvise this scene, realizing Androcles' changing relationship toward the lion.

(18) In *Rosencrantz and Guildenstern Are Dead,* by Tom Stoppard, Rosencrantz and Guildenstern are betting on the flip of a coin. Each toss comes up heads—an impossibility. Rosencrantz pockets each coin as he wins it, betraying no surprise at all. He feels, however, a bit embarrassed in taking so much money from his friend.

(19) In *Butterflies Are Free,* by Leonard Gershe, Don Baker is a good-looking young man who has just moved into an apartment in Greenwich Village. Although Don has been blind from birth, he accepts his blindness as more of an inconvenience than a handicap, and he is fiercely protective of his ability to care for himself. He tells Jill, his next-door neighbor, that part of the reason he does not bump into things around the apartment is because he has "memorized" his room. To prove it, he walks around the room with grace and confidence, calling off each item as he touches or points to it: bed, bookcase, guitar, cane, books, front door, and tape recorder.

In these exercises, remember that your primary task is to discover a specific relationship to the object or objects and to communicate that relationship by a score of psychophysical actions. Objects—properties or props, as they are called in stage lingo—(as well as costumes and scenery) are excellent "performers" when good actors bring them to life.

RELATING TO OTHER ACTORS

When an actor engages in a transaction with another actor by trying to influence his behavior, he can hardly fail to establish a relationship. Both consciously and unconsciously, he will make logical and psychological adjustments to the other person, and such adjustments depend on an awareness of the other's presence and personality. Often the techniques for relating to objects, which you practiced in the previous exercise, are equally useful in accomplishing objectives that require you to relate to another actor. The actor uses these techniques to "transfigure" the other actor into "something that is warmly felt." The nature of the transfiguration depends, of course, on the given circumstances.

We are frequently faced, both in life and on the stage, with the problem of evoking the same responses from two or more people toward whom we feel quite differently or with whom we have dissimilar relationships. Again, the

A moment from the Repertory Theatre of St. Louis production of *M. Butterfly*. Study the portrait for use of costume and prop in characterization, physical involvement, and concentration of attention. (Photo courtesy of the Repertory Theatre of St. Louis.)

opening scene of *King Lear* provides a good example. Lear wants to influence his three daughters to shower him with love, but his relationship with each of them is not the same. He knows that Goneril is shrewd, cold, ambitious, and willing to do whatever is necessary to gain a share of the kingdom. Regan is a follower who wants what Goneril has and will do what Goneril does. Cordelia, on the other hand, is straightforward and honest; he expects her protestation of love to be genuine. Lear's vanity requires a public declaration of love from each of the three, but he uses a different strategy in each case to get it. Toward Goneril he could establish a kind of bargaining relationship: Tell me you love me, and I'll give you a share of my kingdom. Since Regan's response is so predictable, he might approach her with indifference, perhaps even mingled with contempt. To bring about the proper impact of the scene, he will need to seek honest love from Cordelia, for he is depending on her for comfort in the loneliness of his advancing age.

These relationships are merely suggestions. The actor playing Lear establishes those that will work for him by (1) probing his imagination for an answer to the question: "If I were King Lear, what would I do in these circumstances to get Goneril, Regan, and Cordelia to behave as I want them to?" and (2) responding honestly to the immediate attempts of the actresses playing the daughters to influence his behavior. We pointed out earlier that actors' spontaneous responses to each other are the principal sources of vitality in any performance.

Opening the mind and body to these responses, sometimes called *playing off of another actor,* is a technique that aspiring actors should thoroughly explore and practice. Once mastered, this technique allows you to behave toward the other actors as if you believe they are the characters they play and simultaneously to make full use of your sensory and intellectual responses to each as a person. For instance, the wrong approach in playing Lear would be to try to relate to an image the actor had conjured up of the three daughters. This approach traps the actor into "playing by himself" and deprives him of the stimulation that comes from genuine relationships with his fellow performers. He must respond as fully as he can to the palpable qualities of the three actresses with whom he is playing. If he were to play Lear again with different actresses performing the daughters, his performance would take on a new set of nuances, yet each performance would have equal truth and vitality.

EXERCISE

The following activities help develop real connections and responses between the actors. They do not involve imaginary circumstances. They may be done in pairs or in small groups.

(1) Play catch with a real ball. As the game progresses, try to surprise your partner.
(2) Continue the game with an imaginary ball. Use your sensory memory so you can handle the ball as if it were real. Watch carefully when, how, and

where the ball is thrown, and catch it accordingly. Change the weight of the ball, making it a basketball, a medicine ball, a balloon.

(3) Working in pairs or with a group divided into two teams, engage in various games or contests using imaginary athletic equipment. Develop team spirit, and establish a relationship with the other players. Try

Volleyball
Badminton
Ping pong
A tug of war
Shadowboxing

(4) Peter Brook described an exercise that is a variation of shadowboxing. The actors fight in pairs, taking and giving back every blow but never touching and never moving heads, arms, or feet. The movement is from the torso only. Within these limitations, the fight must be carried on with full physical action and with a commitment to win.

(5) Engage in a conversation. If you are not well-acquainted with your partner, find out about his background, family, interests, and hobbies. Encourage him to talk about himself. During the conversation, seek attractive features in the other actor that will promote a pleasant and favorable relationship.

(6) Engage in a conversation on a controversial subject. Seek to get an actual exchange of ideas and opinions. Stimulate the other actor to express himself.

(7) Extend these exercises in relationships into your everyday life. Along with observing other people, analyze your responses to them. Notice carefully how you are responding and what it is about them that produces your responses. This is one way of following Coquelin's practice of "seizing and noting" anything in life that might be useful to you on the stage.

EXERCISE

Return to any of the earlier problems based on scenes involving two or more actors. Establish a specific and real relationship with your partner. Remember that you make the relationship specific by discovering the attitude of your character toward the other characters. You make it real by

(1) letting yourself respond to the imaginary relationship and
(2) actually using the qualities and features (personality, appearance, voice, feelings) of the other actors as if they belonged to the characters they are playing.

The actor turns first to external stimuli—props, costumes, scenery, and other actors—for the place to focus his attention and the source of his creative energy. Techniques for relating imaginatively to these sources, plus the ability to perform believable physical actions with true intentions, are the major *internal* weapons in the actor's arsenal, and his voice and his body comprise his *external* tools. Stanislavski's system of actor training featured an additional *psychological* technique, which proved to be the most controversial part of his method. It shall be the subject of the final chapter of Part II of this book.

NOTES   1. Constantin Stanislavski, *An Actor's Handbook,* ed. Elizabeth Reynolds Hapgood (New York: Theatre Arts Books, 1963), p. 25.

CHAPTER 9

RELATING TO THINGS—
INTERNAL STIMULI

In Chapter 1, we discovered that an actor's inner resources consist of his memory of what he has done, seen, read, and felt. How he uses these resources—how he puts his past experience to work—is a matter of considerable importance to him. Stanislavski called his approach to the use of internal stimuli *affective memory,* which he later divided into *sense memory* and *emotional memory.* This technique was designed to produce within the actor controlled emotional reactions that he could use to color his performance of a role. Taken with the admonition that the actor must first concentrate on relating to external objects and then focus on performing the action, not on feeling the emotion, some technique for producing emotional coloration in a characterization is extremely useful. We shall look at two such approaches.

Fortunately, most of the time our memory serves us spontaneously, onstage as in life. Facts, figures, faces, stories, images we have known in the past—even sensory and emotional experiences—come back automatically as we need them. If the actor performs logical actions, believes in the given circumstances, tries to accomplish commanding intentions, and establishes specific relationships with props, costumes, scenery and other actors, his past experiences will likely be serving him without his giving any thought to it. His actions and his relationships, coming directly from the imaginary circumstances of the play and from connection with the other actors, should automatically tap his inner resources and evoke the proper feeling. If, on occasion, the techniques of physical action, intentions, and relationships do not elicit the desired responses, the actor may need to bring his past experience directly to bear on the situation.

**RELATING
TO PAST
EXPERIENCES**

Although theatre history provides much evidence that actors to some degree have always made conscious use of their experiences as a specific technique, Stanislavski first extensively explored this practice. After several years of experimentation, much of which was adopted as gospel by one or another of Stanislavski's disciples, he ultimately came to realize that emotional recall was an indirect process. We should focus, Stanislavski decided, on recalling the sensory experiences of the situation, and, most of all, we should remember what we did. With these admonitions in mind, and in keeping with the basic thrust of this book, we shall designate this process *physical action memory* and discuss it under five steps:

1. The original experience

2. Retaining the experience

3. Selecting an experience that relates to the problem

4. Recalling the sensory and physical details

5. Using the experience within the given circumstances

You ordinarily go through these steps without thinking about them, but a separate examination of each will help you when you need to make conscious use of the process.

The Original Experience

The original experience may have occurred months, even years, before you recall it and put it to practical use. In fact, events that occurred some time ago are better because you will be able to use them more objectively. Childhood incidents, because they frequently remain in the mind with peculiar vividness, are often especially valuable. Any experience you use must be one you have felt deeply.

Retaining the Experience

Retaining the experience is partly a matter of natural memory and partly a matter of conscious effort. Most people are genuinely aware of what is going on around them and are likely to remember what has happened in the past. Any technique, however, that will aid the actor in retaining the details of an experience vividly in the mind is worth developing.

Here is what we mean. A story has it that the great French actor François Joseph Talma (1763–1826), a favorite of Napoleon and later of Louis XVIII, on hearing the news of his father's death, was shocked to the point of uttering a piercing cry. He immediately noted the nature of his grief, while commenting that the memory of it might be of use to him on the stage. Such behavior might seem cold-blooded, but there is no reason to doubt that Talma's sorrow was sincere. Good actors accumulate "inner resources."

Selecting the Experience

In deciding what experiences to recall, the actor searches his past for happenings most nearly parallel to those of the character he is playing. They may be identical, or they may be far removed. John (Jack) Barrymore described how recall of past experience helped him play the title role in *Peter Ibbetson,* a dramatization of George duMaurier's novel:

> An actor's performance, at best, is the way he happens to feel about a certain character....
>
> I'm a bit of Peter Ibbetson and a bit of Jack Barrymore. At least, I never utterly forget Jack Barrymore—or things he's thought or done—or had done to him....
>
> I leave my dressing room to make Peter's first entrance. I am Jack Barrymore—Jack Barrymore smoking a cigarette. But before I make the entrance I have thrown away the cigarette and become more Ibbetson than Barrymore. By the time I am visible to the audience I am Ibbetson, quite.
>
> That is, you see—I hope to make this clear—on my way to the entrance I have passed imaginary flunkies and given up my hat and coat. Peter would have had a hat and coat—naturally; and would have given them up. And he's a timid fellow. He gives up his imaginary hat and coat to these flunkies just as I, Jack Barrymore—and very timid then—once gave up my hat and coat to flunkies at a great ball given by Mrs. Astor.
>
> Of course I don't always make Peter's entrance with the memory of a bashful boy at Mrs. Astor's ball. That would harden the memory—make it useless. You couldn't keep on conjuring up the same thing. You have to have different things to get the same emotion.... [1]

Barrymore's description is an example of recalling an experience close to the circumstance of the play. The entrance he mentions is Peter Ibbetson's arrival at a great ball given in honor of the Duchess of Towers. Peter, Barrymore's character, is a very timid fellow, painfully embarrassed in the presence of duchesses and liveried footmen.

More often than not, the actor, unlike Barrymore in the previous example, cannot find in his past so close an approximation to the experience of the character. Obviously, his personal experiences will not parallel those of every character he might be called on to play. He thus must often resort to situations in which his feelings were similar to those of the character, although the circumstances that prompted the feelings may have been entirely different.

In playing Macbeth, for instance, an actor must be able to feel Macbeth's vaulting ambition to be king and his willingness to commit any crime in order to realize his desires. But the actor certainly will not find any experience in his past that parallels Macbeth's evil course of action. On the other hand, a young actor could probably recall a time when he was cast as a walk-on when he desperately wanted to play the lead. Might it have flashed across his mind that he wished the actor who was selected for the leading role would suffer a calamity that would render it impossible for him to perform it? If so, this experience—the momentary wish to realize an ambition at the expense of someone else—could enable him to come to grips with the terrible desire that drove Macbeth along his path of blood and crime.

Using experiences different from the given circumstances is called *substitution*. In the suicide in *Redemption,* Jacob Ben-Ami said he substituted the recall of the shock of taking a cold shower for the impact of the bullet. His acting of this scene stunned many playgoers who were fortunate enough to see it. An actress might play some of Alma's scenes in *Summer and Smoke* using the recall of a painful sunburn that caused her to tense and withdraw when anyone started to touch her.

A scene from a student production of *Assassins* by Stephen Sondheim. Note how the company communicates serious subject matter with comic technique. Directed by James Miller, scene design by Patrick Atkinson, costume design by James Miller, lighting by Phillip Klapwyk. (Photo courtesy of University of Missouri-Columbia University Theatre.)

Another situation that is likely to call for the technique of substitution is the potion scene (Act IV, Scene 3) from *Romeo and Juliet*. Secretly married to Romeo, Juliet has been promised by her parents to the Count of Paris. To get herself out of this entanglement, she is about to take a potion to make her appear dead. She then will be placed in the family tomb, and Romeo will rescue her. Juliet is about to do something whose outcome is uncertain and fraught with dreadful possibilities, an action that will surely call for emotions starting with fear and mounting almost to hysteria. During the moments before this horrifying act, she is distracted by imagining all the things that might happen to cause her plan to fail. What if the potion does not work at all? What if it is a poison? What if she should wake before Romeo comes and find herself alone in the tomb with the remains of all her buried ancestors? If you are to play Juliet, you must make these fears personal and believable within the given circumstances.

What experience have you had that might enable you to realize Juliet's fear? Have you been in a situation, no matter how dissimilar in its actual circumstances, that induced a feeling akin to Juliet's? Have you ever been alone, preparing to take some step whose uncertain consequences held possibilities of danger? Unhappiness? Pain? Discomfort? Did you ever prepare to run away from home? Contemplate an elopement? Did you ever prepare to go to the hospital for an operation? To go into the army? To go away to college? To move to a new town where you might be homesick? Have you ever felt trapped while exploring a cave? Perhaps you could recall an instance of fright from your childhood. Almost everybody has experienced something like this:

> When you were ten years old, you spent a weekend with an aunt who lived alone in a large house with no neighbors nearby. On the first evening, before you had become acquainted with your surroundings, your aunt was called to care for a sick friend. You boasted that you were used to staying alone, and because it was impractical to get a "sitter" on short notice, your aunt reluctantly left you to look after yourself for a couple of hours. You settled down in the living room, feeling grown up and independent, and looked happily at a picture book. Gradually you became uneasy. At home, you had activity and noise to calm you, but this place was terribly still. At home, lights all through the house made everything bright and cheerful. Here a lamp with a green shade in the living room and a lamp with a red globe in the hallway cast eerie shadows on unfamiliar surroundings.
>
> Suddenly you were overcome with fear. A noise on the porch started you thinking of thieves and kidnappers. You had no sooner quieted those fears than a noise upstairs started you thinking of ghosts and haunted houses. It seemed impossible to stay on in the house alone, but the outdoors was just as terrifying, and to reach the telephone you had to go down the hall and into the completely dark dining room.

If such an incident is your liveliest experience with fear, it will have to serve, and if you can recall it vividly, it will serve you well in preparing to play Juliet's potion scene.

Recalling the Details

Concentrate on remembering the details of the experience rather than on the emotion itself. Begin by using sensory recall. In the last example, you should attempt to remember as much as you can about the room—the lights with their bright spots and especially the dark corners; the reflection of the light on the dark, polished surfaces of the furniture; the windows, shiny black in the darkness, reflecting the quiet gloom. Remember the chair you sat on, the objects on the table beside the chair, and the pictures you looked at. Recall the odors of the room—lilacs and furniture polish. Recall the stillness and the sounds you heard (or thought you heard).

When returning to such a situation as a source for your performance of the potion scene, you will need to develop a shortcut to the heart of the memory. By breaking the memory down into its individual components, you can usually re-create the sensation of the moment by concentrating on the aspect that provides you with the most vivid connection to the situation. You should be able to get to the sensation of fear by concentrating on a specific sound, a particular odor, or the way your body temperature changed, rather than by attempting to evoke the entire experience every time you need to use it. When you can place this odor, this sound, or this body temperature within the given circumstances of the potion scene, your use of *emotional memory* is complete.

If you are unfamiliar with this technique, you will be surprised (after you give it an honest trial) how many details you will be able to bring back and how much the memory of the way things felt and looked and smelled will help you recapture the essence of the entire experience.

As you are working with the experience during the rehearsal period, try to remember as much detail as possible about what you did in this situation. How did you deal with the cause of your fear—the frightening shadows, the sounds on the porch, the noise upstairs? Perhaps you first pretended you were not afraid. You may have tried to renew your interest in the pictures. Did you brave your way into one of the dark corners for another book? You tried then to reassure yourself by singing as loudly as possible. Gaining a little confidence, you may have gone timidly to the window to investigate the sounds on the porch. What happened physically, when you could not bring yourself to take a good look? Remembering the childhood situation at the level of physical action should give you a range of believable choices for performing Juliet's scene. Adapting them to the given circumstances of the scene you are playing should reinforce your emotional recall.

When you attempt to remember an incident, sit quietly relaxed, free of tensions that might interfere with the flow of memory and feeling. In a sense, this technique is an application to acting of Wordsworth's famous definition of poetry: "Emotion recollected in tranquility."

Using the Experience in the Given Circumstances of the Play

In each instance described, we have admonished you that the final step of the exercise is to make certain that anything you use from your remembered experience is believable within the given circumstances of the scene and your character. You will take yourself out of the play and away from your intention, unless you can use the feelings you have induced to help you play the actions and speak the lines of the character. *You must especially guard against reducing moments conceived by the imagination of a master dramatist to your own personal experiences, which may be drab and smaller in scope.* One of the strongest tendencies of a student actor is to "play everything too small." Don't forget that drama, for the most part, is larger than life.

Unless your director schedules time during rehearsals for such exercises, you should carry on this process during your work on the role at home or during your preparation before rehearsal and performance. The mark of a prepared and competent actor is the ready ability to access his responses during rehearsals and performances upon the demand of the script and the director.

EXERCISE

(1) Return to any of the earlier exercises. Make your playing of them more effective by using the technique of physical action memory, of recalling past experience.

(2) Remember the moments in your life when you most strongly felt some emotion such as anger, hate, love, or fear. Reconstruct in your mind the detailed circumstances that caused you to experience this emotion. Perform an activity related to these circumstances until you can sense the emotion associating itself with the activity.

It should be apparent that emotional memory is a technique better suited to the study and rehearsal periods than to performance. Used correctly, it sharpens your inner resources, especially those needed to perform scenes of intense emotion. Many teachers who use this tool in the classroom spend hours with individual students, attempting to stimulate the believable recall of an emotional experience. Others think this technique offers so much potential for self indulgence and for "playing the emotion" rather than "playing the action" that they have turned away from emotional memory altogether.

If you are serious about becoming an actor, we urge you to spend the time it will take to develop this technique, to make it yours, and to be able to use it on command. If you find that believable, true emotions do not arise from selecting imaginative intentions and concentrating on the external elements of the physical actions you are performing, you will need a technique such as emotional memory in order to muster a complete mastery of the role. Another approach, which has stood the test of use by many great actors through the years, is the use of images.

RELATING TO IMAGES

Most actors find it useful to master the technique of relating to things in the mind, of using *images*. The image technique is familiar because we use it—both voluntarily and involuntarily—in everyday life. To combat the disturbing feelings of being alone in a strange town, we envision specific pictures of home. We see the porch with its comfortable chairs, the living room with its soft lights, and the table set for dinner. We hear voices in the kitchen and smell rolls baking in the oven. Immediately, we are filled with feelings of homesickness. Tired and bored at home, we see pictures of strange, faraway places. We see towering hills, wander in our minds through quaint villages, or hear the tinkle of cowbells on a Swiss mountainside. Immediately, we are filled with a desire to get away. Waiting for someone who is late in arriving, we cannot keep pictures of accidents out of our minds. We see the person we are waiting for struck by a passing car, lying in the hospital, perhaps the victim of muggers. We cannot dispel the feelings of worry and fear. Planning to surprise a friend with a present, we see her unwrapping the package. We see her taking the gift out of the tissue and holding it up to examine it. We see her smile, and we are filled with feelings of happiness and affection.

Imagination shapes the actor's responses and behavior onstage very much like the way it does in life. Sergei Eisenstein, the renowned Russian filmmaker and advocate of the "inner technique," described how an actor might use the technique of images when preparing to play the part of a respected government employee on the point of committing suicide, because he has lost a large amount of government money at cards:

> I believe it would be almost impossible to find an actor of any training today who in this scene would start by trying to "act the feeling" of a man on the point of suicide.... We should compel the appropriate consciousness and the appropriate feeling to take possession of us....
>
> How is this achieved? We have already said that it cannot be done with the "sweating and straining" method. Instead we pursue a path that should be used for all such situations.
>
> What we actually do is to compel our imagination to depict for us a number of concrete pictures or situations appropriate to our theme. The aggregation of the pictures so imagined evokes in us the required emotion, the feeling, understanding and actual experience that we are seeking....
>
> Suppose that a characteristic feature of our embezzler be fear of public opinion. What will chiefly terrify him will not be so much the pangs of conscience, a consciousness of his guilt or the burden of his future imprisonment, as it will be "what will people say?"
>
> Our man finding himself in this position, will imagine first of all the terrible consequences of his act in these particular terms.
>
> It will be these imagined consequences and their combinations which will reduce the man to such a degree of despair that he will seek a desperate end.
>
> This is exactly how it takes place in life. Terror resulting from awareness of responsibility initiates his feverish pictures of the consequences. And this host of imagined pictures, reacting on the feelings, increases his terror, reducing the embezzler to the utmost limit of horror and despair.[2]

As Eisenstein pointed out, the mental process that would actually drive a person to suicide and the creative process that would stimulate a character to the same action on the stage are very similar. A picture of the circumstances that led him to such foolhardiness would be constantly in his mind, and he would be driven to despair by the image of his associates casting him off when the crime was discovered.

The technique of using images, then, begins with pictures of specific circumstances supplied voluntarily by the imagination. These pictures lead in turn to action, to belief, and to feeling. Again, we must recognize that feeling is the end and not the means, that the actor is concerned with *causes,* not with *effects.* He is like the interior decorator who wants to create a beautiful room. He is concerned with color and fabric, with line and form because he knows they are the means to beauty; if properly controlled, they will produce a beautiful effect. But he also understands that trying merely to create beauty without a specific knowledge of how to use his materials would be futile.

In using the technique of images, the actor imprints a series of pictures in his imagination that stimulate him to action. Succinctly stated, *When such an actor acts, he sees a picture.* He keeps the images before him as if they were on a television or a motion picture screen, and he sees them in color, synchronized with sound. He can locate the screen in various positions, depending on the requirements of the moment. If the scene is introspective, he may keep the screen in his mind. If he is trying to influence another character, especially if he wants the other actor to see vividly what he is talking about, he may place the screen on the actor's face, in a position in which he directs the attention of another actor to it. Or he may want to locate the images in the auditorium, sometimes creating a giant screen across the rear wall.

The process of using images as an acting technique is well described in the following passage:

> The actor needs...an uninterrupted series of visual images which have some connection with the given circumstances. He needs, in short, an uninterrupted line not of plain but of illustrated given circumstances. Indeed, at every moment of his presence on the stage,...the actor must be aware of what is taking place outside him on the stage (i.e., the external given circumstances created by the producer, stage-designer, and the other artists) or of what is taking place inside him, in his own imagination, that is, those visual images which illustrate the given circumstances of the life of his part. Out of all these things there is formed, sometimes outside and sometimes inside him, an uninterrupted and endless series of inner and outer visual images, or a kind of film. While his work goes on, the film is unwinding itself endlessly, reflecting on the screen of his inner vision the illustrated given circumstances of his part, among which he lives on the stage.[3]

EXERCISE

(1) These problems are for developing the habit of seeing definite images from word stimuli. For each of the following concrete words, visualize a detailed and specific picture. See yourself in the picture, and think what

you would do if you were there. Let yourself respond. Remember that you can't *make* yourself feel but that you can *let* yourself feel. You can make this exercise more valuable by writing down what you see, or, if you can draw, by making a sketch of it. Describe your picture and your actions to the members of the group, making them see the images as vividly as you do.

fountain	ship
shoe	mansion
chair	fish
sister	trumpet
wedding	courtyard
funeral	shack
palace	automobile
candy	fire
flower	vase
queen	teapot
bench	pie

(2) Repeat the same process for the following abstract words. It is important that the actor learn to realize abstract concepts in meaningful concrete images that can stimulate responses. *Happiness* might be a picture of a child laughingly chasing his shadow. *Injustice* might be a picture of an injured woman denied admission to a hospital because of her color.

power	bliss
speed	misery
love	fame
happiness	grief
poverty	calmness
wealth	indifference
mercy	beauty
elegance	disgrace
cruelty	jealousy
kindness	glamour
injustice	bigotry

In these exercises, you have been creating a "film" of visual images and describing them vividly to the group. In the process, you have unwittingly used another helpful technique called the *inner monologue*. What the actor is thinking —what is in his mind—each moment he is onstage is vastly important to his performance. The technique of the inner monologue controls the actor's thinking and makes it serve his overall purpose. He uses it when he is not speaking the playwright's words; that is, during pauses in his own speeches and during the lines of the other characters. The inner monologue is a key aspect of the interpretative art of acting, because it is not composed by the playwright except in rare instances. The accomplished actor carefully plans his inner monologue, writes it out, memorizes it, and thinks it at each rehearsal and performance, just as faithfully as he memorizes and speaks the playwright's lines.

The most common instances in which the dramatist creates inner monologues are soliloquies and asides that supply thoughts to be spoken to the audience. Hamlet's "To be, or not to be..." and Macbeth's "Tomorrow, and tomorrow, and tomorrow..." are examples of superb inner monologues. Eugene O'Neill experimented with the inner monologue in *Strange Interlude,* in which he wrote "thoughts" for the actors to speak between the lines of regular dialogue.

In telling the group the images you had in your mind in the prior exercises, you were, in a sense, speaking an inner monologue. You were making the inner monologue an *outer* monologue and thus receiving an initiation into this useful technique. The next series of exercises will allow you to make further application of it.

EXERCISE

Perform an action that you do not want anyone to know about, for example: opening someone's mail, searching someone's desk, breaking your diet, drinking secretly. Your inner monologue, which for purposes of practice you will speak as you are carrying out the action, should make use of images and should be an attempt to justify to yourself what you are doing. Be sure you have an intention, an obstacle, and a dramatic structure.

EXERCISE

Plays abound in opportunities to use images. Situations in which you will find this technique useful need not by any means be so desperate as one in which the embezzler was driven to suicide. Work on several of the problems described next. The pictures should be definite and detailed, not vague and general. They should be from life experience, not from the theatre (that is, don't use an image of another actor in a similar circumstance). Describe the image in a monologue, write it out, memorize it, and, along with appropriate psychophysical actions, make it part of an improvisation in which you accept as one of the circumstances that the character speaks his thoughts. Reading the play from which the situation is taken will stimulate your imagination, but don't memorize the playwright's lines. Use your own words, and commit yourself to sharing your images with the group.

(1) In *Getting Out,* by Marsha Norman, Arlie has been released after spending eight years in prison. A vehicle with a loud siren goes by in the street below the bleak apartment where she is trying to make a home. Fitfully

half-asleep, she flashes on a prison memory, leaps from the bed, and begins making up the bed in a frenzied, ritual manner.

(2) In *To Gillian on Her 37th Birthday,* by Michael Brady, 16-year-old Rachel is standing outside scanning the late-summer night sky. As she traces the paths of falling stars with her finger, she slowly begins to visualize the face of her late mother, who would have been 37 that day, had she lived.

(3) In *She Stoops to Conquer,* by Oliver Goldsmith, Mrs. Hardcastle is the victim of a deception planned by her mischievous son, Tony Lumpkin. At night on a country road, she believes she is being confronted by high-waymen. Her imagination calls forth pictures of all kinds of dreadful things that might happen to her.

(4) In *Raisin in the Sun,* by Lorraine Hansberry, Ruth, a young black woman, is preparing with her husband's family to move from crowded quarters into a large house in a white neighborhood. She anticipates the greater comfort their new home will provide as she packs bric-a-brac, accumulated over the years, into a carton. The objects provoke images from the past, and her anticipation evokes images of the future.

(5) In *Lu Ann Hampton Laverty Oberlander,* by Preston Jones, the teenaged Lu Ann sees a picture on the classroom wall of a European castle with a tiny door at its very top. The castle stimulates her to dream about getting out of the small, stifling, Texas town in which she lives.

(6) In *The Rainmaker,* by N. Richard Nash, Noah's older but inexperienced sister has slipped out of the house to the tack room, where a fast-talking stranger who claims to be a rainmaker is sleeping. Noah's visions of what might be taking place between the two of them lead him to take down a gun from the rack and start after them.

(7) In *A Delicate Balance,* by Edward Albee, Tobias recalls an instance several years in the past when a pet cat bit him, after which he took it to the veterinarian and had it killed.

(8) In *The Doctor in Spite of Himself,* a farce by Molière, Martine has been soundly beaten by her drunken husband. She complains, "These cudgel blows set heavy on my stomach" and pictures to herself how she is going to get revenge for the beating she has received.

(9) In *Biloxi Blues,* by Neil Simon, a young soldier named Epstein has filched the notebook in which Eugene has been writing descriptions of all his army comrades. He opens it and reads the section about himself, discovering that Eugene believes Epstein is a homosexual. (*Note:* regardless of the situation in the play, actors may improvise this scene as if they are alone as they read or that they are reading aloud to the entire barracks. They may also assume the given circumstance that Eugene's notion is either true or false.)

(10) In *School for Scandal,* by Richard Brinsley Sheridan, Snake makes his daily visit to Lady Sneerwell to tell her the latest gossip. Both take exquisite pleasure in the vividness and maliciousness with which he recalls—and fabricates—scandalous tales of their acquaintances.

(11) In *Desire under the Elms,* by Eugene O'Neill, the brothers Peter and Simon are planning to run away from the hard life on a New England farm and seek easy wealth in the California gold rush. They picture acres of nuggets and streets paved with gold. This exercise could be done by either one or two actors.

(12) In *The Gentleman Caller,* by Ed Bullins, the Maid has been a model of servitude for many years. She pictures the time when black people will come together and overcome the forces that have oppressed them.

(13) In *The Basic Training of Pavlo Hummel,* by David Rabe, Pavlo is a wide-eyed, totally inept soldier, born and raised in a middle-class environment. He wants to be thought of as a tough street kid, so he conjures up romantic pictures of stealing automobiles and being chased by the police.

(14) In *The House of Blue Leaves,* by John Guare, Bunny is an ever-hopeful, failure-plagued dreamer. She tells her friend Artie a dream she had about a Buick nicknamed the Green Latrine, in which she attempts to give rides to Jackie Kennedy, Bob Hope, President Lyndon Johnson, and Francis, Cardinal Spellman, but they refuse her offer of a ride. A melee breaks out, the Green Latrine blows four tires, and the people rush to separate cabs. Later, on "The Johnny Carson Show," Cardinal Spellman and Bob Hope tell the story, and Bunny, in her dreams, once again feels like the object of the world's ridicule.

(15) In *Serjeant Musgrave's Dance,* by John Arden, Musgrave has a nightmare in which he watches London burn and times the countdown to the end of the world. The inner dialogue of wildly imaginative scenes such as nightmares must be as accurately conceived and recorded as that growing from images of things that actually happened.

(16) In *The Zoo Story,* by Edward Albee, Jerry is an "outsider" in life, a man unable to fit into contemporary society. When he meets Peter, the epitome of the society he both abhors and desires, he tries to lure Peter into conversation. Peter is fascinated and a bit frightened of Jerry but listens while Jerry relates the story of a dog who inhabits Jerry's apartment house. Jerry has tried to befriend the dog and, failing, has resolved to kill him. The dog emerges as an image of all Jerry's frustrated attempts to communicate with other people.

Part II has offered you a basis for developing your own method of acting. It assumes that you establish, from the very beginning, a regimen of physical exercise and vocal study that will place these two tools totally and flexibly at your command. It has concentrated on developing your inner resources so you will be able to create a believable character to communicate with your body and your voice. Your inner technique consists of three stages: (1) discovering the physical actions required in order to perform the role; (2) creating intentions to go with each physical action that are believable and stimulating to the imagination; and (3) learning to respond to both external and internal stimuli provided by the given circumstances of the play. Along the way, we have also helped you learn to relax, to direct your attention to the proper focus of the moment, and to learn to see things in the special, imaginative way an actor views the world. Next, you need to know how to mine the play for the raw materials of the role, and that is the objective of Part III.

NOTES

1. Ashton Stevens, *Actorviews* (Chicago: Covici-McGee, 1923), pp. 64, 66–67. Quoted in Toby Cole and Helen Krich Chinoy, eds., *Actors on Acting,* new rev. ed. (New York: Crown Publishers, 1970), p. 594.

2. Sergei Eisenstein, *The Film Sense,* trans. and ed. Jay Leyda (New York: Harcourt Brace Jovanovich, 1947), pp. 37–38.

3. David Magarshack, "Introduction," *Stanislavsky on the Art of the Stage* (New York: Hill and Wang, 1961), p. 38.

PART 3
THE ACTOR AND THE PLAY

CHAPTER 10

GETTING INTO THE PART

Throughout the preceding chapters, we have been advocating a method that allows the actor to use his intelligence, his life experience, and his senses as raw material for creating a character. Frequently, we have referred to the "circumstances given by the dramatist" that guide the actor in using his resources. When creating exercises derived from plays, we have attempted to include enough of these circumstances to provide practice in developing logical and appropriate behavior. The actor must know how to discover and use the total circumstances of a play when preparing to create one of its characters for performance.

Stage productions that contain living, vital characters result from a melding of the creative talents of the actor and the dramatist. Any argument over which of the two is more important is fruitless because they are completely interdependent. The actor relies on the character created by the dramatist to provide a vital, continuing stimulus and source of inspiration. Without the actor to bring it to life, the dramatist's character will lie dormant on the pages of the script. The creation resulting from the collaboration between actor and dramatist is truly attributable to both. For instance, the audience will see neither Shakespeare's Macbeth nor the actor's Macbeth, but the actor *as* Shakespeare's Macbeth. Each character a dramatist conceives has the potential to sustain a broad range of actions, and for a great character such as Hamlet, that number is practically unlimited. The character's final shape in a particular production will be colored both by the actions the actor selects to perform and by what he finds significant about his personal relationship to the part. Even the skill to imagine characterizations when reading plays is dependent on the same interpretative skills as those used by the actor.

An actor's performance of a character consists of both an *inner characterization* and its *outer form*. To create the outer form—the way the character looks, moves, gestures, and speaks—the actor draws "from his own experience of life or that of his friends, from pictures, engravings, drawings, books, stories, novels, or from some simple incident—it makes no difference."[1] If the actor is to perform a believable, three-dimensional characterization, he must also create its inner life. He accomplishes this portion of his task by adopting the character's thoughts, emotions, and states of mind, drawing wherever possible on similar experiences in his own life. When everything works correctly, the actor establishes a direct connection between the character's external anatomy and its inner characterization. That is his goal, and he dedicates his study of the play and the role, as well as the designated period of rehearsals, to achieving it.

To a very considerable degree, the actor must always "play himself." He can create another person only by drawing on his own experiences, actual or vicarious. No matter how he may alter his outward appearance, no matter how he may change the sound of his voice (and this outer form is necessary to complete characterization), his ability to communicate the essential truth of his role—which is, after all, the core of any performance—is dependent on what he is able to bring to it from his inner resources. Even though study and observation in the preparation of a specific part may greatly enlarge these resources, what is essentially "you" remains the same from one character to another. The way to get to any character is through yourself.

The final product of the actor's art, "the actor in the part," is a unique creation that cannot be duplicated. No two actors will relate in the same way to the same part because they have not had a lifetime of identical experiences. The characterizations of two actors performing the same role have the same father (the dramatist) but a different mother (the actor). David Magarshack extended this analogy:

> Every artistic stage character is a unique individual creation, like everything else in nature. In the process of its creation there is a "he," that is "the husband," namely the author of the play, and a "she," that is "the wife," namely the actor or actress.... There is "the child"—the created part. There are in this process, besides, the moments of the first acquaintance between "him" and "her," their first friendship, their falling in love, their quarrels and differences, their reconciliations, and their union.... During these periods the producer, Stanislavsky points out, helps the process of the birth of the man-part by playing the role of matchmaker.[2]

To say that the actor becomes a creative artist in his own right in this process neither minimizes nor falsifies the creativity of the dramatist. *John Gielgud's* Hamlet is different from *Laurence Olivier's* because each actor finds meaning in *Shakespeare's* Hamlet in light of his own experience. In so doing, each is true to Shakespeare and to himself.

To this point in the book, we have concentrated on helping the actor learn how to be true to himself. It is now time to consider how he can be true to the dramatist.

DISCOVERING THE DRAMATIST'S CONCEPT OF THE CHARACTER: THE MOTIVATING FORCE

A successful actor, while creating a characterization that is unique and personal, realizes and readily accepts the great responsibility he owes to the dramatist. His first step toward fulfilling that obligation is to study the play until he has gleaned all evidence that discloses what the dramatist intended the character to be. Jerzy Grotowski explained that the actor must allow the role to "penetrate" him. By definition, *penetrate* means to "enter by overcoming resistance," so Grotowski is admonishing the actor to yield freely to the physical and psychological demands of the part as he prepares to play it. Some teachers have suggested that the actor "have an affair with the script," that they read it as if it were a sensual, "juicy" story. He must open his senses to the character, reading the script over and over, each time for a different purpose.

At a very early stage in his preparation, the actor will also want to familiarize himself with the accessible critical commentary for the play on which he is working, and, for the standard classics, this is no simple task. He will also discuss everything—especially any problems he encounters—with his director and with others whose insight and judgment inspire his confidence. In short, he searches incessantly for every suggestion that can help him understand any aspect of the character.

When the actor turns to the script, his study is guided by two basic questions. He needs to know:

1. What primarily does the character want?

2. What is he willing to do to get it?

A certain character, for instance, may want more than anything else to be rich and may be willing to employ any means to satisfy his desire. He may be willing to forego all ordinary pleasures, even to sacrifice his health and the happiness of his family. He might break any law—legal or moral—that he found to be an obstacle. Another character may also want to be rich but might not be willing to obtain his wealth by gambling with the happiness and security of his family or by taking advantage of friends and associates. A certain character may want to find love, and she might be willing to sacrifice everything, even her pride and virtue, to gain what she wants. Another with the same basic desire might be too proud to compromise her reputation. Still another might be too shy to let her desire be known.

If you know what your character wants and what he is willing to do to achieve it, you have the key to creating an honest performance. Answering these two questions provides you with the *motivating force* behind what your character does and says, so this task completely dominates your initial study of the play. Failure to understand the desire that motivates the character's behavior means failure to understand the dramatist's intention. This, in turn, means failure to interpret the play truthfully.

Studying a script is a process of analysis and synthesis, of taking apart and putting together. The actor analyzes, or takes apart, the character, studying his behavior in relation to the other characters and to the play as a whole. Then, guided by his sensitivity and imagination, he reassembles the parts, organizing them to form an artistic creation.

The actor's analysis should finally lead him to an unequivocal decision about "what a character wants," at which time he must be able to state it in specific terms. Finding a name for the motivating force is an important step in creating a character. The name must designate a desire true to the author's intention, and it must also stimulate the actor to action. A motivating force that does not suggest action is worthless.

NAMING THE MOTIVATING FORCE

Stanislavski emphasized the importance of choosing the right name, recalling his analysis of Argan, the principal character in Molière's *The Imaginary Invalid*. As the title suggests, Argan is a hypochondriac, a person who suffers from imaginary ailments. Stanislavski wrote:

> Our first approach was elementary and we chose the theme "I wish to be sick." But the more effort I put into it and the more successful I was, the more evident it became that we were turning a jolly, satisfying comedy into a pathological tragedy. We soon saw the error of our ways and changed to: "I wish to be thought sick." Then the whole comic side came to the fore and the ground was prepared to show up the way in which the charlatans of the medical world exploited the stupid Argan, which was what Molière meant to do.[3]

Stanislavski's name for Argan's motivating force was clearly true to Molière's intention. Equally important, this specific desire had the potential to stimulate him to action when playing the role. Argan wanted people to think he was sick because the attention he thus received from his family and his physicians gratified his enormous vanity. This desire was so strong that, attempting to satisfy it, he became the victim of a horde of unscrupulous doctors. He was even willing to sacrifice his daughter's happiness by marrying her to a simpering physician so a medical man would be in his own household to attend him constantly.

Stanislavski provided another example from his preparation to play the hero in Goldoni's *The Mistress of the Inn*. He wrote:

> We made the mistake of using "I wish to be a misogynist," and we found that the play refused to yield either humour or action. It was only when I discovered that the hero really loved women and wished only to be accounted a misogynist that I changed to "I wish to do my courting on the sly" and immediately the play came to life.[4]

Besides not being in accord with the dramatist's conception, "I wish to be a misogynist" was a weak choice because it was insufficiently specific. "I want to hate women" defines a general attitude but fails to suggest action. Such statements as "I want to avoid women" or "I want to take advantage of every opportunity to embarrass women" would have been better. For this character, however, they would still have been unacceptable because he did not hate women at all. And what splendid possibilities for action are suggested by "I want to do my courting on the sly."

A good motivating force will be stated as a *specific desire that the character can attempt to satisfy through action.* Examples of unsatisfactory statements that cannot motivate specific action are

I want to be unhappy.
I want to be popular.

Examples of better statements are

I want to play on everybody's sympathies.
I want to ruin my neighbor's reputation in the community.
I want to make people laugh.

The rules for naming the motivating force for the character's behavior throughout the play are the same as those for stating the intention for a smaller sequence of actions, which we discussed in Chapter 4. Begin the statement with "I want to" or "I wish to," and follow with an *active* verb expressing the basic desire of the character. Don't follow with the verb *to be* or a verb expressing feeling, because *being* and *feeling* are conditions, not actions, and consequently cannot be acted.

Another cardinal rule is that the statement must involve the actor with other characters. As we recognized earlier, a play is a conflict. Your motivating desire must demand something of the other characters and bring you in conflict with them. And it is through conflict in motivating desires that plot unfolds and character is revealed.

Last, the character's motivating force must mean something personal to the actor. It must arouse in him a real desire to accomplish his aims. To *think* is not enough; the actor must truly *want.* Michael Chekhov explained that the actor must be "possessed" of his objective.[5]

ANALYZING THE ROLE

During the period of analysis and study of the script, the actor has several sources for discovering the character's motivating force. The most important are

What the character does
What the character says
What the other characters in the play say about him (always taking into consideration the speaker's purpose in saying it)
What actions are suggested in the character's lines
What comments and descriptions the playwright offers in the stage directions

By way of illustration, let us analyze the roles of the Young Man and the Girl (Emily) in William Saroyan's one-act play *Hello Out There.* (*Note:* this play is printed in its entirety in the Appendix of this book.)

William Petersen and Cherry Jones in the Goodman Theatre's production of *The Night of the Iguana* by Tennessee Williams. Study the actors' faces as an example of actors thinking onstage. (Photo by Liz Lauren.)

The plot of this short drama is simple. The Young Man has been thrown in a small-town Texas jail for raping a married woman, a charge he denies. He strikes up a conversation with Emily, who cooks for the prisoners and cleans the jail. He tells the naive teenager he wants to run away with her, and Emily hurries home to get the Young Man a gun. Before she can return, the husband of the woman involved in the altercation the evening before returns and shoots the Young Man, despite his insistence that the wife has duped them both. Emily, in the empty jail, is even lonelier than before.

The following example, cast in the first person, shows how much information an actor's study of the role of the Young Man reveals.

What I do:

I try to contact somebody who can help me.
I entice the girl to keep talking to me.
I convince the girl that I want her always with me.
I sympathize with the girl's plight.
I plot to escape with her.
I fight for my life.

I say that

I want something substantial to eat.
I am lonesome and friendless.
I am a drifter and a gambler.
I long for San Francisco.
I will marry the girl and take her with me if I escape.
I was set up by the woman who cried "rape."
I want to make a lot of easy money, but I don't want to work for a living.
I need a steady woman.
I want a cigarette.
I lie when it will do somebody some good, but I am not lying now.

The other characters say that

I have a whole gang of people worked up over what I did.
I am in jail in Matador, Texas, having been brought here from Wheeling.
They are thinking about taking me to another jail for safe keeping.
I raped a woman last night.
I "liked" Emily when I talked to her in my sleep.

The dialogue suggests these physical actions:

I nervously pace the floor and beat on it with a spoon.
I rub the place where somebody hit me on the head.
I kiss "Katey's" hand.
I kiss "Katey."
I fall to my knees when I am shot.
I lose consciousness (die?).

The comments supplied by the dramatist are

I call out dramatically.
I am "kidding the world."

Two aspects of this analysis deserve special comment. First, because of the confined setting of the play, the Young Man's actions are mostly bound up in speech. Still, the actor playing this role must find active verbs to describe what the Young Man does. "To talk," "to argue," or "to convince," for instance, will not provide the actor with sufficient understanding to decide on a *motivating desire*. Second, the playwright gives the actor very little assistance in the stage directions of this play. Please note that he does not even give the "Young Man" a name, although he later allows him to tell us that his nickname is Photo Finish. Saroyan certainly had a reason for this vagueness, but the actor must not be trapped into equally vague decisions. He must be specific as he imaginatively surrounds the given circumstances with facts of his own invention.

We also will need to decide when this play takes place. The young woman says the time of day is "about ten" in the evening. The skilled actor finds many ways to use the time when an action takes place either as an inspiration for the selection of intentions or as a reason for giving a certain emotional coloring to the playing of an intention. Time is also an important part of the environment of the play; it is crucial for the actor to fix its attributes firmly in his imagination. Somehow the dimly lighted space and the darkness daring the couple to come outside must be a part of the given circumstances. We must also remind ourselves of the date. Saroyan wrote the play in 1942, and since he does not specify otherwise, we shall accept that as the year when the action occurs. This decision will have an impact on many choices we must make as we analyze the play.

After listing and studying the given circumstances outlined in the example, the actor can proceed to "name" the motivating desire. In this drama, in which the characters present psychological complexities, the problem is not simple. The actor must take pains to consider all the possibilities, finally stating the desire specifically and in terms that will stimulate him to action.

Obviously, the Young Man's motivating desire will have something to do with getting himself out of his current predicament. One way to state it might be "I want to escape this confinement." To make such a selection would be to limit the actor's imagination, for this motivating desire would not help the actor account for much of his dialogue.

Before deciding on the motivating desire, the actor—probably with the help of the director—will have to decide how sincere the Young Man is about marrying the young girl. If he is totally sincere, his motivating desire will be something like "I want to find a lifelong companion" or "I want to share my life" or "I want to make somebody happy." But, if the actor takes a closer look at the dialogue, he will find much evidence that the Young Man is not entirely sincere in what he tells Emily, that much of what he says is a "line" calculated to get her to help him escape. Still, he convinces *her,* and one has a lingering belief that he really would take her with him if she could spring him free, especially after he learns about the stultifying conditions of her life.

The strongest factor influencing the Young Man's behavior appears to be his desire to get back at the world, to set it straight by his own admittedly skewed standards. Thus we may state the Young Man's motivating desire as "I want to hurt those who hurt me." Obviously, this is not the only motivating desire for the Young Man that the play will support. One could argue that the strongest factor influencing his behavior springs from his desire to be left alone, to live in peace, or to find happiness. Clearly, such a decision will result in an entirely different characterization than our choice, which bears repeating: "I want to hurt those who have hurt me."

An analysis of Emily reveals that she is seventeen years old, born and reared in Matador. She works at the jail, cleaning and cooking, for a pittance of a wage, which her father takes from her. She is lonesome, bored, and naive, but she also has a spark of desire and life in her. She is so desperate for kindness and romance that she falls in love with the Young Man, and she has enough spunk to agree to help him escape. A good statement of her motivating desire might be "I want to find someone to love me." Again, the script will support other interpretations. Imagine, for example, how different the character would be performed if the choice for a motivating desire were "I want to disappear from this town, this state, this life."

By now it must be apparent that discovering the motivating force is the key to getting into the part. Important as it is, actors frequently fail to understand the basic motivation clearly, to name it accurately, and to feel it fully. This failure stems from two causes: (1) Many actors don't study the play with enough care and imagination, and (2) the motivating force—especially for a long and complex role—is frequently difficult to find.

You should not give up if you do not know the motivating desire when you begin rehearsal; instead, keep searching while you work on the role. During this stage, you can play smaller objectives and realize the character's intentions from scene to scene without knowing for certain how they relate to the motivating desire. In fact, you may never be convinced that you have the absolute, final answer for some characters; however, the search must not be abandoned, because the effort itself is of great value. Because of the ongoing nature of this process, your statement of the motivating desire you are working with at any particular moment is always hypothetical. You must continue to explore it, test it, and be willing to change it as your understanding of the character and the play increases.

During the early stages of the analytical process, the actor must also determine how important his character is relative to the other characters and to the communication of the playwright's meaning. Coquelin called this task discovering the plane on which his character should be placed; that is, whether he was in the foreground of the play, the background, or the middle ground. Deciding that a relatively minor character should receive more than his appropriate share of attention would obscure the meaning of the play. A good actor is not guilty of such overemphasis.

The actor must also see his character objectively. Some actors tend to "whitewash" their characters, making them more sympathetic than the playwright intended. The actions of foolish characters must appear foolish, those of greedy characters greedy, and those of evil characters evil. As we have already shown, this sort of objectivity would be especially important in analyzing the role of the Young Man in *Hello Out There*. The actor should search for reasons that make the character the way he is, including all qualities that are essential to the playwright's meaning, even if they make him out to be an unfulfilled, destructive fool. The actor should also not be afraid to search for what is foolish, unfulfilled, and destructive in himself, so he can nail down a solid connection with the role.

EXERCISE

Select a role from a standard one-act or full-length play. Make a list of what he does, what he says about himself, what others say about him, and what the dramatist says about him. State your initial idea of the character's motivating desire in terms that are true to the dramatist's conception and that could stimulate you to action in playing the part. Most of the plays used as examples in this text contain interesting characters for study and analysis. The following are some additional examples from the past two decades:

Caryl Churchill: *Top Girls*
Christopher Durang: *The Marriage of Bette and Boo*
Harvey Fierstein: *Safe Sex*
Maria Irene Fornes: *Promenade*
Michael Frayn: *Noises Off*
Athol Fugard: *"Master Harold"... and the Boys*
Charles Fuller: *A Soldier's Play*
Frank Galati: *John Steinbeck's The Grapes of Wrath*
William M. Hoffman: *As Is*
Tina Howe: *Coastal Disturbances*
_____: *One Shoe Off*
Wendy Kesselman: *My Sister in This House*
James Lapine: *Twelve Dreams*
Craig Lucas: *Prelude to a Kiss*
Ken Ludwig: *Lend Me a Tenor*
Terrence McNally: *The Lisbon Traviata*
David Mamet: *Speed-the-Plow*
Jane Martin: *Talking With...*
William Mastrosimone: *Shivaree*
Mark Medoff: *Children of a Lesser God*
John Ford Noonan: *A Coupla White Chicks Sitting Around Talking*
Marsha Norman: *'night, Mother*
_____ and Lucy Simon: *The Secret Garden*

Eric Overmyer: *On the Verge*
Wallace Shawn: *Aunt Dan and Lemon*
Sam Shepard: *A Lie of the Mind*
Robert Schenkkan: *The Kentucky Cycle*
Larry Shue: *The Foreigner*
Neil Simon: *Lost in Yonkers*
Alfred Uhry: *Driving Miss Daisy*
Wendy Wasserstein: *The Heidi Chronicles*
_____: *Isn't It Romantic*
_____: *The Sisters Rosensweig*
Michael Weller: *Loose Ends*
August Wilson: *Fences*
_____: *The Piano Lesson*
Lanford Wilson: *Burn This*
_____: *Redwood Curtain*

NOTES   1. Constantin Stanislavski, *Building a Character* (New York: Theatre Arts Books, 1949), p. 7.

2. David Magarshack, "Introduction," *Stanislavsky on the Art of the Stage* (New York: Hill and Wang, 1961), p. 77.

3. Constantin Stanislavski, *An Actor Prepares* (New York: Theatre Arts Books, 1936), pp. 257–58.

4. Stanislavski, *An Actor Prepares*, p. 258.

5. Michael Chekhov, *To the Actor* (New York: Harper & Row, 1953), p. 69.

CHAPTER 11

GETTING INTO CHARACTER

The job of acting demands that you be able to command the technique of accessing your inner resources while performing truthful physical actions, playing logical intentions, and establishing believable relationships—all within the circumstances supplied by the dramatist. Chapter 10 introduced methods for discovering the dramatist's concept of the character and illustrated how to state the concept in the form of a basic motivating desire. Unfortunately, some actors never progress beyond the point we have now reached in molding a technique of creative acting. If so, they stop short of understanding their work completely, for they have not learned how to put it all together. The successful actor knows how to bring everything he knows to bear on the actor's most fundamental contribution to the production of a play: the creation of a complete, well-rounded character. That process comprises our next lesson.

To learn this lesson, you will not need to add a new technique. Everything you have learned from the beginning has anticipated this moment. All acting begins with the question, "What would I do if I were the person prescribed by the dramatist in these given circumstances?" and each time you answer it, you are preparing to solve the preliminary problems of characterization.

The techniques you have developed so far have made you aware that a character is much more than what the audience *sees and hears,* even though you will certainly make use of all sorts of externals when you perform your character in a fully realized production. Some you will develop yourself during the course of the rehearsals: mannerisms, dialects, accents, for example. Others will be given to you as the production design takes shape: wigs, beards, special props, and costumes. Like all good actors, you will learn to use these resources with telling effect. You have also learned, however, that characterizations emerge from an *inner technique* that allows you to establish a convincing relationship with other characters by playing believable actions with meaningful intentions. Everything you have learned has reinforced the idea that the actor emphasizes doing, not being, because onstage, as in life, what a person does and what he avoids doing defines who he is.

DOING A LITTLE AT A TIME

One common error in characterization is to attempt to create the whole character at once, to grasp it with all its complexities at the very beginning. Such an actor is like a starving man who tries to cram whole handfuls of food into his mouth instead of taking bite-sized morsels he can readily chew and swallow. Good actors learn to perfect each piece of the character before shaping the whole performance.

One good way for the actor to begin building a character is to choose, out of the entire play, the scene or the sequence of physical actions he can most readily believe. It may or may not be the first scene in which the character appears, and it may or may not be an important scene. It must, however, be a scene that the actor understands relative to the dramatist's concept. Furthermore, it must be one that contains actions he has in his own experience, one that stimulates his imagination, and one in which he can readily become "possessed" of the intention.

Having chosen one small segment, the actor must learn to perform all its actions believably and to relate them to the character's motivating desire. Let us suppose you are preparing to play the Young Man in *Hello Out There* and you choose to begin with the scene in which the Young Man first asks "Katey" if she has access to the keys to his cell. Everything he has said to her prior to this moment has been in preparation for this request. Does he have a chance? Can she help him? Here is a scene for which an actor can recall a corresponding, if not identical, situation from his own experience. Surely he will have actually tried to get somebody else to help him accomplish something he desperately wanted to do, but, if not, he should easily be able to imagine himself doing so.

The excitement attending this situation is readily comprehensible. The possibility that his request will not be granted is ever present. The scene certainly cannot be played in a casual manner, yet it must be performed so the actor is prepared for failure as well as success. In fact, the Young Man gets a response that is even more devastating than failure: He learns that local officials consider his plight so dangerous that they are talking of moving him to a jail in another town.

The Young Man is able to ask for "Katey's" assistance because he has previously impressed her with flattery about her appearance and has touched her with his loneliness and despair. From the lines, we learn that the Young Man's method of flattering her is to sweet talk her and compliment her on her good looks and that his method of playing on her sympathy is to tell her vignettes from his life in which his "bad luck" always causes him to come out a loser. From the stage directions, we learn that his predicament leaves him pacing the floor like an animal. These details, supplied by Saroyan, help the actor solve the problem of how to perform the scene.

The actor's basic responsibility in preparing a role is to find, one by one, the numerous intentions and actions that taken together constitute his "part." Each is carried out to satisfy an explicit desire of the character, and each has a precise relation to the character's total behavior. Most actors call the "distance from the beginning to the end of an intention" a beat,[1] an important term for which Charles Marowitz has provided an illuminating definition:

> [A beat is] a section of time confined to a specific set of continuous actions, or perhaps the duration of a mood or an internal state. As soon as our actions graduate to the next unit of activity, we can be said to be in the next beat of the scene.... A beat...is a unit of time bounded by a common preoccupation with related actions. It is characterized by one overriding emotional colour and distinguishes itself from units of action which come before and after it.[2]

The actor and the director break down each scene into these units so they can more precisely discuss the role and prepare its performance, in much the same way a conductor uses a "measure" to focus the attention of the individual members of the orchestra on a particular part of a score. The beats of a play are comparable to the measures of a musical score in another way: They are primarily useful as rehearsal aids and should never be evident to the audience. Harold Clurman explained the importance of finding the beats:

> The analysis of the play's beats, the characters' actions, can and should be made before the actual staging of the play is begun. The actors derive a basic direction from such analysis and from *the notation of the beats in their part-books,* a guiding line that is the foundation for their entire work in the play. Without such groundwork, we may get a display of "general emotion" but not the meaning of the play.... The actor's talent becomes evident in the manner in which he carries out these actions. But talent or not, they must be clearly presented for the play to become an intelligible, coherent whole.[3]

Stanislavski usually referred to beats as *units of action* and also stressed the necessity of seeing the role as a series of units. As soon as the particular intention or desire that fires a unit is satisfied, another desire arises that forms the basis for another beat. In earlier chapters, when we asked you to structure your work by clearly delineating a beginning, a middle, and an end, we were in effect dividing the exercise into beats.

Objective is another analytical term that some teachers use to refer to the sum of an actor's intentions in a series of beats; however, for our purposes, it will suffice to consider objectives and intentions as synonymous terms. The important concept for us to understand is that, for the actor, every analytical unit of the play must be developed around a need or a want. To attempt to provide different names for various sized units is confusing, at best, so we shall use the terms intention and objective interchangeably. Once an objective or intention has been determined, it stands as the chief motivating force until the character successfully achieves it or until the circumstances of the play force the character to move to a new unit and a new goal.

When the beats have been selected so they form a rational progression and the intentions or objectives determined so they progress logically throughout the play, the raw materials of the inner characterization are in place. The movement from one unit to the next provides the *basic direction* (Clurman) or the *through-line* (Stanislavski) that guides the actor's performance. Taken together, all beats and objectives lead to the *super-objective* or *super-intention* that describes the character's larger, overriding goal for the entire play. This super-objective at least flows from and often coincides identically with the

A moment from the Missouri Repertory Theatre's production of *A Moon for the Misbegotten* by Eugene O'Neill, starring Richard McWilliams, Robert Elliott, and Lyn Greene. Study the faces as examples of actors thinking onstage. (Photo courtesy of the Missouri Repertory Theatre.)

motivating force, which we learned to discover and name in the previous chapter.

All actions ought to help to disclose the character's super-objective to the audience. If an action, much less a beat, is not related to this purpose, it should be eliminated. The audience understands the play by following a series of logical and expressive units. This understanding is facilitated when an actor thinks a logical progression of thoughts and performs a believable and consistent set of actions, all of which grow from the given circumstances of his role.

The seeming illogic of some contemporary plays—especially those identified as theatre of the absurd—is deceptive. The dramatist has written the play for a specific purpose and has given the characters some pattern of behavior. To express the absurdity he finds in contemporary life, he may require from the actor a series of illogical actions. But by using speech and actions illogically, by introducing the fantastic and the ridiculous, his purpose is to express the absence of truth and meaning in modern society. As in the case of any drama, it is the actor's job to discover a super-objective in the seemingly illogical pattern and to communicate it to the audience as clearly as possible.

Creating a character requires, more than anything else, the ability to follow a through-line of action. To do so, the actor must carefully perform each beat, always attempting to realize his intention and to relate each beat clearly to the one that follows it, even though in some instances the relation may be that no relation exists. A definite "terminal point" at the end of each unit and a firm "attack" at the beginning, marking clearly that something new is starting, give the play a sense of forward movement. *Hello Out There,* constructed for the most part with clear cause-and-effect relationships between the beats, illustrates the kind of analytical problem with which the actor will be confronted in most plays, both classic and contemporary. The following beats and causal relationships provide a basic road map for playing the Young Man from the beginning of the play to the entrance of the young girl:

1. The Young Man calls out dramatically to the "world." His intention is *to relieve the tension of being alone in the cell.*

   Progress to next beat: The young girl's answering voice leads him into the next beat.

2. The Young Man's intention in this beat is *to find out who is there.*

   Progress to next beat: Realizing this intention leads the Young Man into the next one. Having determined that she is somebody who works at the jail, he now wants to keep her talking to him.

3. The Young Man engages her in a variety of small talk in which his intention is *to size her up, to learn more about her.*

   Progress to next beat: His banter produces several valuable facts about "Katey," but she produces an obstacle to his fully realizing his intention by raising the issue of why he is in jail.

4. The Young Man's new intention is *to set her right about the incident*.

   Progress to next beat: He never knows for certain if this intention succeeds, for discussing the events of the previous evening leads him back into the state of fear and loneliness in which the scene began.

5. The Young Man's next intention is *to draw her closer to him*. His lonely call of "Hello out there" is now personalized, and the sincerity of his feelings entices her into his world.

   In analyzing Emily/"Katey," we discover the following units and causal relationships in the same section:

1. Emily answers the Young Man's call because its urgency demands a reply and because she enjoyed what he said to her when he was talking in his sleep. Her intention is *to find out if he is awake and alert*.

   Progress to next beat: Emily clearly liked what he said to her earlier. She is more than a little intrigued by the opportunity to have a conversation with a "man of the world."

2. Emily's new intention is *to find out what she can about him without getting too close*.

   Progress to next beat: Note that her beats do not necessarily begin and end at the same place as those of the Young Man. She succeeds, somewhat, in this intention, until he forces her to start talking about herself. She is not yet comfortable with self-disclosing talk, so she devises a strategy to gain control of the conversation.

3. Emily's new intention is *to confront him with his crime*.

   Progress to next beat: The one thing that has troubled her about the Young Man is that he is accused of something so horrible she can hardly comprehend it. She is relieved, but not totally satisfied, that he denies it.

4. Her new intention is *to take a chance on getting closer*. She responds to the sincerity of his call and to their mutual longing. Her entering his world is, for her, a brave act.

EXERCISE

(1) Study the breakdowns of the play carefully. Make a list of all the physical actions you can discover in the script that occur during the performing of each beat. Remember, speech is an action, so try to describe what the character is *doing* during each unit of dialogue contained in the beat.

(2) Prepare a beat analysis of the entire play for either the Young Man or for Emily.

(3) The importance of learning to divide a role into beats or units, of clearly playing each intention, and of firmly attacking the beginning of each unit cannot be overemphasized. Since accomplishing these tasks is the key

both to building character and to developing plot, you should not try to proceed further until you can make effective application of this technique.

Return to the character you studied in Chapter 10 to find the motivating desire. Divide the role into beats, and state the intention for each beat. Make a score of physical actions. Select a beat you can completely believe in, and play it, relating it carefully to the character's basic motivation.

Characterization, then, begins with discovering the character's motivating desire and proceeds by breaking the role into small units, each with a clearly understood intention that moves the character toward accomplishing the larger purpose. Discovering, enriching, and playing these units is a constant challenge throughout the rehearsals and performance. Few actors, even of the highest professional caliber (and after playing a role a great number of times), would claim they succeed in believing, with equal conviction, every beat. That, however, is the aim of creative actors, whether they are professionals or performing nonprofessionally in an educational or community theatre, and they work to accomplish it at every rehearsal and performance. But they realize that failure to achieve complete belief at every moment does not indicate a bad actor any more than failure to return every ball indicates a bad tennis player. A good actor succeeds in believing a large proportion of what he does, just as a good tennis player succeeds in returning a large proportion of balls. Both the actor and the athlete work to improve their techniques in order to increase the proportion of their successes.

SUPPLYING AN IMAGINARY BACKGROUND

The dramatist provides enough detail for the actor to understand the motivating desire and the essential traits of a character, but the actor must almost always supply an imaginary background to round out the essentials gleaned from the text. In playing the part of Emily, for instance, the actor needs to know what she went through in deciding to stick around after everybody else had left and her job was completed. She states that she hoped for a chance to talk to the Young Man and that he said he liked her when he was talking in his sleep. It is important for the actress to realize that coming into contact with the Young Man is a part of Emily's plan, that it happens not from the pure chance of her being there performing her duties but through her deliberate calculations.

The actor playing the Young Man, on the other hand, must be careful not to jump to the conclusion that some "magic moment" has caused his character to fall in "love at first sight" with Emily. It is clear from his dialogue that he is a "ladies' man," that he revels in the company of women, that he is unhappy unless he has a woman to share his life. His casualness in deciding to marry Emily and his haste in rushing to a relationship suggest that he has done this many times before. This conclusion will lead the actor to imagine a lifetime of broken, brief relationships that lead to the moment this play begins. He simply cannot step into this role without fleshing out in his imagination the given circumstances provided by the playwright.

The Young Man's selection of the name "Katey" provides another opportunity for imagined circumstances. Why did he select this particular name? Has he known a Katey in the past, or is this a name he associates with the "woman of his dreams," who is always there for him, who shares his world? Does it come to mind because he travels about the country by hopping freight cars, and the line he rode into Texas was the MKT—the "Katey?" Whether or not the actor selects this imaginary circumstance as truth, he will certainly want to re-create in his mind—if not actually improvise—how the Young Man came to be in the town of Wheeling, Texas, as well as how long he had been there before the incident of the night before. Saroyan is especially stingy in his description of the character; therefore, the actor has an even greater responsibility to furnish the missing facts.

The actor can often prepare for this technique of supplying an imaginary background for specific events in the script by writing an autobiography as if he were the character, narrating events that the play does not include. To be valid, it should contain only details that logically extend from those provided by the dramatist, and, to be useful, it should contain only those details of specific behavior that can guide the actor's choice of intentions and relationships.

In many of the great classic dramas, vital matters of interpretation depend on supplying an imaginary background. Consider *Othello,* for instance. What relationship, before the beginning of the play, had existed among the characters that prompted the Moor to prefer Cassio over Iago as his principal officer and, at the same time, to trust Iago with knowledge of his personal affairs, of which he kept Cassio ignorant? What is Roderigo's background that he aspires to win Desdemona, has access to her only through Iago, and has the wealth to satisfy Iago's extravagant demands on his purse? Finding answers to such questions help determine the behavior of a character.

The following is an example of a possible autobiography for Emily:

My name is Emily Smith, and I am almost seventeen years old, the oldest child in a family of six. My father has not worked for years, and our family is dependent for its livelihood on his small relief check, my tiny salary I earn cleaning up and cooking at the jail, and what few odd jobs such as cleaning, washing, or ironing my mother can get from the few families in our community who have any money.

I finished the eighth grade, but I could not afford to go to high school. I like to read, and I borrow romantic novels and *True Story* magazines from a woman on the other side of town who my mother sometimes works for. These books and magazines help me know a little bit about what it is like in the outside world. I rode the school bus to Wheeling, and once we visited my grandfather in San Antonio, but I was very young and don't remember anything about the trip.

I want more than anything in the world to leave Matador and see the world. I think I might be pretty if I had nice clothes and my hair fixed. Sometimes the boys around town whistle at me and try to get me to talk to them, but I can't stand them. I know most of them will grow up to be just like my father, and I want more than that out of life.

I don't really know how I learned about sex, and I actually don't know much about it. My mother was embarrassed when she had to explain to me why I was having my period. She told me it meant I could have babies, but she wouldn't talk about it any more than she had to. I wouldn't want any of the boys around here to be interested in me that way, but I do long to know what it would be like to be kissed and held and touched by a handsome man of the world.

I will not give up. I know my chance will come to get out of this town. I will leave my family without regret, because I know I have love to give, if I can only find somebody who can teach me how to give it and who will love me in return.

An autobiography will put you on closer terms with the character you are playing. Make preparing one a regular part of your analysis procedure.

USING OFFSTAGE ACTIONS

When an actor writes a theoretical autobiography, he is using his imagination to construct a history, a past life of the character. Although such work is necessary for creating a believable person who can live and act within the given circumstances of the play, the actor must concentrate his efforts on those moments in the character's life the playwright chooses to dramatize. Closely related to these events are other actions, some of which are extremely important to the development of the plot, that take place offstage. The actor can make use of these actions by writing a narrative version of the entire story, curtain to curtain, from the point of view of his character, and by improvising actions that happen offstage.

Although *Hello Out There* is a compact one-act play, events that take place offstage still affect the outcome of the story. The actor playing Emily will certainly want to know what happened in the brief interval she was offstage the first time she started to look for the gun. She comes back scared and almost crying. In order to play this important moment convincingly, she will need to continue the action without interruption from the time she leaves until she returns. Later, she does leave and unsuccessfully searches for the gun. When she returns, she will want to bring the excitement and drama of her mission onstage with her. She tells about avoiding the crowd gathering outside by coming in through a back window. What an adventure! Has she actually searched for the gun? Did she hear the crowd and, fearing the worst, return to see if she could help? Was she almost discovered by some member of her family? Remember, we noted that the time of the play was the evening—she must perform these actions in the dark. Does she care if she is discovered? How can she justify the gun in her romantic mental picture of involvement with the Young Man?

In writing the story of the play from the point of view of the woman who enters during its final moments, the actress would need to fill in a complete account of what took place the night before and what has happened since that time. She has only a brief, climactic scene in which to establish her character, and she will surely fail if she does not know everything about the events that bring her into the jail where the scene happens. It will also be important for her to consult with the director and the rest of the cast before working out the details of her life. Whether or not the events of the night before took place as the Young Man says they did, or as she says they did, is absolutely crucial to the way both she and the Young Man perform the scene.

EXERCISE

We have referred more than once to the necessity of deciding where the truth lies in the story of the incident that precipitated the action of this play. Be prepared to justify one side or the other, based on a careful and detailed reading of the script. Would our decision to set the play in 1942 influence your contention? Why?

The actor playing the woman's husband may have an even greater need to understand his character's offstage actions. He certainly gives every indication that he suspects the Young Man is telling the truth about his wife, and to play the rage and hate that allows him to pull the trigger will take some strong emotional recall work as well as a precise knowledge of the character's intentions and motivations. Writing a detailed narrative of his life, especially during the actual time of the play, curtain to curtain, will immensely help the actor believe the onstage actions of this character.

EXERCISE

Select one of the following characters, and write a narrative of the character's life that includes offstage events during the actual time covered by the play. Select an important offstage event, construct it as a unit, break it into beats, and improvise it either alone or with a partner. For instance, in the first example, the actress might choose to improvise the scene in which Abigail pushes a needle into her stomach in order to cast suspicion on Elizabeth Proctor.

(1) Abigail in *The Crucible,* by Arthur Miller.
(2) Jack in *The Importance of Being Earnest,* by Oscar Wilde.
(3) Austin in *True West,* by Sam Shepard.
(4) Joseph Surface in *School for Scandal,* by Richard Brinsley Sheridan.
(5) Lizzie in *The Rainmaker,* by N. Richard Nash.
(6) Tilden in *Buried Child,* by Sam Shepard.
(7) Horner in *The Country Wife,* by William Wycherley.
(8) Meg Brockie in *Brigadoon,* by Alan Jay Lerner and Frederick Loewe.
(9) Mariane in *Tartuffe,* by Molière.

(10) Babe in *Crimes of the Heart,* by Beth Henley.
(11) M'Lynn in *Steel Magnolias* by Robert Harling.
(12) "Froggy" LeSeur in *The Foreigner* by Larry Shue.
(13) Lieutenant Commander Joanne Galloway in *A Few Good Men* by Aaron Sorkin.
(14) Cephus in *Home* by Samm-Art Williams.

CHARACTERIZING THROUGH EXTERNALS

Earlier, we mentioned that *externals* can be an invaluable aid to characterization. To refresh your memory, externals are exactly what the term implies: manifestations of character the audience sees and, in the case of departures from the actor's natural speech, hears. Examples of externals are costumes, makeup, wigs, padding, dialects, foreign accents, and hand properties such as fans, pipes, canes, snuffboxes, and cigarette holders. The term also refers to physical attributes such as posture, a manner of walking or sitting, a distinctive gesture, or any such physical abnormality as being lame or hunchbacked. *Externalizing* a character is one of the actor's most important responsibilities. We have already noted that the audience believes what it sees, so the actor must find outward forms that will help the audience believe the character he is playing.

Externals may also greatly help the actor believe in a character. A vivid imagination is required to find outward forms to express inner character traits, and these outward forms are often used to reinforce an actor's conviction in the truth of his creation. An especially erect posture, with chin held high and nostrils pinched, as if constantly trying to locate a slightly offensive odor, might aid an actress in characterizing the overpowering Lady Bracknell in Oscar Wilde's *The Importance of Being Earnest.* A mannerism of sucking his teeth might help an actor in believing the vulgarity of Mr. Burgess in George Bernard Shaw's *Candida.* Elia Kazan's notebook for *A Streetcar Named Desire* outlines effective externals for the crude, simple, naive, sensual character of Stanley Kowalski. He sucks a cigar. He annoyingly busies himself with other things while people are talking to him. Note that Kazan was also the first director of this play: A good director is worth his weight in gold to the actor in developing externals for his character.

If the actor playing the Young Man wears clothing that he can believe the character originally splurged on because it made him stand out in a crowd but that is now torn and dirty, and if wearing it makes him feel angry about what has happened, he is making proper use of an external to aid him in believing the character. Another use of an external might be to imagine that the Young Man is famished. Saroyan has the character complain about the quality of the food, and the actor's centering on the gnawing pains of hunger could add a believable dimension to the desperation with which the Young Man wants to get out of his cell.

Dramas abound with opportunities for actors to use externals as a means of deepening and extending their characterizations. For instance, the actor doing

Willy Loman in Arthur Miller's *Death of a Salesman* should examine the effect of carrying heavy sample bags on the physique of an elderly man. The rounded shoulders, the body leaning forward to balance the weight of the samples, the feet hurting from too much pressure, the eyes looking at the ground to search for obstacles—all these external manifestations can help create a truthful characterization of the exhaustion of Willy Loman.

The late distinguished actor, Sir Laurence Olivier, often used makeup to help find the character. For example, he once told of developing the right type of nose as a key to a role. From this center, he could create a whole physical presence. However, Olivier would have been the first to emphasize that the external approach must be used in conjunction with internal motivation in order to develop a complete characterization.

When using externals as a means to characterization, the actor must observe two cautions:

1. He must beware of clichés, the stereotyped mannerisms or properties that have been so frequently repeated they would occur immediately to even an unimaginative mind. For the audience, clichés no longer express individuality but only general types. For the actor, they are often the imitation of an imitation, worn-out devices that he can execute mechanically. Consequently, they are powerless to aid him in believing the character.

2. He must be sure that the externalization either results from or leads to a specific need he can relate to the character's motivating desire.

RELATING DETAILS TO THE MOTIVATING DESIRE

The caution we registered about making externals serve the motivating desire may be repeated with similar emphasis for all aspects of the characterization. Everything the actor does, says, or wears on the stage should help either create the motivating desire or satisfy it. The more clearly the actor understands how a particular detail relates to his goal, the more significant it will be both to him and the audience. The Young Man's hunger, his nervousness, his smooth talk, and his intense loneliness all stem directly from or strengthen his desire to hurt those who have hurt him.

The motivating desire is the unifying factor in selecting both internal and external details of characterization. Anything that does not relate to it is extraneous and should not be permitted. In fact, the actor should even avoid introducing details that are merely neutral; that is, details that perhaps do not hinder but bear no inherent relationship. Neutral items of characterization are deadwood, excess weight from which no benefit is received. Whether the actor wears a slouch hat or a homburg, whether his socks are plain-colored or striped, or whether he gulps his coffee or sips it slowly should all be determined by the motivating force behind the character's actions. The way an actress does her hair, the way she sits, and the way she says "Good morning" should all be similarly determined. Every detail should make a positive contribution to the total characterization.

EXPANDING
THE
CHARACTER

Once an actor has sufficient insight into a character to believe and perform a single intention, he is ready to proceed to a second unit of action that may have appeared more difficult in the beginning. Let us assume you have arrived at this point in playing the Young Man. The second intention you choose to concentrate on might be near the closing of the play, when the Young Man desperately tries to convince the husband that they have been equally duped by the wife.

The imaginary background we have already supplied will, of course, help us believe the general actions of this unit, but we must return to the play for important information about its specific demands.

1. Saroyan tells us that the Young Man ignores the implications of the sounds of the approaching automobiles and slamming car doors, suggesting that he is reluctant to accept the reality of the situation. "If I ignore it, perhaps it will go away."

2. The Young Man suddenly shouts at the husband, which can be seen as a ruse on his part to try to get the upper hand, to dominate the scene. Treating the man as if he thought he was the jailer is another ramification of his attempt to postpone the inevitable.

3. When he is forced to relate to The Man as the husband, he continues to delay the real confrontation by indignantly debasing him for hitting him over the head the night before.

4. He degrades the wife in an action calculated to establish a common denominator between the two men that might lead the husband to divert his anger.

These circumstances place the Young Man in a position in which he has a chance to achieve his motivating desire through an action that will also provide him with a chance to escape from his predicament. It is a calculated risk, but it is the only chance of a desperate man. All the autobiographical work you have done, especially that which has filled in the details of the encounter with the woman on the night before, will be necessary in order for you to believe strongly in this difficult and important unit. It is the climax of the play and the moment that will define the remainder of the character's life.

Return to the exercise in which you prepared beats for one of the characters in *Hello Out There,* and think about how you might analyze each unit in the same detailed manner we have provided. Do not seek shortcuts. You must gain a thorough understanding of your character's actions and responses, moment by moment, beat by beat.

In summary, the beginning steps in preparing to perform a character are

1. Analyze the role to discover the character's motivating desire.

2. State the desire in the form of a basic want that will stimulate specific action.

3. Break the role into beats that will help you accomplish the motivating desire.

4. State the intention of each beat.

5. Supply an imaginary background to supplement the information about the character given by the dramatist.

This scene is from the Long Wharf Theatre production of *National Anthem* by Dennis McIntyre, starring Kevin Spacey, Mary McDonnell, and Tom Berenger. Study the picture and write inner monologues for these three characters. (Photo © T. Charles Erickson, 1991.)

6. Select externals that will help you believe the motivating desire.

7. Choose one unit whose intention you can readily justify.

8. Make a score of physical actions for the unit.

9. Rehearse the actions until you can believably repeat them at will.

10. Continue steps 8 and 9 through each beat of the role.

---

1. Robert Lewis, *Method—Or Madness?* (New York: Samuel French, 1958), p. 33.

2. Charles Marowitz, *The Act of Being* (New York: Taplinger, 1978), pp. 29–30.

3. Harold Clurman, "The Principles of Interpretation," in *Producing the Play,* ed. John Gassner (New York: Holt, Rinehart, 1941), p. 287. Italics ours.

NOTES

CHAPTER 12

GETTING INTO THE PLAY

Creating a character is the actor's important and particular responsibility in a theatrical production. But a single character is part of a much larger whole, and the actor must relate his performance to the entire play. He must discover why the dramatist wrote the play, what he wanted it to say, what experience he wanted the audience to have while watching it, and what thoughts and feelings he wanted the audience to take away with them when they leave the theatre. Ideally, the entire company of actors should agree on what they believe the dramatist intended the total meaning of the play to be, so each individual can honestly communicate to the audience his share of the playwright's ideas.

In Chapter 10, which discussed the technique of getting into the part, we learned that the actor must analyze a character with considerable care to determine the motivating force behind his actions. In this chapter, we shall discover that a dramatist employs a group of characters, all motivated by different and often conflicting desires, for the purpose of expressing in the play a single or total meaning. Further, we shall be concerned with how each actor's role can help to realize the author's intention.

Several sources help the actor prepare to learn about the play. He will want to know something of the playwright's life and of the circumstances under which the play was written. Knowing that *The Tempest* was probably Shakespeare's last play and that in Prospero's farewell to his art—the practice of white magic—Shakespeare was saying farewell to his supreme artistry as a dramatist and a poet might help an actor realize the calm, the dignity, and the finality of the overall tone of this play. An actor in Moliére's plays may be able to use the knowledge that this playwright had a young wife and that, in his several plays in which an old man is married to a young girl, his observations came from his own experience. Some of O'Neill's plays are almost completely autobiographical, and knowing about his relation with his parents and his older brother and about his life as a young man in New London, Connecticut, might well help actors select actions to illuminate O'Neill's characters and help them communicate the nature of his world.

Good drama always reflects, if it does not deal directly with, the social, economic, and moral values of its time. It follows that actors need to learn about the prevailing social conditions at the time a play in which they are performing was written. An actor could hardly succeed in Congreve's *The Way of the World* without learning as much as possible about the amoral behavior of upper-class society in Restoration England. On a more modern note, it might help an actor preparing to perform in one of Bertolt Brecht's intriguing dramas to know that the enigmatic German playwright was ideologically a Communist and that most of his works protest against a capitalistic society. For the corpus of dramas written about the war in Vietnam, such as David Rabe's *The Basic Training of Pavlo Hummel* or Sean Clark's *Eleven-Zulu,* the actor needs to learn about the conditions in training camps, the prevailing moral values in the combat zones, and the breach that combat experience is likely to cause between a returning soldier and his family.

One of the fascinating aspects of being an actor is the constant need to understand what makes people from all walks of life "tick." Depending on the production in which he is working at the moment, he may have to learn about conditions among the coal miners in Pennsylvania or among sharecroppers in the South, or about the treatment of American Indians. He may have to learn about proper procedure in a courtroom, in a hospital, or on a battleship. For instance, in order to perform *Hello Out There,* the play on which we have been working, the actor will need to know what life was like in small Texas towns in the early 1940s.

To understand and perform in period plays, the actor must find out about the clothes worn at the time. He must know not only how to wear them and move in them but also why a certain fashion prevailed. Why were stocks and farthingales worn in the Renaissance? Paniers and powdered wigs in the eighteenth century? How did Restoration gentlemen use a walking stick or Victorian ladies use a fan?

Where does an actor find answers to questions about the playwright's life; the social, economic, and moral values of a play's time; or the details of behavior and dress of a period? First, he must be a voracious reader, concentrating on both the fiction and nonfiction of the period during which the play takes place. He should study biographies of his playwright and of famous actors and other people from the period. Pictures from the period—paintings, engravings, magazine and newspaper photos—are excellent sources for makeup and costume, but they also indicate attitudes and atmosphere of the times. Good pictures arouse strong feelings, and good actors find ways to use the flavor of pictures in defining a believable character. For more recent periods, motion pictures, both fictive and documentary, provide excellent sources of behavior and social detail. Finally, the actor can use theatre history, especially the stage history of the play he is performing. Although an actor should not—and could not—duplicate another performance of the role, he may find details he had overlooked. To know too much about the play, the period, and the character is impossible.

Knowledge of such matters as period and style, an invaluable source of actions, intentions, and relationships—what the actor can perform—is also essential to a full understanding of the playwright's meaning. Consequently, the actor finds it doubly important to obtain this information; indeed, he cannot afford to ignore it. It helps him prepare to read more intelligently his chief source for interpreting the play—the script, itself.

FINDING THE DRAMATIST'S BASIC MEANING

All actors in the performing company must agree on what a play is about, what meaning the dramatist had in mind, before each individual can fulfill his particular function in the cooperative effort of a dramatic production. Stanislavski wrote about this necessity: "The main theme must be firmly fixed in the actor's mind throughout the performance. It gave birth to the writing of the play. It should also be the fountainhead of the actor's artistic creation." He called this main theme the *super-objective of the entire play:*

> In a play the whole stream of individual, minor objectives, all the imaginative thoughts, feelings, and actions of an actor, should converge to carry out the *super-objective* of the plot. The common bond must be so strong that even the most insignificant detail, if it is not related to the *super-objective,* will stand out as superfluous or wrong.[1]

Harold Clurman stated emphatically that "no character of the play can be properly understood unless the play as a whole is understood." He recognized that understanding the play resolves itself into one question:

> What is the *basic action of the play*? What is the play about from the standpoint of the characters' principal conflict?...What is the play's core? For Gordon Craig, *Hamlet* is the story of man's search for the truth. Saroyan's *My Heart's in the Highlands,* to its New York director, was the story of people eager to give things to one another—lovers all, in a sense. For me, Odets' *Night Music* had to do with the search for a home.
>
> Whether these formulations are correct or not, the point is that the director's most important task is to find the basic line of the play. I call it the *spine* of the play because my first teacher in this field, Richard Boleslavsky, used the word.[2]

Although finding the basic action is one of the director's most important tasks and sharing it with his cast is one of his most important responsibilities, the actor, if he is to be a creative artist in his own right, needs to understand the meaning of the play through his own efforts. Only then can he be certain that it is *his,* that it has possessed every fiber of his imagination. How does he discover this basic meaning, the wellspring of his characterization?

In *Hello Out There* we found the Young Man's motivating desire to be "I want to hurt those who hurt me." We decided that Emily's motivating desire was "I want to find someone to love me." The conflict in this play results from the outside forces that keep either of them from achieving their desire, although one might speculate that at the final curtain Emily is even more motivated to continue her quest. To understand Saroyan's basic meaning, what it was that "gave birth" to the play, we must study the script with both characters' motivating desires and the ultimate conflict of the action in mind.

The meaning of a play cannot be determined solely from a study of its events. Story is rarely the unique feature of a dramatic work, for essentially the same story may be used to express a variety of meanings. People who are interested only in the "story" of a play are missing a good deal of its value, and a production that offers the audience nothing more than story is realizing only a part of its possibilities.

The story of *Hello Out There* could actually be summarized in three short sentences. Two people meet. They find a common bond in their trapped

Steel Magnolias by Robert Harling forces the actresses to find a single, believable source for the pathos of the central situation and the natural comedy of much of the dialogue. (Photo © Carol Rosegg/Martha Swope Associates.)

existence. One of them is killed before they can escape together. Simple, right? In fact, if this story is all the play offers, it cannot be distinguished from half of all the dramas ever written.

Even a cursory reading of this script, however, will reveal the importance of a second dramatic element—character. These are not any two people. They are the Young Man with his idealism, his jaded worldliness, and his threatening predicament, and Emily with her naiveté, her romantic dreams, and her youth. So, in addition to telling the story, the action allows us to get to know these two interesting persons.

Story and character combine to form plot, and these two elements working in concert with each other allow the dramatist to make an observation on life. We have emphasized many times that revealing this observation is the actor's basic purpose when the play is produced on the stage.

What observation has Saroyan made in *Hello Out There*? The play cannot be merely a story of two people getting to know each other under desperate circumstances. Such an action has little point unless it is directed toward some further end. What purpose does the action of the play serve? Of course, we become engaged by the story of these two people and empathize with their needs and emotions, but that does not relieve us from the responsibility of trying to determine Saroyan's purpose. To be significant, any production of the play must attempt to make clear Saroyan's observations as interpreted by the artists associated with that particular performance.

Follow our reasoning process as we attempt to discover a defensible interpretation of Saroyan's major purpose or observation in this play about two people who meet under unusual circumstances. After several readings of the play, two points emerge as important factors:

1. The Young Man is literally trapped by his environment. He is in jail.

2. To both the Young Man and Emily, escaping from their environment is a serious matter. They must escape before they can possibly accomplish their motivating desires.

The play, then, must be about people who find themselves trapped within complex circumstances from which they need to escape.

But, why these particular characters? What do this drifter and this innocent young girl have to do with each other? What is it about their lives that allows them to find a common bond of understanding? Both take considerable risks during the action of the play. Emily risks her reputation to try to help the Young Man. She could easily be found out by her family or people who know her in the town. The Young Man risks his life, literally, in an attempt to save it. The only chance he has to escape is to tell The Man a convincing story, to forge a bond of understanding between the two of them. He fails.

From this brief summary of our study of the script, how would you characterize the major point Saroyan wants to make about life? We decide to state our choice as follows: *Loving people—trusting people—is a risky business.*

But, we must not stop there. Even though in this play Saroyan does not appear to be clear about whether or not it is a risk worth taking to love and trust other people, we will certainly have to take a position on this question before we can proceed with our interpretation. At this point we return to the background reading we did for this production. Our examination of the other works by Saroyan disclosed that he consistently writes about the "little" people, the "gentle people," and their struggle to find love, life, and significance in a harsh world. We conclude that it would be most in line with the spirit of the playwright and the play to emphasize in our production that love and trust are worth the effort.

Once we agree on it, we must be unwavering in our commitment to this major purpose. We will set it up by the way we present the events leading up to the climax of the play, and the actress playing Emily must find a way to "nail it down" in the production's final moment. Our single and unwavering goal will be to see that this meaning is comprehended by the spectators, for the through-line-of-action is complete only after the audience absorbs it. If our production is successful, the spectators should take away with them the realization of how risky but how important it is to take a chance on caring about another human being. We want them to empathize with the plight of the main characters but be uplifted by the chances they took on each other.

The next step in interpreting the script is for the actors (and the director) to determine the basic action that grows out of its meaning, for it is this action that provides the play's dramatic conflict and through which the playwright makes clear his message. Harold Clurman referred to this overarching action that embodies the meaning as the *spine*. It serves as a constant guide to the director and the actors, because it is the unifying factor for the superobjectives of all characters; indeed, for all details of the performance. We may say the spine of *Hello Out There* is "to take a chance on love."

The playwright's basic observation and the play's "spine" are such key concepts that we shall illustrate them further by examining *Romeo and Juliet*. The play opens with a violent outbreak of the rivalry between the Montagues and the Capulets. Starting with a comic quarrel between the servants of the two houses, it next involves Benvolio and Tybalt (the younger generation), and finally the old men themselves—old Capulet calling for his sword and old Montague calling Capulet a villain. They are restrained from combat only by the jibes and pleadings of their wives. The unseemly brawl is finally brought to an end by the prince of Verona; it is a nasty fight, and it sickens us with its violence and its pointlessness.

In subsequent scenes we see the Capulets and the Montagues not as enemies but as parents. We see they are not ogres but are concerned with their children, the Montagues with finding the cause of Romeo's depression and the Capulets with finding a suitable husband for Juliet. We wonder about this mixture of filial concern and violent hatred; that we first see Romeo and Juliet in relation to their parents is significant to understanding the play.

The conflict develops rapidly. In quick succession we see the meeting of the lovers, the balcony scene (death to Romeo if he should be discovered), the marriage, the killing of Mercutio and Tybalt, Romeo's banishment, and the death of the lovers in the tomb. We glory in the greatness of their love, but we loathe the senseless "canker'd hate" that brought about their tragedy. We are filled with wonder at their sacrifice and grateful that the ancient rivalry has ended. But how unnecessary! The parents are left with golden statues instead of living children, and they are faced with a realization of the awful price Romeo and Juliet have paid.

What is Shakespeare's key observation that informs the facts of his story? It can probably be stated in some embodiment of the old bromide that "love conquers all." If we communicate it clearly, the audience should be sickened by the hatred between the families and rejoice for the love that overcame such bitterness. We want them to know that cankered hate brings tragedy and suffering and that it must ultimately yield to the force of love. The play's spine—the basic action that embodies the meaning we have just interpreted—could be stated as "to overcome all obstacles in the path of love." A production that used this spine to guide the actors and the director throughout rehearsals and performance could provide an unforgettable experience for the audience.

Beginning actors sometimes have a mistaken notion that careful analysis destroys spontaneity. This attitude is difficult to defend. Acting, like any other art, is a conscious process. Spontaneity is fruitful only after careful study directs it toward the accomplishment of a purpose. The resistance to analysis may be especially strong in the case of comedy, where it is natural for the actor to assume that the purpose is simply to "be funny." Actually, a dramatist's basic intention is no different in comedy than in the so-called serious types of drama; the difference, if any, lies in the treatment. The successful actor accepts without question the responsibility to know the meaning and spine of every play he undertakes.

INTERPRETING THE PLAY: THE DUAL PERSONALITY OF THE ACTOR

In discharging his responsibility of communicating the play to an audience, the actor assumes a dual personality. Figuratively, he splits himself into two parts. One part is the actor in the character, and up to now this has been our primary concern. The other part remains outside the character as a *commentator,* continually pointing out the significance of each action in relation to the total meaning of what the character is doing and saying.

The actor should never "lose himself in the part." George Bernard Shaw's maxim is frequently quoted: "The one thing not forgivable in an actor is being the part instead of playing it." Shaw would have stated the case more accurately if he had said: "In addition to being the part, the actor must also play it"; then his statement would warn against losing oneself yet recognize the necessity of the divided personality.

Let us state the actor's twofold function again. He must create the character, yet to make his creation fully express the dramatist's observation, he must also find a way to tell the audience what the dramatist (and, very possibly, what he himself) thinks and feels about the character's behavior. This subtle finishing touch to developing a characterization often marks the difference between a work of art and merely playing a role. All great actors find a way to provide this comment without detracting in the least from the believability of their performance. *If such comment is handled well, it allows the audience to glimpse inside the mind of both the actor and the playwright.*

Again *Hello Out There* will serve as an illustration. In playing the Young Man, the actor devotes a part of himself to creating a character in which he and the audience can believe. The other part is devoted to saying that the Young Man is an incurably idealistic ne'er-do-well. As a commentator, the actor must leave no doubt that the Young Man's braggadocio is a front, that his philosophizing is hollow, and that his concern about Emily is a bid for attention so she will help him escape. In playing Emily, the actress-as-commentator must

Ron Liebman and Jessica Walter in the New York production of *Rumors*. This play creates a reality that stretches from high comedy to naturalism. Performers must find ways to accommodate this ever-shifting world. (Photo by Martha Swope.)

communicate her character's lack of worldliness. Since she is totally without the necessary experience to judge whether or not she could experience happiness with this man, would her life actually be better if she could run away with him? The actress-as-commentator must help the audience understand that the impulse of the character to help this loser is primal.

In other words, the actor has the added task of guiding the audience in forming an opinion of his character. By this means, he leads them to an understanding of the play's basic meaning. The comment may say that a character is weak but essentially good; that although it may not be possible to approve of his actions, he is entitled to sympathetic understanding. It may say that another character is vain and selfish, undeserving of sympathy, and that still another is living fully and happily according to sound principles.

The comment comes from the omniscience of the actor who knows the character better than the character can know himself. The Young Man does not recognize that he is a loser: The actor has to recognize it and tell it to the audience by emphasizing certain details of his characterization.

The actor must commit himself to expressing the dramatist's intention as nearly as it is possible to discover what that intention is. To make the audience dislike a character whom the playwright intended to be received with sympathy would alter essential values. Obviously it would be very wrong in our interpretation of *Romeo and Juliet* for the long-standing feud to seem justified and the love between the two young people to be seen as a breach of family loyalty. As a result of their comment, the actors will set the beauty and rightness of their love in contrast with the ugliness and wrongness of the obstacles against it.

Aware of his dual personality, a part of the actor's preparation is to decide how his performance can best express the meaning of the play and whether his comment should be made obvious or subtly detectable. His decision will be based on the type of play the dramatist has written and the kind of production the director has planned. Factors in his decision may include one or more of the following:

1. The period in which the play was written (a classic Greek play is not acted like a modern play)

2. The type of play (a farce is not acted like a tragedy)

3. The theatricality of the play and the production (a naturalistic play is not acted like an absurd play)

Books abound on the differences between dramatic genres such as comedy and tragedy or realism and expressionism, and the dedicated actor will want to become acquainted with them. Nevertheless, since beginning actors (especially in a college or university) are as likely to be working with Elizabethan tragedy as with modern comedy, we must at least discern some of the varying demands they are likely to encounter.

The approach to the internal and external preparation of a role is essentially the same for all periods and types of plays. Performance choices will definitely vary, depending to which extent the audience is allowed to be aware of the actor-as-commentator and to which extent the actor is allowed to show that he is aware of the presence of the audience. When a production purports to be realistic or illusionistic, it is more than likely based on the tradition of the proscenium theatre, which presupposes a "fourth wall" through which the audience sees the actors but through which the actor must not appear to see the audience. When viewing plays produced in this tradition, audiences should have the impression that they are privileged to observe the action onstage, but that it would go on in the same way whether or not they were there. This concept of theatre is called *representational,* because the actor is attempting to represent action as it happens in life. He makes no direct contact with his observers because to do so would destroy the illusion. Any adjustments he makes to the presence of the audience (speaking in a voice loud enough to be heard, holding his lines for the laughs, and performing actions so everyone may see them) must appear "natural" or lifelike; they must be clearly motivated by the desires of the character he is playing.

It is in this kind of theatre that the actor's paradox is most readily apparent. He must forget the audience, yet he must always keep them in mind. He must develop a technique that allows him to immerse himself in the imaginary world of the play and, at the same time, consciously adapt to the audience that is outside this imaginary world. He makes direct contact with the other actors while he makes indirect contact with the audience, and his connection with both is reciprocal. His relationship to the spectators is always a challenge, because the real essence of theatre is what happens between the actor and the audience.

In earlier periods and in an increasing number of modern plays, the approach is *presentational,* or nonillusionistic. Instead of representing events as they would happen in life, the actor frankly accepts the contrived circumstances under which the plays are given. He presents the play directly to the audience without attempting to conceal the theatrical devices he is using.

The ultimate in presentationalism is the traditional Chinese theatre, in which both the performers and their audience recognize that the conditions of the theatre are not real and consequently find no necessity for creating an illusion of reality. An actor astride a pole suffices as a general on horseback. The property man sits at the side in full view and provides hand props as the actor needs them. The magic of the Chinese theatre comes from the formal manner in which it presents truthful observations of life without attempting to represent life. Chinese actors distinguish to a much greater extent than we do the difference between *truth* and *actuality.*

In some respects the classic plays—the plays of Sophocles and Shakespeare and Sheridan and Moliére—are closer to the Chinese theatre than to the more modern illusionistic stage. They are presentational, in that they do not attempt to represent life in a realistic environment. They are not as theatrical as the Chinese plays are with their visible property men, but they permit the actor a greater frankness in recognizing the presence of the audience. Soliloquies may allow the actor to speak the character's thoughts directly to the house, and "asides" may allow him to comment freely on the action of the play, although it is important to note that both are done *in character*. Some modern plays provide an interesting mixture of representational and presentational theatre. As an example, consider the following stage direction from Robert Patrick's play, *Kennedy's Children:*

A performance of the Free Street Theatre, directed by Patrick Henry, at Chicago's Civic Center Plaza. In this improvisational situation notice how each actor in his own person is making direct contact with the audience. (Photo by Al Ashe.)

Wanda leans back wearily, checks the time on her travel alarm, puts her pencil down, and begins to speak. As with all the characters in the play, it is her thoughts we are hearing, and we have come in not at the beginning, but in the flow of an endless stream of revery. In no way does any character ever acknowledge the fact that another is speaking.[3]

A scene from the Harold Prince production of *Candide.* To accommodate this multi-level production, a floor of the Brooklyn Academy of Music was gutted, and the set was designed in a way that allowed the actors to surround part of the audience while other members of the audience surrounded the playing space. (Photo by Martha Swope.)

Her actions, her attention to detail, are clearly taken directly from the realistic, representational, theatre. Speaking her thoughts is just as clearly a presentational technique.

One of the most exciting aspects of the contemporary theatre is that it has opened the door to plays and performances that establish almost every conceivable relationship, both social and physical, between the actor and the audience. One example is *improvisational theatre,* in which the actors create their own play, often attempting to include the audience in the improvisation. Other similar approaches are often termed *environmental theatre* or *alternative theatre.* Augusto Boal, an infectious teacher and director from Brazil who is committed to this approach to performance, describes it as: "*theatre* in [the] most archaic application of the word. In this usage, all human beings are Actors (they act!) and Spectators (they observe!). They are Spect-Actors."[4]

Performers in this kind of theatre often advocate a social cause they strongly believe in and just as often do not create characters. Their technique is to reach the audience directly in their own persons, a method frequently called nonacting. Physical relationships are equally varied; performers often come into the aisles and walk between the rows of spectators, talking to them directly on a person-to-person basis. Other times they work in large open rooms, "found spaces," in which the differentiation between the space used for performance and the space used for the audience is blurred if not totally erased. Since a major objective is to break down any barrier between actor and audience, this concept minimizes the duality of the actor.

SUMMARY

Different types of plays and productions, of course, demand differences in acting, but they rarely are mutually exclusive. In improvisational and "nonacted" theatre, some sequences always present an opportunity for actors to behave in accordance with imaginary circumstances. In the most realistic play, on the other hand, the actor is always to some degree visible within the character, and the audience responds to the actor as a performer as well as to the behavior of the character he has created. In addition, the actor plays his role to express the total meaning of the play; that is, he shapes his character to point out this meaning. We have termed this shaping, this relationship the actor establishes with the audience, *commenting.* In comedy the actor figuratively holds up the character to the audience for them to ridicule and enjoy. He himself enjoys the ridiculousness of the character, and he has a keen sense of sharing his enjoyment. Sometimes, as in realistic drama, the comment is subtle; the audience is never consciously aware of it. Sometimes, as in farce or in a nonrealistic production, the comment is very obvious.

Most of all, it is important to recognize that whether an actor is creating an imaginary character behaving logically in circumstances given by a dramatist, playing an absurd drama in which the behavior is illogical, or contacting the spectators directly in advocation of a social cause, his objective remains the same: to affect the audience by carrying out specific tasks that will communicate a meaning.

The idea of the actor's dual personality may seem hopelessly complicated and obtuse, but in reality it is not. A good actor incorporates the level of presentation demanded of the role into his given circumstances. But he still must be able to believe in his performance; changing relationships with the audience merely changes the nature of the transaction. When the audience is brought more openly into the "secrets" of the theatre, they become a part of the reality from which the actor selects his actions. His job remains the same: to convince the audience that he is who he pretends to be, that what he is doing and saying is what he ought to be doing and saying, and that how he is doing and saying it is in keeping with the play and the demands of the production. Acting is believing so the audience can believe.

EXERCISE

(1) Return to one of the plays you worked on in a previous chapter, and determine the basic meaning (the observation of life) that you believe was the unifying factor in the dramatist's mind. State the meaning briefly and clearly.

(2) Now determine the spine from a study of how the dramatic action embodies the meaning. State it clearly in terms that will stimulate action, and make clear how each character is related to the basic idea. (Remember that when a group is working together on a production, general agreement is necessary. Obviously no unity would be possible if each actor were working toward a different purpose. The most desirable means of arriving at an agreement, thus, is through group discussion under the guidance of the director, each actor having prepared an independent analysis.)

(3) List your character's traits that are important to the total meaning, and decide to what extent you might need to comment on them to make that meaning clear.

(4) Read a number of plays to increase your understanding of different types and styles of drama. The following is a suggested list for a beginning:

Edward Albee: *The American Dream* and *The Zoo Story*
Antonin Artaud: *Jet of Blood*
Samuel Beckett: *Waiting for Godot*
Bertolt Brecht: *Mother Courage*
Charles Busch: *Psycho Beach Party*
Jean-Claude Carrière: *The Mahabarata*, based on the Indian classic epic; translated by Peter Brook.
Anton Chekhov: *The Three Sisters* and *Wild Honey* (in a version by Michael Frayn)
e. e. cummings: *him*
Hamilton Deane and John L. Balderston: *Dracula*

David Edgar, adapter: *The Life and Adventures of Nicholas Nickleby*
Lonne Elder III: *Ceremonies in Dark Old Men*
Euripides: *Alcestis*
Federico García Lorca: *Blood Wedding*
Oliver Goldsmith: *She Stoops to Conquer*
Christopher Hampton: *Les Liaisons Dangereuses*
Peter Handke: *Insulting the Audience*
Vaclav Havel: *Largo Desolato*
Lillian Hellman: *The Little Foxes*

A scene from a production of *True West* by Sam Shepard, directed by Larry D. Clark with scenery by Patrick Atkinson. Fight scenes call for acute physical control and heightened concentration on the part of the actors. (Photo courtesy of University of Missouri-Columbia Department of Theatre.)

David Henry Hwang: *M. Butterfly*
Henrik Ibsen: *A Doll's House*
Eugene Ionesco: *Rhinoceros* and *Exit the King*
LeRoi Jones: *Dutchman* and *The Death of Malcolm X*
George Lillo: *The London Merchant*
Arthur Miller: *Death of a Salesman*
Moliére: *The Imaginary Invalid*
Eugene O'Neill: *Long Day's Journey into Night*
Harold Pinter: *The Caretaker* and *The Homecoming*
David Rabe: *The Basic Training of Pavlo Hummel* and *Sticks and Bones*
Elmer Rice: *The Adding Machine*
William Shakespeare: *King Lear* and *The Taming of the Shrew*
Sam Shepard: *Red Cross* and *The Tooth of Crime*
Richard Brinsley Sheridan: *The Rivals*
Sophocles: *Antigone*
Tom Stoppard: *Travesties*
August Strindberg: *The Stronger*
Jean-Claude van Itallie: *America Hurrah* and *The Serpent*
Peter Weiss: *Marat/Sade*
Tennessee Williams: *The Glass Menagerie*
George C. Wolfe: *The Colored Museum*

NOTES

1. Constantin Stanislavski, *An Actor Prepares* (New York: Theatre Arts Books, 1936), pp. 256–58.

2. Harold Clurman, "The Principles of Interpretation," in *Producing the Play,* ed. John Gassner, (New York: Holt, Rinehart, 1941), p. 277.

3. Robert Patrick, *Kennedy's Children* (New York: Random House, 1973), p. 5.

4. Augusto Boal, *Games for Actors and Non-Actors,* tran. Adrian Jackson (London and New York: Routledge, 1992), p. xxx. Italics in the original.

CHAPTER 13

INTERPRETING THE LINES

At some point in the development of a character, the actor must be concerned with *interpreting,* rather than merely speaking, his lines. In spite of such old adages as "Seeing is believing" and "Actions speak louder than words," one of the actor's prime responsibilities is to communicate the dramatist's lines to the audience. How to speak most lines emerges easily once the actor understands the meaning and spine of the play and has committed himself to a logical series of believable actions. Nevertheless, difficulties arise. The actor must know how to dissect the proper interpretation of a line, and he must be prepared to do so speech by speech if necessary.

The basis for effective interpretation is a good voice. Even though trying to estimate the relative value of an actor's various attributes is like trying to determine which of the four wheels is most important to the automobile, perhaps Tyrone Guthrie's blunt analysis of the minimum requisites of an actor's voice and speech will bring their importance into focus. He wrote:

> The following are not "tips" but facts, of which intending actors should be, but seldom are, aware:
>
> 1 A well-trained actor should be able to manage, at moderate speed and sufficiently loudly to "carry" in a large theatre, SEVEN lines of blank verse. Untrained, unpractised speakers are "pumped" after one and a half lines.
>
> 2 A well-trained voice should easily cover a range of two and a half octaves. In normal conversation we rarely use more than one.[1]

These are vigorous demands, but the effectiveness and range of an actor largely depend on the extent of his ability to use his voice and shape his speech. To the extent his voice is not as good as it could be, he is a less effective actor than he could be, and we have stated before that one of our basic assumptions is that all serious student actors will be undertaking organized voice training at the same time they are studying the principles of acting proclaimed by this book.

The past few decades have seen a tremendous increase in the number of master voice teachers specializing in the problems of the actor. Primarily through the influence of such seminal thinkers and teachers as Arthur Lessac, Edith Skinner, and Kristin Linklater, the training of the actor's voice (as well as his body) is considered a continual and fundamental priority in good acting programs everywhere. These teachers have shown that, assuming the absence of physiological defects, no voice is so poor that it will not respond to proper training and that no voice is so fine that it could not be better if given the advantage of proper exercise. Whatever program of voice training the actor undertakes, he should try to accomplish several objectives. For instance, in training his voice, he should seek to acquire:

1. *Volume,* so the actor's voice may be heard without difficulty; even quiet, intimate scenes must be heard in the rear of the balcony. Jerzy Grotowski emphasized this objective: "Special attention should be paid to the carrying power of the voice so that the spectator not only hears the voice of the actor perfectly, but is also penetrated by it as if it were stereophonic."[2]

2. *Relaxation,* so his voice will not tire unduly during a long performance and so that he will not involuntarily raise his pitch during climactic scenes. *Relaxation* means that the column of air carrying the sound flows freely, unconstricted by tension in the throat or the jaw. Voice tension creates undesirable empathic responses in the audience, impairs the actor's expressiveness, and can cause permanent damage to his vocal mechanism.

3. *Quality* that is pleasant to hear and capable of expressing varying emotional states. A voice that is pleasant to hear is one of the actor's most prized attributes and is to a large extent a matter of resonance.

4. *Flexibility,* so his voice is capable of a variety of volumes, qualities, and pitches. A good voice is capable of adapting to a large range of demands with maximum ease.

5. *Energy,* so the voice commands attention and makes others want to listen. It is especially important to guard against a habit (common among young actors) of "fading out"—letting the energy diminish—at the ends of grammatical units. In speaking, as in golf or tennis, one must learn to "follow through."

    Speech training should improve:

1. *Articulation,* so the actor can be readily understood, even in passages requiring rapid speech. Good articulation, achieved primarily through careful attention to forming the consonants, is essential to clear speech. A story is told of a very great British actress who evaluated the work of an aspiring student with the comment, "Poor dear, no consonants."

2. *Pronunciation* that is free from slovenliness and provincial influences. This objective is becoming increasingly important. Television and motion pictures that reach audiences all over the country cannot use actors whose speech identifies them with a particular region, unless regional speech is essential to

the characters they are playing. Absolute absence of colloquial speech is necessary for classic plays, which emphasize the universality of the characters, not their individual idiosyncrasies.

3. *Artful control of tempo and rate* in order to convey satisfactorily the psychological and physiological connotations of human discourse. Perhaps no other factor of speech relates so closely to the actor's sensitivity to the complexities of his material. Tempo also is established by proper cue pickup so the performance moves at a pace appropriate to that of the audience's comprehension.

Most of the notable vocal training techniques we have recommended quite rightly focus on these aspects of voice and speech. Interpreting the character's lines falls more in the realm of acting technique, so we shall consider that subject at this point in our overview. The art of *interpretation,* meaning what the actor expresses and why, is a necessary part of the study of acting, no matter what vocal training technique one employs.

In earlier chapters we noted that a character speaks for the same reason that he acts—to satisfy some basic desire. The question always in the actor's mind as he seeks to interpret his lines is "Why does the character say what he says at this particular moment?"

FINDING THE UNDERMEANING OF THE LINES

To find the undermeaning of his lines, the actor must discover what the character wants to result from what he is saying, what he wants another character to do—the motivation beneath the speeches. In seeking the motivation, the actor must consider (1) how a line helps the character accomplish his intention and (2) how a line relates to its context, especially to the preceding line. A line that does not help the character accomplish his purpose will be one of those details that Stanislavski said will stand out as "superfluous or wrong." A line that is not related to its context will baffle the audience because it will seem pointless and illogical.

We must understand that the real significance of a line rarely is in the meaning of the words themselves or in the literal information they convey. Such a simple dialogue as

A: What time is it?
B: It's eleven o'clock.

has no dramatic significance until the meaning beneath the lines is known. Why does one character ask the time? What is in the other character's mind when he answers?

These words can convey a number of different meanings, depending on the circumstances under which they are spoken. In a melodrama, A might be in the death cell awaiting execution, so the lines might mean

A: How much longer do I have to live?

B: Exactly an hour. You are to be executed at midnight.

The speakers might be listening to a dull and seemingly endless lecture, so the lines (no doubt whispered) might mean

A: When is this thing going to end?

B: The bell will ring any second.

Or the speakers might be engaged in some engrossing activity, and the meaning might be

A: We've completely lost track of the time.

B: We're already late for our appointment with Mr. Higgins.

An actor must know and think his subtext. The *subtext* is what the line means to the character who is speaking, which frequently is not what the line says on the surface. Directors often admonish actors with "I hear what you're saying, but I don't know what you mean by saying it." Clearly perceptible subtext deepens the experience of the audience with the play and helps engage other characters in strong transactions. It is through the subtext that an actor attempts to affect the behavior of other characters in the scene and to add insight and meaning to his performance.

An actor's success in communicating his personal interpretation on a role lies to a very considerable extent in his choice of subtext. He must speak the text that the dramatist has written, but the subtext is his own contribution. It demonstrates his insight into the role and sensitivity to the play. Subtext is grounded in the motivating desire and in the objectives of the beats, both of which have been explored in the last few chapters. In fact, subtext is the vehicle through which imagination and interpretation connect with performance.

An example of how subtext affects meaning (in this case not just of a single speech but of an entire play) is Katharina's famous "advice" at the end of *The Taming of the Shrew,* in which she describes the responsibilities of a dutiful wife. Katharina is a headstrong, willful woman who has been "tamed" by and wed to Petruchio. He wants to complete the taming by having Katharina show her obedience at the wedding banquet. With one choice of subtext, the speech makes it plain that he has brought Katharina to submission. With another choice, we know she is not tamed at all but has learned to carry on the battle of the sexes in a more subtle way. For this second choice, Petruchio's response—his inner monologue while she is speaking—also has a significant effect on the total meaning. If he does not understand her subtext but takes the words for their surface value, the tables will have been turned completely, and it will now be Katharina who will dominate their relationship. If, on the other hand, he understands her subtext, even though the other characters do not, he and Katharina will clearly have a lively marriage.

In *The Zoo Story,* by Edward Albee, the confrontation between Jerry and Peter over a park bench leads to Jerry's suicide. The opening moment of the play demonstrates how important a clear subtext is to its successful performance. As the play begins, Peter is seated on a bench reading a book. Jerry's intention in his opening line, "I've been to the zoo. I said I've been to the zoo. *MISTER, I'VE BEEN TO THE ZOO!*" is more than "to become louder until he notices me." That would distort the author's purpose and create a willful, self-centered hoodlum who might frighten Peter immediately and cause him to leave. Instead, the actor playing Jerry wants to keep Peter there, so his subtext must include the pain and desperation of a person at the end of his rope. What Jerry thinks is as important as what he says.

Stanley's subtext in the scene with Lulu from *The Birthday Party,* by Harold Pinter, prepares the audience for the visit by the mysterious Goldberg and McCann. If his reason for refusing to leave the house is not specific and substantial, the word games with Lulu and his offer to take her anywhere will lose all importance. The actor must know that Stanley is in danger and that his options of hiding in the house or running away are ways of avoiding a dreaded confrontation. The net result of the scene would be mere mental gymnastics without the underpinning of fear, which can be established only through subtext.

In *Cat on a Hot Tin Roof,* Maggie is determined to have a child by Brick. The child is an economic necessity, but a Maggie whose subtext is based only on her own survival becomes a shrew, which is not the playwright's intention. Maggie is also full of positive life force, and her desire to achieve security is reinforced by her honest caring for Brick. If the actress misses this love, the pain of Brick's rejection would be hollow and unmoving. If we are to care for Maggie, the subtext has to contain the love along with the ambition.

People go to the theatre to "hear" the subtext; they can read the text in greater comfort at home.

EXERCISE

A helpful exercise is to find different subtexts for the same line and to speak the subtext immediately after you have said the text. You can create your own simple lines, but here are two examples to get you started:

Don't go. (I command you to stay.)
Don't go. (Please stay if you care anything about me.)
Don't go. (It's not safe for you to go out now.)
Don't go. (I warn you, you'll be sorry if you leave me.)

I love you. (But not in the way you want me to.)
I love you. (If you force me to say it, I will.)
I love you. (How can you treat me this way?)
I love you. (I don't ever want you to doubt it.)

Find at least two possible subtexts for each of the following lines. Speak each line, followed by your first choice of subtext. Then speak it without the second choice, making clear its different meaning. Have a partner or the entire class check your success.

> I'm going to do it.
> That's just fine.
> Thank you.
> I'm dying.
> What's the matter?
> I'm an awful person.
> Time goes so fast.
> Who says?
> Don't cry.
> It's so expensive.
> Baby.
> You've changed your mind.
> I haven't seen him for a long time.
> He's been gone twenty minutes.
> It's easy to understand why.
> I don't believe a word of it.

FINDING THE VERBAL ACTION

The previous examples should make it clear that finding the undermeaning or subtext of a line is not the same as paraphrasing it or restating the words of the author in the words of the actor. Paraphrasing may be necessary when surface meaning is not immediately clear; indeed, the actor may find it especially worthwhile to restate in his own words the lines of a verse play. But the paraphrase will not tell him what is beneath the line and how it relates to the dramatic action and to the character's motivating desire. Finding the undermeaning begins with understanding the character's purpose in saying the line. We will call the purpose of each line a *verbal action,* in order to emphasize that lines as well as actions help a character accomplish his intention. Hamlet's famous "To be or not to be," for example, may be paraphrased as "To live or not to live." His verbal action is to decide whether or not to kill himself.

When A asks, "What time is it?" meaning "How much longer do I have to live?" the verbal action is to hold back the time. When he means "When is this thing going to end?" his verbal action is to get out of a dull lecture or to make the time go faster. And when he means "We have completely lost track of the time," the inherent action is to break off what he is doing and go to his appointment.

To summarize, then, the significance of a line is not on the surface but beneath it; the real meaning is the undermeaning or subtext. It is the undermeaning that makes the character say the words, and it is the undermeaning that carries the actor's interpretation of the role. When the actor speaks a line, he must think simultaneously of the words he is saying, their undermeaning, and their inherent verbal action.

Let us illustrate this crucial point with examples from Oscar Wilde's famous satire on snobbery, *The Importance of Being Earnest*. When the haughty Lady Bracknell speaks slightingly of the family background of Cecily Cardew, Cecily's guardian, Jack Worthing, replies,

> Miss Cardew is the granddaughter of the late Mr. Thomas Cardew of 149 Belgrave Square, S.W.; Gervase Park, Dorking, Surrey; and the Sporran, Fife-shire, N.B.

To give the addresses of Mr. Thomas Cardew's three residences is not Jack's purpose. Rather, the undermeaning is

> My ward is a person of excellent family connections that may be quite as acceptable in English society as your own are, Lady Bracknell!

The verbal action is to put Lady Bracknell in her place.

Earlier, Jack has been informed that Lady Bracknell hardly approves of him either. He says, "May I ask why not?" His subtext is, "I am sure I don't see why she doesn't approve of me. I am every bit as good as she is." His verbal action is to assert his equality.

The choice of the subtext determines to a considerable degree the overall effect of a line—whether it will be comic, pathetic, or melodramatic. These lines from *The Importance of Being Earnest* are, of course, comic. Their subtexts must help point up the ridiculous seriousness with which the characters take themselves.

EXERCISE

Create subtexts that will allow you to speak the line "Don't shoot" with as many different effects (satirical, melodramatic, tragic, etc.) as possible.

RELATING THE LINES TO THE MOTIVATING DESIRE

The undermeaning and the verbal action, both significant in interpreting a line, do not by themselves disclose its significance. The actor determines this by relating the meaning to the motivating desire of the character he is playing. By understanding how each line serves to help the character get what he wants, the actor will have a better chance of making the motivating desire clear to the audience.

Although, in any circumstances, the character may be motivated in one of several ways, the actor must make a clear and unequivocal commitment to a motivating desire before he can give a line its full value. Recall the situation in which A is in the death cell. The actor might decide that the condemned man feels only the primal urge to live, that he is hoping for a reprieve from the governor, or even hoping blindly for a miracle. With such a motivating desire, his asking for the time will be essentially a cry for help. He might also decide that the man has accepted his death as inevitable, in which case his motivating desire might be to seek redemption, and his line might be a plea for more time in which to make atonement. Another interpretation might be that even at the point of death, the man was filled with the same bitterness that led him to commit the crime and was determined to give no one the satisfaction of seeing any sign of remorse. In this case, the line would reinforce his motivating desire to refrain from making any repentance. In any case, once the motivating desire has been decided, the actor must stick to it and follow it wherever it takes him as he interprets the lines.

B will need to go through the same process in order to communicate the meaning of such a simple line as "It's eleven o'clock." If she is A's devoted and loyal wife, her motivating desire will be to comfort her husband, and her line will be an expression of love and faith. But if, to imagine a melodramatic situation, B is a rival spy wishing to coerce A to reveal vital information before he dies, the line might be a threat to harm his family if he refuses the request.

Examination of an interesting interpretation problem from *Hello Out There* may provide further help in understanding the issue of relating a line to a character's intention and his motivating desire. At several points in this play, the Young Man (and, later, Emily) must repeat the line: "Hello, out there." Just as we demonstrated in our simple improvisation about asking for the time, these repetitions will have no dramatic significance until the meaning underneath the line is known. The line first appears at the very beginning of the play:

YOUNG MAN: Hello—out there! *(pause)* Hello—out there! Hello—out there! *(long pause)* Nobody out there. *(still more dramatically, but more comically, too)* Hello—out there! Hello—out there!

To repeat. This is the opening of the play. We are just getting acquainted with his character and the surroundings. The subtext here is fairly consistent with the line. He is saying: "Is anybody here except me?" "Answer me, damn it!" And, later: "I must sound foolish, standing here yelling at the walls." His verbal action is to cajole someone into answering. The line appears again in the very next sequence.

(A GIRL'S VOICE is heard, very sweet and soft)

THE VOICE: Hello.

YOUNG MAN: Hello—out there.

THE VOICE: Hello.

YOUNG MAN: Is that you, Katey?

THE VOICE: No—this here is Emily.

YOUNG MAN: Who? *(Swiftly)* Hello out there.

THE VOICE: Emily.

The Young Man's verbal action is to find out who is there. The first subtext is "Did I hear somebody?" and the second is "Say that again." We have already discussed the Young Man's enigmatic selection of "Katey" in his response to The Voice. Once the actor portraying this role concludes how that selection fits into the biography of the character, choosing a proper subtext for the line in which he first speaks the name will help him convey that decision to the audience. And remember, everything is flowing from the Young Man's motivating desire we selected earlier: "I want to hurt those who hurt me." Choose another motivating desire, and you would need to reexamine the subtext.

EXERCISE

The cumulative effect of Saroyan's repetition of the line "Hello out there" is to create a spoken invitation to examine the play's theme. Unfortunately, this is a dramaturgical device, and even the knowledge of what the playwright is up to will not help the actor find a believable action for these lines. Find each time in the script that the line occurs. Study the circumstances, and write the character's intention and subtext for each repetition. Make certain each fits his motivating desire.

Confusion often arises from the use of a variety of terms to describe the actor's relationship to the role and the relationship of the role to the whole play. For clarity, let us review the definitions of those terms as we employ them:

1. *Motivating desire* is the term for that which gives the character a sufficient reason to pursue the course of action demanded by the play. The motivating desire for the play and the intention for each scene must be entirely compatible.

2. *Spine* is the theme or basic line of the play and is synonymous with its *super-objective*. In this context it is a directional term. In addition, each role has a spine that must be compatible with the overall spine of the play. If the spine of *Hello Out There* is the risky business of trusting and loving people, all the roles must be related to this objective.

3. The *through-line-of-action* is the progressive movement from one unit of the play to the next. It assumes a series of consistent and logical actions, a pattern of behavior that is the route an actor takes to the super-objective. The attempt to fulfill the objectives of the character against a series of obstacles moves the play to a conclusion, and the through-line-of-action is the thread that links all the character's actions.

The actor also must know how his lines serve the dramatist's basic intention and how they aid in communicating the play's central idea to the audience. This problem has been anticipated in such previous steps as (1) finding the character's motivating desire—a process in which the lines were an important consideration, (2) relating this fundamental desire to the meaning of the play as a whole, and (3) finding the undermeaning and the verbal action, which, as we have seen, emerge only after the lines have been related to the motivating desire.

After completing these steps, the actor will likely understand how the dramatist intended each line to aid in expressing his meaning. Knowing that the central idea of *Hello Out There* has to do with people who take a chance on caring about other people, the actors will emphasize the riskiness of their encounter. They also will make certain the audience understands that their need is great enough to justify the chance that they take, that both characters *must* take the chance, risky as it is. Saroyan's lines and suggested activities, especially during the scene where Emily decides to try to find the Young Man a gun, strongly support this interpretation. Recall that this scene takes place immediately after the tender contact of the kiss.

YOUNG MAN: Come here. *(THE GIRL moves close and he kisses her.)* Now, hurry. Run all the way.

THE GIRL: I'll run. *(THE GIRL turns and runs. The YOUNG MAN stands at the center of the cell a long time. THE GIRL comes running back in. Almost crying.)* I'm afraid. I'm afraid I won't see you again. If I come back and you're not here, I—

YOUNG MAN: Hello—out there!

The actors' performance must also make it clear that even if Emily and the Young Man get together, the odds are great that they will not find happiness. Nevertheless, their brief moment of coming together must be filled with hope, love, and beauty. Saroyan paints a picture of a bleak world, but those who grab for even a moment of contact have something that those who sit idly in their own "jails" can never experience.

Loneliness itself is reason enough for stretching out the hand of contact. The Young Man makes it clear that, at least in his mind, such was his motivation for going home with the woman the previous night.

YOUNG MAN: I thought she was lonesome. She *said* she was.

THE GIRL: Maybe she was.

YOUNG MAN: She was *something*.

THE GIRL: I guess I'd never see you, if it didn't happen, though.

Every beat of the play must be carefully examined in the context of the playwright's basic meaning as interpreted by each particular production. No element of the production is excused from this basic demand. The actor's task is

**RELATING
THE LINES
TO THE
DRAMATIST'S
MEANING**

to hold to the agreed-on interpretation with an unyielding grip and to make everything he says or does flow from some variation on the theme. He must turn the interpretation into action, and subtext is one of his major tools for doing so.

Once again, Oscar Wilde's *The Importance of Being Earnest* can serve as a contrasting example of the problem of relating the lines to the dramatist's meaning. This play is a satire on the snobbish upper classes at the close of the last century, who sought to relieve their boredom by concentrating on inconsequentials. Wilde saw the comic possibilities in the affectations of such people, and he ridiculed them good-naturedly in this farce. The plot has to do with two young ladies whose virtually sole requirement for a husband is that his name be Ernest, a requirement that compels both Jack and Algernon to arrange to be rechristened. The actors in this play must see that their lines serve Wilde's purpose of having fun at the expense of these people.

The following dialogue drips with Jack's boredom and underscores the eagerness with which Algernon engages in trivial pursuits. Discuss with your teacher and the class ways of performing these scenes in order to make certain the lines reinforce Wilde's meaning. How could they be performed so as to subvert or run counter to the author's meaning?

ALGERNON: ... may I dine with you tonight at Willis's?

JACK: I suppose so, if you want to.

ALGERNON: Yes, but you must be serious about it. I hate people who are not serious about meals. It is so shallow of them.

And later:

ALGERNON: ... Now, my dear boy, if we want to get a good table at Willis's, we really must go and dress. Do you know it is nearly seven?

JACK: Oh! it always is nearly seven.

ALGERNON: Well, I'm hungry.

JACK: I never knew you when you weren't....

ALGERNON: What shall we do after dinner? Go to a theatre?

JACK: Oh no! I loathe listening.

ALGERNON: Well, let us go to the Club?

JACK: Oh, no! I hate talking.

ALGERNON: Well, we might trot round to the Empire at ten?

JACK: Oh, no! I can't bear looking at things. It is so silly.

ALGERNON: Well, what shall we do?

JACK: Nothing!

ALGERNON: It is awfully hard work doing nothing. However, I don't mind hard work where there is no definite object of any kind.

Incidentally, this scene offers an excellent example of the verbal actions of two characters being in conflict. Algernon's objective is "to get ready for dinner," and Jack's objective is "to remain inert." The undermeaning will flow from how they resolve these contradictory goals.

Many times a dramatist makes his basic intention clearer and stronger by using contrasting elements. In such cases, the relationship of certain characters' lines to the total meaning is one of *contrast* with the central theme. The meaning is thus pointed more sharply, just as colors appear brighter when contrasted with other colors.

Several examples of the use of contrasting elements appear in *Romeo and Juliet.* Remember that we found its theme to be the triumph of young love over "canker'd hate." Although Romeo and Juliet both meet a tragic death, their love is triumphant. Because of it, the Montagues and the Capulets end their ancient feud, and civil brawls no longer disturb the quiet of Verona's streets.

Triumphant love is expressed throughout the play in Juliet's and Romeo's lines:

> My bounty is as boundless as the sea,
> My love is as deep—the more I give to thee
> The more I have, for both are infinite.

and

> O my love! my wife!
> Death that has suck'd the honey of thy breath
> Hath had no power yet upon thy beauty.
> Thou art not conquer'd—Beauty's ensign yet
> Is crimson in thy lips and in thy cheeks,
> And Death's pale flag is not advanced there.

The final beauty of their love is moving and memorable because it stands out in relief against the hatred of old Montague and old Capulet, the Nurse's vulgarity, Mercutio's mockery, Tybalt's malice, and Lady Capulet's coldness. The lines of these characters are related to the total meaning through contrast, and it is important that the actors understand this relationship. For instance, Romeo's romantic love appears stronger because it rises above the jibes and cynicism of Mercutio's mocking lines. Tybalt's malicious lines put Romeo's new-found love to a test and bring about the duel that causes Romeo's banishment. Throughout the play, Juliet's warmth and generosity stand out against her mother's unyielding practicality. Lady Capulet rejects Juliet with:

> Talk not to me, for I'll not speak a word,
> Do as thou wilt, for I have done with thee.

These particular lines underscore the desperation of Juliet's predicament and propel her toward her final course of action.

Although the Nurse's character is vastly different from that of Lady Capulet, she serves a similar purpose in providing dramatic contrast—her bawdiness against Juliet's sweetness and purity. Her advice to marry the Count Paris for practical reasons, when Juliet is already secretly married to the banished Romeo, is revolting to a person of Juliet's innocence:

> I think it best you marry'd with the County.
> O, he's a lovely gentleman!
> Romeo's a dishclout to him. An eagle, madam,
> Hath not so green, so quick, so fair an eye
> As Paris hath. Beshrew my very heart,
> I think you're happy in this second match,
> For it excels your first, or if't did not
> Your first is dead—or 'twere as good he were,
> As living here and you no use of him.

In such instances, relating the lines to the dramatist's intention means making them provide dramatic contrasts. Knowing when this is so and how various relationships unfold demands a complete understanding of the play, as a whole. No individual line can be interpreted without a complete command of the play's global meaning. Even difficult lines will yield to honest interpretation once this meaning has been mastered.

EXERCISE

Study carefully the lines of a character you selected in one of the previous exercises. For each line, determine

(1) Its undermeaning
(2) Its verbal action
(3) Its relationship to the character's motivating desire (That is, relate what the character wants as a result of having said the line to realizing his basic motivating desire.)
(4) Its relationship to the meaning of the play as a whole

Write out this information, as it will complete your score of physical actions.

EXERCISE

Choose a play from the list at the end of Chapter 10, and make a similar study of the lines of one or more of the characters.

The lines are composed of two elements, both of which are vital:

1. The content: what the lines say, including both their surface and their undermeanings.

2. The form: the manner in which the content is expressed, including grammar and vocabulary.

We have just been exploring how the actor detects the content of the lines, so we shall now consider the problem of believing the manner in which the character speaks.

Different speakers may express the same meaning in a variety of ways:

I hope it ain't gointa rain an' spoil the picnic we was plannin' fer so long.
I trust inclement weather will not mar the outing we have been anticipating for
    such a time.

These two lines are alike in content, and their surface meanings are identical. Their undermeanings could be the same, and both lines could bear the same relation to the speaker's motivating desire. But neither is expressed in a manner that the average actor would find "natural." The actor's problem is to understand the background of the character's speech so he can believe the manner of speaking in the same way that he believes in the character's actions. For our purposes, we shall say that the manner of speaking includes vocabulary, grammar, pronunciation, and articulation.

For the most part, the dramatist imposes the character's manner of speech by choosing the vocabulary and the grammar, both of which should be accepted as given circumstances by the actor. Occasionally, as a part of the externalization of his character, the actor may introduce variations in pronunciation and articulation. For instance, he might play a character with a dialect, a stammer, or baby talk. Like all good externalizations, such characteristics should support inner traits and help both the actor and the audience believe them. Baby talk, for example, might be helpful in characterizing a woman who had been pampered by her parents and whose motivating desire is to get the same attention from her husband. Such decisions about the speech of the character are subject to the same intense scrutiny as are other character externals and are justified only if they enable the actor to realize the dramatist's intentions.

The actor studies a character's speech habits in the same way he studies other traits provided by the dramatist: He tries to find justification for them in the play. He also may need to supply, as he did when justifying actions, imaginary circumstances true to the playwright's conception that help explain why the character speaks the way he does (see Chapter 11).

If the manner of speaking is similar to the actor's or if he has frequently heard others speak in a similar way, he will have little difficulty. The speech background of Gene Garrison and his mother, Margaret, in *I Never Sang for My Father,* by Robert Anderson, is so immediately comprehensible that it presents no problem to an American actor. The following dialogue is typical. Gene is at Pennsylvania Station meeting his mother and father, who are returning from a vacation in Florida:

GENE: Hello, Mother.

MARGARET: *(Her face lights up)* Well, Gene. *(She opens her arms but remains seated. They embrace)* Oh, my, it's good to see you. *(This with real feeling as she holds her son close to her)*

GENE: *(When he draws away)* You look wonderful.

MARGARET: What?

GENE: *(Raises his voice slightly. His mother wears a hearing aid)* You look wonderful.

MARGARET: *(Little-girl coy)* Oh ... a little rouge.... This is your Easter orchid. I had them keep it in the icebox in the hotel. This is the fourth time I've worn it.

GENE: You sure get mileage out of those things.

MARGARET: *(Raising her voice slightly)* I say it's the fourth time I've worn it.... Some of the other ladies had orchids for Easter, but mine was the only white one. *(She knows she is being snobbishly proud and smiles as she pokes at the bow)* I was hoping it would last so you could see it.[3]

On the other hand, the speech in Preston Jones's *Lu Ann Hampton Laverty Oberlander* presents a problem. Lu Ann and Billy Bob are high school seniors in a small, rural, West Texas town.

LU ANN: Well, ah thought ah would die! Ah jest thought ah would curl up and die right there on the gym floor. When the coach introduced the basketball team and you-all come out there with your hair all dyed green. Well, sir, mah eyes liked to jumped plumb outta mah head! Why, Mary Beth Johnson jest hollered. That's right, jest hollered right out loud.

BILLY BOB: It was Pete Honeycutt's idea.

LU ANN: Why, ever'one jest laughed and shouted and carried on so. Eveline Blair came runnin' over to me shoutin', "Look at the basketball boys, look at the basketball boys!"

BILLY BOB: It was Pete Honeycutt's idea.

LU ANN: *(Gestures to porch—they go out.)* After the assembly we cheerleaders all got together and decided we'd do somethin' funny too.

BILLY BOB: Aw, like what?

LU ANN: Now wouldn't you like to know? Mr. Green-headed Billy Bob Wortman.

BILLY BOB: Aw, come on, Lu Ann, what are you-all fixin' to do?

LU ANN: Oh, ah don't know, somethin', somethin' real neat.

BILLY BOB: You cain't dye you-all's hair. Pete Honeycutt already thought that one up.[4]

The average actor will find it difficult to believe this manner of speaking in terms of his own experience. The actor may have no doubt that the speech is right for the character. He may understand the regional factors that have produced this unique, musical language. Still, he is aware that his own speech is quite different, and such a difference is not always easy to reconcile.

Often, much of the actor's early efforts toward believing a variation from his normal speech is mechanical and imitative. The actor records and listens to himself as he tries to form the sounds in accordance with the dramatist's attempt to represent the character's speech on the printed page. Some playwrights are remarkably skillful in their use of phonetic spellings to indicate speech variations. George Bernard Shaw, for example, was adept in representing Cockney English in this way. The actor, also, may listen to recordings or imitate actual models if he is fortunate enough to know someone whose speech is similar.

If this external approach is to serve its purpose, however, it must lead the actor to believe the character's speech. And believing the speech should, in turn, increase his belief in the character. In other words, as the actor becomes convinced he has developed a true manner of speaking, he will have a greater conviction in his total characterization. *Diction*—the way of expressing oneself—is one of the actor's principal resources in creating a character.

Gene and Margaret and Billy Bob and Lu Ann are modest folk who use their abilities to express their thoughts and feelings as best they can, as colorful as their speech often is. As you probably recall, we meet people in *The Importance of Being Earnest* with quite a different background. Algernon Moncrieff is, by his own admission, "immensely overeducated." He speaks not only to express his ideas but also to impress his hearers with his cleverness and his aptness of phrasing. We have known for some time that speech is an action; now we see that the manner of speaking can carry with it its own dramatic intention.

All of the characters in *The Importance of Being Earnest* exhibit a kind of "speech embroidery" indicative of their elegance and earnest artificiality. The following lines of Gwendolen Fairfax are an example. She is talking to Cecily Cardew, whom she has learned is Jack Worthing's ward. Gwendolen and Jack have recently become engaged.

GWENDOLEN: Oh! It is strange he never mentioned to me that he had a ward. How secretive of him! He grows more interesting hourly. I am not sure, however, that the news inspires me with feelings of unmixed delight. *(Rising and going to her)* I am very fond of you, Cecily; I have liked you ever since I met you! But I am bound to state that now that I know that you are Mr. Worthing's ward, I cannot help expressing a wish you were —well, just a little older than you seem to be—and not quite so very alluring in appearance. In fact, if I may speak candidly—

CECILY: Pray do! I think that whenever one has anything unpleasant to say, one should always be quite candid.

GWENDOLEN: Well, to speak with perfect candour, Cecily, I wish that you were fully forty-two, and more than usually plain for your age. Ernest has a strong upright nature. He is the very soul of truth and honor. Disloyalty would be as impossible to him as deception. But even men of the noblest possible moral character are extremely susceptible to the influence of the physical charms of others. Modern, no less than Ancient History, supplies us with many most painful examples of what I refer to. If it were not so, indeed, History would be quite unreadable.

Taking command of these lines will provide quite a test for young American actresses. Just learning to "say" them will not be enough. They must understand the ostentation and snobbery that produced such a vocabulary and structure. Only then can they begin to believe the speech and actions of the characters, and they must believe them before they can make an adequate "comment" on their ridiculousness.

Believing a character's manner of speaking is a matter of understanding the influences in his background that have determined his way of speech, of justifying the character's speech in terms of his background. The actor is constantly faced with such questions as

Why does one character have such an extensive vocabulary, whereas another speaks almost entirely in words of one syllable?

Why does one character speak in long, involved sentences, whereas another speaks in halting fragments?

Why does one character speak with faultlessly correct grammar, whereas another says "he don't" and "we was"?

Why does one character say "you gentlemen," whereas another says "you guys"?

Why does a character say "poosh" for push and "haouse" for house?

EXERCISE

(1) Study the speech of the character you are working on, and justify the manner of speaking in terms of background. Continue your study until each detail of speech seems right and true.

(2) From another play, choose at least one character whose manner of speaking varies from your own. Study the speech, and practice the lines until you believe you are truthfully reproducing the character's manner of speaking. If possible, use actual models, sound recordings, or phonetic transcriptions.

(3) Find instances in *Hello Out There* in which the character's background influences his or her choice of words and manner of speaking.

So far in this discussion of interpreting the lines, we have concentrated on the importance of *motivation,* of relating the lines to the character's basic desire and understanding how each line helps the character get what he wants. For the most part, we have been thinking of lines no longer than a sentence or two. Long speeches frequently pose exceptionally difficult problems of interpretation. Usually, the best way to approach them is to break such speeches into small parts, find the undermeaning of each segment, and relate it to the character's motivating desire. In other words, long, complicated speeches should be treated as if they were a series of shorter, more manageable, lines. You should avoid the temptation to motivate all speeches as a single unit. Some long, complex speeches may contain several beats.

When discovering and arranging the beats of a longer speech for performance, remember that each unit should have a clearly stated verbal action. In many long speeches, the actor can easily detect the familiar, classical, three-part structure—the beginning, the middle, and the end. Other speeches may have only two parts, and still others may have five, or seven. The actor should never divide a speech into so many units that he cannot keep its overall pattern in mind; otherwise, it will appear to the audience to lack structure or form. Sometimes, of course, speeches are broken off, either by the speaker or by another character, before they reach a structural ending.

A speech from *Golden Boy,* by Clifford Odets, will serve as an illustration. Joe Bonaparte, on the eve of his twenty-first birthday, is telling his father he wants to break away from the restraints of home so he may have "wonderful things from life." He thinks he can find what he wants by becoming a prize fighter. But Mr. Bonaparte, a humane and kindly man, wants Joe to find happiness as a violinist and has paid a lot of money for a fine violin that he plans to give Joe for his birthday. Others present in the scene are Frank, Joe's older brother who travels about a good deal, and Mr. Carp, a neighbor who owns an *Encyclopaedia Britannica.*

MR. BONAPARTE: Sit down, Joe—resta you'self.

JOE: Don't want to sit. Every birthday I ever had I sat around. Now'sa time for standing. Poppa, I have to tell you—I don't like myself, past, present, and future. Do you know there are men who have wonderful things from life? Do you think they're better than me? Do you think I like this feeling of no possessions? Of learning about the world from Carp's encyclopaedia? Frank don't know what it means—he travels around, sees the world! *(Turning to Frank)* You don't know what it means to sit around here and watch the months go ticking by! Do you think that's a life for a boy my age? Tomorrow's my birthday! I change my life!

Joe's purpose in this speech is to make his father see that he is going to change his way of life and that the change will mean a difference in their

MOTIVATING THE LONGER SPEECH

relationship. His verbal action is to break away from his home and his father. He is excited and resentful, but the speech does not come easily and he cannot say it all at once. Once said, he also feels it necessary to defend his decision. Through all this, his relationship with his father creates a psychological obstacle to every verbal action in every beat.

The speech may be divided into three structural units:

1. Verbal action: *to assert his independence from his father.*

   Don't want to sit. Every birthday I ever had I sat around. Now'sa time for standing.

2. Verbal action: *to defend his decision to break away from his father.* This is the middle part, the development leading to the climax. Joe gives several reasons for his decision, and he plays each reason with increasing intensity:

   Poppa, I have to tell you—I don't like myself, past, present, and future. Do you know there are men who have wonderful things from life? Do you think they're better than me? Do you think I like this feeling of no possessions? Of learning about the world from Carp's encyclopaedia? Frank don't know what it means—he travels around, sees the world! *(Turning to Frank)* You don't know what it means to sit around here and watch the months go ticking by! Do you think that's a life for a boy my age?

3. Verbal action: *to defy his family.* This is the climax of the speech.

   Tomorrow's my birthday! I change my life!

EXERCISE

The following speeches provide material for practice in interpreting lines. Read the plays they have been selected from, because the significance of any speech lies in its relationship to the play. Determine the motivating desire of the character. Break the speech into units. Find the verbal actions. Make a score of physical actions. Memorize the speech. As you rehearse it, look for the separate motivation for each unit, and relate its meaning to the intention of the speech as a whole. If the language is different from your own, study the speech background of the character.

(1) Sparger in *Kennedy's Children,* by Robert Patrick[5]

> *(Sparger is twenty-six, described by Patrick as being "languid, dressed with personal chic," an aspiring actor. This play takes place in a New York bar. All characters speak their "thoughts" without regard to other characters. It is a play of soliloquies, so to speak. Sparger has been drinking brandy.)*
>
> SPARGER: *(Sloppy drunk)* The fact of the matter is, I *wasn't* always like this. Maybe people just weren't meant to live in the present. Meant? By

whom? Who cares? Sure, I used to live in the present. According to science we all used to live underwater, too. But we adapted! We just haven't adapted to the present yet. Not till we grow asbestos filters in our nostrils. And learn to live on monosodium glutamate. And survive six inches of steel shoved up us in every other doorway. And ignore the pangs of dread and empathy and guilt that *paralyze* us whenever we see some human being, reduced to a lump of mucus, come wobbling towards us with his ragged, flaking hand held out, muttering and blubbering and slobbering, "Help me! Help me! Help me! For God's sake, somebody please help me!" Uh-oh. I'm thinking about things I don't want to think about. I'm too drunk too early. I'm trying to stay off drugs. I haven't got anything left to stop up the back of my brain, and I'm having a memory hemorrhage! I can't help it! I can't stop it! I'm remembering it all again! I'm remembering! I'm having an attack of the truth! It's coming at me, and it is me, the truth, the truth, I'm sitting here in a public place, seeping and sopping and soaking and reeking with truth. And the end—the end—the end of truth—is *death!*

(He runs off urgently to the mens' room)

(2) Biff Loman in *Death of a Salesman, by Arthur Miller* [6]

(Biff has returned home after knocking aimlessly about the country for a number of years. He has no object in life and no certain sense of values. He is talking to his brother.)

BIFF: *(with rising agitation)* Hap, I've had twenty or thirty different kinds of jobs since I left home before the war, and it always turns out the same. I just realized it lately. In Nebraska when I herded cattle, and the Dakotas, and Arizona, and now in Texas. It's why I came home now, I guess, because I realized it. This farm I work on, it's spring there now, see? And they've got about fifteen new colts. There's nothing more inspiring or—beautiful than the sight of a mare and a new colt. And it's cool there now, see? Texas is cool now, and it's spring. And whenever spring comes to where I am, I suddenly get the feeling, my God, I'm not getting anywhere! What the hell am I doing, playing around with horses, twenty-eight dollars a week! I'm thirty-four years old, I oughta be makin' my future. That's when I come running home. And now, I get here, and I don't know what to do with myself. *(After a pause)* I've always made a point of not wasting my life, and every time I come back here I know that all I've done is to waste my life.

(3) Babe Botrelle in *Crimes of the Heart,* by Beth Henley [7]

(The small town of Hazlehurst, Mississippi, is scandalized because Babe has shot her big-wig politico husband in the stomach. She tells her sisters the incident that brought it all about.)

BABE: And we were just standing around on the back porch playing with Dog. Well, suddenly Zackery comes from around the side of the house. And he startled me 'cause he's supposed to be away at the office, and there he is coming from round the side of the house. Anyway, he says to Willie Jay, "Hey, boy, what are you doing back here?" And I say, "He's not doing anything. You just go on home, Willie Jay! You just run right on home." Well, before he can move, Zackery comes up and knocks him once right across the face and then shoves him down the porch steps, causing him to skin up his elbow real bad on that hard concrete. Then he says, "Don't you ever come around here again, or I'll have them cut out your gizzard!" Well, Willie Jay starts crying—these tears come streaming down his face— then he gets up real quick and runs away, with Dog following off after him. After that, I don't remember much too clearly; let's see…I went on into the living room, and I went right up to the davenport and opened the drawer where we keep the burglar gun…I took it out. Then I—I brought it up to my ear. That's right. I put it right inside my ear. Why, I was gonna shoot off my own head! That's what I was gonna do. Then I heard the back door slamming and suddenly, for some reason, I thought about Mama…how she'd hung herself. And here I was about ready to shoot myself. Then I realized—that's right, I realized how I didn't want to kill myself! And she—she probably didn't want to kill herself. She wanted to kill him, and I wanted to kill him, too. I wanted to kill Zackery, not myself. 'Cause I—I wanted to live! So I waited for him to come on into the living room. Then I held out the gun, and I pulled the trigger, aiming for his heart but getting him in the stomach. *(After a pause)* It's funny that I really did that.

(4) Christy Mahon in *The Playboy of the Western World,* by John Millington Synge[8]

(A young Irishman named Christy Mahon, having run away from home, is befriended by Pegeen Mike and her father, who owns a public house. Up early in the morning, Christy is polishing Pegeen's boots and counting the jugs behind the bar. He is speaking to himself.)

CHRISTY: Half a hundred beyond. Ten there. A score that's above. Eighty jugs. Six cups and a broken one. Two plates. A power of glasses. Bottles, a school-master'd be hard set to count, and enough in them, I'm thinking, to drunken all the wealth and wisdom of the County Clare. *(He puts the boot down carefully.)* There's her boots now, nice and decent for her evening use, and isn't it grand brushes she has? *(He puts them down and goes by degrees to the looking-glass.)* Well, this'd be a fine place to be my whole life talking out with swearing Christians, in place of my old dogs and cat, and I stalking around, smoking my pipe and drinking my fill, and never a day's work but drawing a cork an odd time, or wiping a glass, or rinsing out a shiny tumbler for a decent man. *(He takes the looking-glass from the wall and puts it on the back of a chair; then sits down in front of it and begins washing his face.)* Didn't I know rightly I was handsome, though it was the divil's own mirror we had beyond, would twist a squint across an angel's brow; and I'll be growing fine from this day, the way I'll have a soft lovely skin on me and won't be the like of the clumsy young fellows do be ploughing all times in the earth and dung. *(He starts.)* Is she coming again? *(He looks out.)* Stranger girls. God help me, where'll I hide myself away and my long neck naked to the world. *(He looks out.)* I'd best go to the room maybe till I'm dressed again. *(He gathers up his coat and looking-glass, and runs into the inner room.)*

(5) Alisa in *Long Time Since Yesterday,* by P. J. Gibson[9]

(Alisa is a married African-American woman of 39, a physical therapist. She and a group of former college friends have gathered to attend the funeral of another member of the group who has committed suicide. As they drink and talk after the services, they begin to tell each other things about themselves that they have previously kept secret. This speech comes after Alisa, who has turned the investment of "a dollar bill" in a governmental "new home-buying program" into a real estate area known as "Reynolds Landing," is asked whether her success resulted from "spontaneity or luck." The names in parentheses refer to the friends to whom she is speaking.)

ALISA: *(Reflects on the phrase.)* Spontaneity and luck.... Always amazes me how other people see things. Distance does that. *(Crosses to the window.)* Luck.... *(Turns to PANZI.)* I was about...ten, my sister Joyce nine, Raymond fourteen, when our parents looked into our faces, looked around the room; the small kitchen, the livingroom with second-hand furniture, the house and family who'd gotten too much for them.... They made a decision to leave. *(BABBS sits.)* Just like that.... Leave. And they did. They placed a box of Cheerios and Kellogg's Corn Flakes on the table, a half gallon of milk we'd just gotten from the Borden's milk man and left. Never came back. We waited, Raymond, Joyce and I...We waited, but they never.... Raymond called a family meeting over the Monopoly game we'd started to pass the time. The topic, our next move. Another pang of reality after hopeless periodical peeks at the clock and front door. Raymond said, after seven long days of waiting and seven longer nights.... said we were going to keep the family together. And we did.... Throughout the *whole* summer, until the fall, until school, nosy neighbors and teachers had the welfare agency at our door.... We were placed in separate foster homes.... *(to THELMA)* Separate new families.... *(to PANZI)* Until that lucky morning I put a dollar bill on a piece of real estate and put together what the neighbors call

'Reynolds Landing.' Maybe it should be called 'Meyers-Reynolds Landing' 'cause I reunited Joyce and Raymond...and that's all of us up there.... All of us. *(silence)* So much for 'luck'.... Why should you [have known]? Why should any of you? All of you coming from respectable families. What was I suppose to do? Announce I had dogs for parents? No, not dogs, turtles.... Turtle mothers drop their eggs and then walk away. Was I suppose to tell you that? No. I let you believe what you wanted to believe. In the long run it was better for everyone. I hated my parents less and got on with living and learning you do the best you can with what you get.

(6) Edmund in *Long Day's Journey into Night,* by Eugene O'Neill[10]

(Even though he has tuberculosis and is soon to go to a sanatorium, Edmund has been walking late at night on the beach. He also has been drinking, and his father has just told him he should have more sense. Edmund is bitter because he blames his father for an intensely unhappy family situation.)

EDMUND: To hell with sense! We're all crazy. What do we want with sense? *(He quotes from Dowson sardonically.)*

"They are not long, the weeping and the laughter,
Love and desire and hate:
I think they have no portion in us after
We pass the gate.

They are not long, the days of wine and roses:
Out of a misty dream
Our path emerges for a while, then closes
Within a dream."

(Staring before him.) The fog was where I wanted to be. Halfway down the path you can't see this house. You'd never know it was here. Or any of the other places down the avenue. I couldn't see but a few feet ahead. I didn't meet a soul. Everything looked and sounded unreal. Nothing was what it is. That's what I wanted—to be alone with myself in another world where truth is untrue and life can hide from itself. Out beyond the harbor, where the road runs along the beach, I even lost the feeling of being on land. The fog and the sea seemed part of each other. It was like walking on the bottom of the sea. As if I had drowned long ago. As if I was a ghost belonging to the fog, and the fog was the ghost of the sea. It felt damned peaceful to be nothing more than a ghost within a ghost. *(He sees his father staring at him with mingled worry and irritated disapproval. He grins mockingly.)* Don't look at me as if I'd gone nutty. I'm talking sense. Who wants to see life as it is, if they can help it? It's the three Gorgons in one. You look in their faces and turn to stone. Or it's Pan.

You see him and you die—that is, inside you—and have to go on living as a ghost.

(7) Juanita in *Blues for Mister Charlie,* by James Baldwin[11]

(Juanita is a black student whose lover has been senselessly murdered by a white man.)

JUANITA: *(Rises from bed; early Sunday morning.)* He lay beside me on that bed like a rock. As heavy as a rock—like he'd fallen—fallen from a high place—fallen so far and landed so heavy, he seemed almost to be sinking out of sight—with one knee pointing to heaven. My God. He covered me like that. He wasn't at all like I thought he was. He fell on—fell on me—like life and death. My God. His chest, his belly, the rising and the falling, the moans. How he clung, how he struggled—life and death! Life and death! Why did it all seem to me like tears? That he came to me, clung to me, plunged into me, sobbing, howling, bleeding, somewhere inside his chest, his belly, and it all came out, came pouring out, like tears! My God, the smell, the touch, the taste, the sound, of anguish! Richard! Why couldn't I have held you closer? Held you, held you, borne you, given you life again? Have made you be born again! Oh, Richard. The teeth that gleamed, oh! when you smiled, the spit flying when you cursed, the teeth stinging when you bit—your breath, your hands, your weight, my God, when you moved in me! Where shall I go now, what shall I do?...Mama was frightened. Frightened because little Juanita brought her first real lover to this house. I suppose God does for Mama what Richard did for me. Juanita!...Mama is afraid I'm pregnant. Mama is afraid of so much. I'm not afraid. I hope I'm pregnant. I *hope* I am! One more illegitimate black baby—that's right you jive mothers! And I am going to raise my baby to be a man. A *man,* you dig?...Did this happen to Mama sometime? Did she have a man sometime who vanished like smoke? And left her to get through this world as best she could? Is that why she married my father?...You're going crazy, Juanita. Oh, Lord, don't let me go mad. Let me be pregnant! Let me be pregnant!

(8) Salieri in *Amadeus,* by Peter Shaffer[12]

(Salieri, a composer of some note, has just met the cocky, irritating Mozart. He has instantly disliked him but just as instantly has recognized and is jealous of his incredible genius. He addresses his God.)

SALIERI: *Capisco!* I know my fate. Now for the first time I feel my emptiness as Adam felt his nakedness.... *(Slowly he rises to his feet.)* Tonight at an inn somewhere in this city stands a giggling child who can put on paper, without actually setting down his billiard cue, casual notes which turn my most considered ones into lifeless scratches. *Grazie, Signore!* You gave me the desire to serve You—which most men do not have—then saw to it the service was shameful in the ears of the server. *Grazie!* You gave me the desire to praise You—which most men do not feel—then made me mute. *Grazie tanti!* You put into me perception of the Incomparable—which most men never know!—then ensured that I would know myself forever mediocre. *(His voice gains power.)* Why?... What is my fault?... Until this day I have pursued virtue with rigor. I have labored long hours to relieve my fellow men. I have worked and worked the talent You allowed me. *(Calling up) You know how hard I've worked!* Solely that in the end, in the practice of the art which alone makes the world comprehensible to me, I might hear Your Voice! And now I do hear it—and it says only one name: MOZART!... Spiteful, sniggering, conceited, infantine Mozart—who has never worked one minute to help another man! Shit-talking Mozart, with his botty-smacking wife! *Him* You have chosen to be Your sole conduct! And *my* only reward—my sublime privilege—is to be the sole man alive in this time who shall clearly recognize Your Incarnation! *(Savagely) Grazie e grazie ancora! (Pause)* So be it! From this time we are enemies, You and I! I'll not accept it from You—*do you hear?... They say God is not mocked. I tell You, Man* is not mocked!... *I am not mocked!...* They say the spirit bloweth where it listeth: I tell You NO! It must list to virtue or not blow at all! *(Yelling) Dio ingiusto*—You are the Enemy! I name Thee now—*Nemico Eterno!* And this I swear: To my last breath I shall *block* You on earth, as far as I am able!

(9) Blanche in *A Streetcar Named Desire,* by Tennessee Williams[13]

(Blanche DuBois is telling her sister Stella why the family home Belle Reve has been lost because of debts.)

BLANCHE: I, I, I took the blows in my face and my body! All of those deaths! The long parade to the graveyard! Father, mother! Margaret, that dreadful way! So big with it, it couldn't be put in a coffin! But had to be burned like rubbish! You just came home in time for the funerals, Stella. And funerals are pretty compared to deaths. Funerals are quiet, but deaths—not always. Sometimes their breathing is hoarse, and sometimes it rattles, and sometimes they even cry out to you, "Don't let me go!" Even the old, sometimes, say, "Don't let me go." As if you were able to stop them! But funerals are quiet, with pretty flowers. And, oh, what gorgeous boxes they pack them away in! Unless you were there at the bed when they cried out, "Hold me!" you'd never suspect there was the struggle for breath and bleeding. You didn't dream, but I saw! *Saw! Saw!* And now you sit there telling me with your eyes that I let the place go! How in hell do you think all that sickness and dying was paid for? Death is expensive, Miss Stella! And old Cousin Jessie's right after Margaret's, hers! Why, the Grim Reaper had put up his tent on our doorstep!... Stella. Belle Reve was his headquarters! Honey—that's how it slipped through my fingers! Which of them left us a fortune? Which of them left a cent of insurance even? Only poor Jessie—one hundred to pay for her coffin. That was all, Stella! And I with my pitiful salary at the school. Yes, accuse me! Sit there and stare at me, thinking I let the place go! I let the place go? Where were you! In bed with your—Polack!

(10) Ardell in *The Basic Training of Pavlo Hummel,* by David Rabe[14]

(A black soldier in Vietnam watches as Private Pavlo Hummel, a victim of a hand grenade, is placed on a stretcher by the body detail.)

ARDELL: He don't die right off. Take him four days, thirty-eight minutes. And he don't say nothin' to nobody in all that time. No words; he just kinda lay up and look, and when he die, he bitin' on his lower lip, I don't know why. So they take him, they put him in a blue rubber bag, zip it up tight and haul it off to the morgue in the back of a quarterton where he get stuck naked into the refrigerator 'long with the other boys killed that day and the beer and cheese and tuna and stuff the guys who work at the morgue keep in the refrigerator except when it inspection time. The bag get washed, hung out to dry on a line out back a the morgue. *(Slight pause.)* Then ... lemme see, well, finally he get shipped home and his mother cry a lot and his brother get so depressed he gotta go out and lay his chippie he so damned depressed about it all; and Joanna, she read his name in the paper, she let out this little gasp and say to her husband across the table, "Jesus, Jimmy, I used to go with that boy. Oh, damn that war, why can't we have peace? I think I'll call his mother." Ain't it some kinda world? *(And he is laughing.)* Soooooooo ... that about it. That about all I got to say. Am I right, Pavlo? Did I tell you true? You got anything to say? Oh, man, I know you do, you say it out.

NOTES

1. Tyrone Guthrie, *Tyrone Guthrie on Acting* (New York: Viking, 1971), p. 14.

2. Jerzy Grotowski, *Towards a Poor Theatre* (New York: Simon & Schuster, 1968), p. 147.

3. Robert Anderson, *I Never Sang for My Father* (New York: Random House, 1968), pp. 7–8. Reprinted by permission of International Creative Management, Inc. Copyright 1968 by Robert Anderson.

4. Excerpt from *Lu Ann Hampton Laverty Oberlander* in *A Texas Trilogy,* by Preston Jones. Copyright 1974 by Preston Jones. Reprinted by permission of Farrar, Straus and Giroux, Inc.

5. Robert Patrick, *Kennedy's Children* (New York: Random House, 1976), pp. 26–27.

6. Arthur Miller, *Death of a Salesman* (New York: Viking, 1949), pp. 22–23.

7. Beth Henley, *Crimes of the Heart* (New York: Viking, 1982), p. 41.

8. John Millington Synge, *The Playboy of the Western World* (Boston: John W. Luce & Company, 1911), pp. 43–44.

9. P. J. Gibson, *Long Time Since Yesterday* (New York: Samuel French, Inc., 1984), pp. 47–49.

10. Eugene O'Neill, *Long Day's Journey into Night* (New Haven, CT: Yale University Press, 1956), pp. 130–31.

11. James Baldwin, *Blues for Mister Charlie* (New York: Dial Press, 1964), pp. 93–95.

12. Peter Shaffer, *Amadeus* (New York: Harper & Row, 1981), p. 51. Copyright 1980, 1981 by Peter Shaffer. Reprinted by permission of Harper & Row, Publishers, Inc. *CAUTION: Amadeus* is the sole property of the author and is fully protected by copyright. All rights, including professional, amateur, motion picture, recitation, lecturing, public reading, radio broadcasting, and the rights of translating into foreign languages are strictly reserved. All inquiries should be addressed to the author's agent: The Lantz Office, Inc., 888 Seventh Avenue, New York, NY 10106.

13. Tennessee Williams, *A Streetcar Named Desire* (New York: New Directions and Curtis Brown, 1947), pp. 25–26.

14. David Rabe, *The Basic Training of Pavlo Hummel* and *Sticks and Bones* (New York: Viking, 1973), p. 99.

CHAPTER 14

COMMUNICATING THE LINES

Many actors assume that if they understand the general meaning of a line and have an idea of its overall purpose, they will read the line correctly without further conscious effort. This assumption is probably tenable for an intelligent actor speaking straightforward prose dialogue. But many plays (all classics and a considerable number of contemporary works) are not written in simple prose. They nearly always employ a range of rhetorical and poetic devices, and their vocabulary is frequently baffling. In these plays, an actor must pay attention to both content and form if he is to communicate the full value of the dialogue to an audience.

To engage in a comprehensive study of the uses of rhetorical and poetic devices demands much more space and time than we can give it here. We need, however, to explore the more common means dramatists use to make their dialogue effective. Understanding these strategies will stimulate you to examine the dramatist's lines more closely. Only by such careful scrutiny can you detect all subtlety of meaning and aptness of form. Since communication is the actor's primary responsibility and since language is a major means of communication, it goes without saying that the successful actor constantly deepens his sensitivity to words and sharpens his ability to communicate their meaning.

An actor must know what the words he is speaking mean! This advice is so obvious you may resent having it said. Yet it is not uncommon for an actor to go into rehearsals not only ignorant of what his lines mean but also ignorant of his ignorance. Every actor should own a good standard dictionary and use it frequently, even looking up words of which he thinks he knows the meaning. He also needs access to special sources: Dictionaries of slang and colloquial speech are two prominent examples. For almost all period plays, he will also need a glossary and a well-annotated edition of the text.

UNDERSTANDING THE WORDS

Actors need to study conscientiously such sources in order to discover the meaning of the play's words. Let us return to *Romeo and Juliet* for an illustration. Juliet's first line in the balcony scene (Act II, Scene 2), spoken to herself after she has just met Romeo at the Capulet ball and fallen in love with him, is

> O Romeo, Romeo! wherefore art thou Romeo?

Without having a complete understanding of the words, actresses will inevitably misread the line by emphasizing *art* and thus making it mean "Where are you, Romeo?" with some such subtext as "I yearn to know where you are, what you are doing, whether you are longing for me as I am longing for you." But a simple check of the dictionary will disclose that *wherefore* does not mean *where;* it means *why*. *Wherefore* then becomes the emphatic word, and the correct subtext is "Why do you, whom I have come to love, have to be called Romeo, the son of our great enemy?" This reading leads logically to the next line:

> Deny thy father, and refuse thy name;
> Or, if thou wilt not, be but sworn my love,
> And I'll no longer be a Capulet.

In analyzing the meaning of Juliet's first line, note also the absence of a comma between *thou* and *Romeo*—Romeo is not being addressed. Attention to punctuation helps greatly in finding the meaning of a speech.

Incidentally, Juliet uses *wherefore* in the same sense in expressing her alarm when Romeo reveals his presence in the Capulet orchard:

> How cams't thou hither, tell me, and *wherefore?*

She means *how* did you manage to get in here and *why* did you come?

Several other usages in the same scene further illustrate the necessity of paying close attention to the meaning of the words. After Juliet has said her famous "that which we call a rose/ By any other name would smell as sweet," she continues:

> So Romeo would, were he not Romeo call'd,
> Retain that dear perfection which he *owes*
> Without that title.

A few lines later, fearing Romeo will think she is too forward in declaring her love, she says:

> In truth, fair Montague, I am too *fond*.

If your edition of the script has a good glossary, you will discover that *owes* in Shakespeare usually means *owns* and that *fond* usually means *foolish*. Juliet is not saying, "I love you too much," she is saying, "I am foolish to declare my love to someone I have known only an hour and whose family is an enemy to my family." This feeling is expressed more fully later in the lines:

> I have no joy in this contract tonight:
> It is too rash, too unadvis'd, too sudden;

Words that look familiar but that the dramatist uses with an unfamiliar meaning can be particularly deceiving.

Let us move to a related problem of interpretation. After Juliet has warned Romeo that he will be killed if any of her kinsmen find him in their orchard, he says:

> My life were better ended by their hate,
> Than death *prorogued,* wanting of thy love.

The word *prorogued* is not likely to be in the average student's vocabulary. It means *postponed* or *delayed.* Romeo is saying, "It is better to be killed at once by your kinsmen than to endure a living death without your love." To make this meaning clear, six words in the line must have some degree of emphasis:

> My *life* were better *ended* by their *hate,*
> Than *death prorogued,* wanting of thy *love.*

Selecting the word or words to emphasize is important when interpreting the lines. The selection is determined by the meaning of the words and by the context in which they are used. We will call these words the *operative* words. In this sense, operative means "exerting the force necessary to produce an appropriate effect," and we choose this term because it suggests the active influence that certain words have in communicating a meaning. Think of the simple sentence "I gave him the revolver." If we exclude the article, any one of the four words might be operative, depending on the meaning intended. Operative words are not, of course, chosen arbitrarily. Although different actors will make different choices, the choices the actor makes should reveal his understanding of the playwright's text and his sensitivity to the uses of language.

Of course, vocabulary needs attention in all plays, not just verse plays from other periods. Not every actor will be immediately familiar with many terms used by emerging black playwrights. And most actors will need help with the meaning of this Cockney dialogue in Edward Bond's *Early Morning:*

LEN: We'd bin stood there 'ours, and me guts starts t' rumble. 'Owever, I don't let on. But then she 'as t' say "I ain arf pecky."

JOYCE: Thass yer sense a consideration, ain it! I'd 'eard your gut.

LEN: I 'ad an empty gut many times, girl. That don't mean I'm on the danger list. But when you starts rabbitin' about bein' pecky I.... You're a rabbitin' ol' git! 'Ear that?[1]

In fact, practically every play demands close examination of its particular idiom. Michael Weller's *Moonchildren* depends heavily on the audience's familiarity with college slang of the 1960s; *Short Eyes,* by Miguel Piñero, makes heavy use of ethnic and prison slang (the term *short eyes* itself is prison slang for a child molester); and one would have to know a whole range of homosexual terms in order to extract nuances of meaning from many of the lines in today's growing body of gay drama.

HANDLING THE SENTENCE

An actor who is ignorant of the basic rules of grammar cannot possibly interpret and communicate a playwright's lines. No matter what the role or the play, he needs to be able to recognize subjects and predicates, modifying words, phrases, and clauses, and he must understand the principles of subordination and pronoun reference. Jerzy Grotowski wrote:

> The ability to handle sentences is important and necessary in acting. The sentence is an integral unit, emotional and logical, that can be sustained by a single expiratory and melodic wave. It is a whirlwind concentrated on an epicentrum [focal center] formed by the logical accent or accents. The vowels at this epicentrum should not be shortened but rather prolonged slightly in order to give them a special value, taking good care not to break up the unity of the sentence with unjustified pauses....
>
> In poetry too, the sentence must be considered as a logical and emotional entity to be pronounced in one single respiratory wave. Several lines (one and a half, two, or more) often constitute the sentence.[2]

Understanding the sentence as a structural unit, recognizing the relationship and relative importance of its different parts, determining the operative words (or logical accents as Grotowski called them), and keeping the sentence moving toward its epicentrum is one of the actor's principal concerns in dealing with the language of a play. Grotowski's warning against unjustified pauses should be heeded, because unnecessary pauses, whether for an intake of breath or for any other reason, obscure the relationship of the parts of the sentence and destroy its rhythmic flow. Doing the former blurs the meaning, and maintaining the latter is essential to the form. Good actors handle sentences so the words are constantly moving forward toward a focal point. The problem can be more complex than Grotowski suggests. In *The Tempest,* Prospero's "Farewell to his Art" (Act V, Scene 1) has a sentence that is seventeen-and-a-half lines long, and Juliet's potion speech (Act IV, Scene 3) has a sentence of eighteen lines. We provide some sentences, less complex than those just mentioned, that illustrate this problem.

In *Major Barbara,* by George Bernard Shaw, Lady Britomart is answering the protest that she treats her grown-up offspring like children.

I have always made you my companions and friends, and allowed you perfect freedom to do and say whatever you liked, so long as you liked what I could *approve* of.[3]

Here is a sentence of thirty-one words that can be handled as a "single melodic wave," culminating in the operative word *approve.* To select *approve* as the operative word does not mean that other words in the sentence do not have a degree of importance and should not receive some manner of emphasis.

But *approve* is a correct choice. It is logical because in Lady Britomart's mind her approval is more important than the freedom she claims to allow. It helps reveal her dominating character, and it highlights the comic contradiction of the line by suggesting that she is blameworthy of the very charge she is denying.

The following line from Arthur Kopit's *Indians* presents a similar, but more difficult, problem. John Grass, a young Indian, is testifying before a group of senators sent by the president of the United States, the Great Father, to investigate charges of mistreatment. He is talking about the futile and bungling attempts of a missionary bishop to help the situation:

> But when we told him we did not wish to be Christians but wished to be like
> our fathers, and dance the sundance, and fight bravely against the Shawnee
> and the Crow! And pray to the Great Spirits who made the four winds,
> and the earth, and made man from the dust of this earth, Bishop Marty
> *hit* us![4]

This is a group of fifty-nine words, punctuated as two sentences but constituting a single logical and emotional entity, always moving toward the operative word *hit*. Grammatically, "Bishop Marty hit us" is the principal clause, and *hit* is the main verb of the entire unit. Logically, it is John Grass's purpose to impress on the senators the mistreatment the Indians have received, in spite of what (to them, at least) has been a reasonable attitude. Emotionally, he feels very deeply about the physical abuse they have suffered. Kopit's choice of the word *hit* is peculiarly expressive of John Grass's uncomplicated earnestness and naiveté.

In *Blues for Mister Charlie,* by James Baldwin, a mature white man tells about his youthful love for a black girl:

> I used to look at her, the way she moved, so beautiful and free, and I'd wonder
> if at night, when she might be on her way home from someplace, any of
> those boys at school had said *ugly things* to her.[5]

The speaker realized that at the school they attended, a black girl's permitting any kind of relationship with a white boy subjected herself to a good deal of cruel comment. This is the concern he is expressing, and, consequently, the whole sentence must move forward to *ugly things*. This speech also affords the actor a chance to observe the principles of subordination, to pick out the main structure, the "skeleton," and to relate the less important parts to it. Here is the skeleton of this sentence:

> I used to look at her ... and I'd wonder if ... any of those boys ... had said ugly
> things to her.

The other parts must be made subordinate.

EXERCISE

Select a speech of at least twelve lines spoken by a character in a play on which you are working. Look up all the words (with the exception, perhaps, of articles and conjunctions) in order to make certain you understand the possible range of meanings of the passage. If necessary, do a prosaic, line-by-line paraphrase—especially if the speech is from a verse play. Find the operative words.

Remember, each sentence may have more than one operative word, but each sentence should be unified into a single structure with its parts related to the whole through the proper use of subordination.

Memorize this speech, and rehearse it until you have control of both its meaning and its form.

This kind of hard work and attention to detail is essential and demonstrates the truth of the saying: "Art is 90 percent perspiration and 10 percent inspiration."

LOOKING FORWARD

In the previous section, we stressed the importance of finding the operative words and of directing the rest of the sentence toward them—if not like a whirlwind, as Grotowski suggested, at least in some form of progression. We must feel when an actor is speaking that his lines are "going somewhere," and following this progression keeps the audience listening. The actor, like the traveler, must keep moving toward some predetermined destination, and he has to structure his dialogue with this direction in mind.

Besides the examples already cited, dramatists have other ways of giving direction and forward movement to their lines. The simplest is a series of two or more parts, in which each part receives increasing emphasis as the series progresses. One of the best-known lines in dramatic literature, the beginning of Antony's funeral oration for Julius Caesar, is such a series:

> Friends, Romans, countrymen, lend me your ears
> (Act III, Scene 2)

In *Romeo and Juliet* Shakespeare uses a similar construction when the Prince of Verona breaks up the street brawl between the Montagues and the Capulets:

> Rebellious subjects, enemies to peace,
> Profaners of this neighbour-stained steel—
> Will they not hear? What ho! you men, you beasts....
> (Act I, Scene 1)

In *The Lady's Not for Burning,* by Christopher Fry, Jennet has told how her father, an alchemist, once accidentally turned base metal into gold and how he died trying to rediscover the formula. The cynical Thomas Mendip answers that if he had been successful

> ... you
> Would be eulogized, lionized, probably
> Canonized for your divine mishap.[6]

Effective handling of such structures requires looking forward to the end and building the series to a climax.

Dramatists may also use a *ladder* device, in which the idea is "stepped up," like ascending the rungs of a ladder, by a careful progression of words. Starting at the bottom, one must look forward to the top rung. Claudius makes the following toast to Hamlet before the duel he has plotted between Hamlet and Laertes:

> And let the *kettle* to the *trumpet* speak,
> The *trumpet* to the *cannoneer* without,
> The *cannons* to the *heavens,* the *heavens* to the *earth:*
> "Now the king drinks to Hamlet!"
>
> (Act V, Scene 2)

Hamlet's mother is overcome with grief when he makes her aware of her guilty behavior:

> Be thou assur'd, if words be made of *breath,*
> And *breath of life,* I have no *life* to *breathe*
> What thou hast said to me.
>
> (Act III, Scene 4)

A delightfully complex example of this device occurs in *As You Like It,* when Rosalind tells Orlando how Celia and Oliver fell in love:

> … For your brother and my sister no sooner *met,*
> but they *look'd;* no sooner *look'd,* but they *lov'd;*
> no sooner *lov'd,* but they *sigh'd;* no sooner *sigh'd,*
> but they ask'd one another the *reason;* no sooner knew
> the *reason,* but they sought the *remedy.* And in these
> degrees have they made a pair of stairs to marriage,
> which they will *climb incontinent,* or else *be* incontinent
> before marriage.
>
> (Act V, Scene 2)

Another way dramatists "progress" the lines is by piling, one on top of another, details that accumulate to create a total effect. This is called a *periodic* structure. Here, the term *periodic* means "consisting of a series of repeated stages," which well describes this method. The repeated stages build to a climax, with no trailing subordinate elements afterward to minimize their effectiveness. Again, this structure is easily recognized when read silently but requires careful handling when spoken. From the very beginning, the actor must look forward to the end and keep moving toward it. Shakespeare often used periodic structure, and a classic example is John of Gaunt's soaring description of England in *Richard II:*

> This royal throne of kings, this scept'red isle,
> This earth of majesty, this seat of Mars,
> This other Eden, demiparadise,
> This fortress built by Nature for herself
> Against infection and the hand of war,
> This happy breed of men, this little world,
> This precious stone set in a silver sea,
> Which serves it in the office of a wall
> Or as a moat defensive to a house
> Against the envy of less happier lands;
> This blessed plot, this earth, this realm, this
> England....
>
> (Act II, Scene 1)

This great speech actually contains several more "stages" before the final climax. Speaking it well is a strong challenge for even the finest actor, but practicing it will prepare you to deliver simpler usages of this structure with ease.

And prepare you must, for all good playwrights use periodic structure, although not always so formally as the ringing example from *Richard II*. Sean O'Casey uses it in *Juno and the Paycock,* when Mrs. Madigan describes how "her man" used to court her:

> "That'll scratch your lovely, little white neck," says he, ketchin' hould of a danglin' bramble branch, holdin' clusters of the loveliest flowers you ever seen, an' breakin' it off, so that his arm fell, accidental like, roun' me waist, an' as I felt it tightenin', an tightenin', an tightenin', I thought me buzzom was every minute goin' to burst out into a roystherin' song about
>
> > "The little green leaves that were shakin' on the threes,
> > The gallivantin' buttherflies, an' buzzin' o'
> > the bees!"[7]

Arthur Kopit uses this structure in *Indians* when Wild Bill Hickok is standing over the beautiful Teskanjavila:

> Hickok, fastest shooter in the West, 'cept for Billy the Kid, who ain't as accurate; Hickok, deadliest shooter in the West, 'cept for Doc Holliday, who wields a sawed-off shotgun, which ain't fair; Hickok, shootinest shooter in the West, 'cept for Jesse James, who's absolutely indiscriminate; this Hickok, strong as an eagle, tall as a mountain, swift as the wind, fierce as a rattle-snake—a legend in his own time, or any other—this Hickok stands now above an Indian maiden....[8]

It is interesting to note how, for comic effect, Kopit has Teskanjavila ruin the climax of Hickok's splendid speech, forcing him to weaken the periodic structure by adding subordinate elements:

TESKANJAVILA: I'm not an Indian and I'm not a maiden!

HICKOK: Who's not an Indian and not a maiden, but looks pretty good
anyhow....

EXERCISE

Other examples of all these approaches to structure abound. As you read,
collect samples for study and practice.

LOOKING BACKWARD

Paradoxically, though the actor needs constantly to build forward toward a
culminating point, he must also at times look backward, referring to what has
already been said. We will call this particular usage *back reference*. Actors
frequently overlook or do not understand this construction and consequently
choose to "operate" on a word or phrase that has already been emphasized,
rather than to select words that will advance the idea. In Hamlet's soliloquy "To
be, or not to be" (Act III, Scene 1), he states

> Whether 'tis nobler in the mind to suffer
> The slings and arrows of outrageous fortune,
> Or to take arms against a sea of troubles,
> And by opposing end them?

"Sea of troubles" refers back to and, in this case, is synonymous with "outrageous fortune." The operative words that carry the idea forward thus are
take arms.

Portia's famous mercy speech in *The Merchant of Venice* (Act IV, Scene 1)
begins with a back reference. After all legal recourses to save Antonio's life have
been fruitless, she declares that Shylock must be merciful. But he retorts with

> On what compulsion must I? tell me that.

And Portia answers

> The quality of mercy is not strained,
> It droppeth as the gentle rain from heaven
> Upon the place beneath....

Strained means *forced* or *compelled* and is a back reference to Shylock's
compulsion.

A back reference may be to something that has been said several lines
before or even in a previous scene. In George Bernard Shaw's *Major Barbara,*
the spineless Stephen Undershaft, who after an expensive education has lived
always on his mother's income, declares he may go into politics. Later, after
Stephen admits he is unequipped for almost every profession but claims that he
at least knows the difference between right and wrong, his father observes

> ... he knows nothing but thinks he knows everything. That points clearly to a
> political career.

The operative word, of course, is referring back to Stephen's earlier declaration. Back reference of this sort is often used for comic effect.

MAKING CONTRASTS

The choice of operative words is often determined by the playwright's use of *contrast emphasis,* in which he emphasizes either the difference between two terms or the possibility of two or more alternatives. When one recognizes this device in a line, it is almost impossible to read it without correctly emphasizing each of the different terms or alternatives. This mode of expression is apparent in such well-known sayings as "It is more blessed to *give* than to *receive"* or by the double-contrast emphasis in "To *err* is *human;* to *forgive, divine."* The lines quoted from the "To be, or not to be" soliloquy as an example of back reference are also an example of contrast emphasis. The emphatic contrasting words are *suffer* and *take arms,* and the alternatives are to endure the slings and arrows of outrageous fortune or to take a positive stand against them.

The actor should be alert to the frequent occurrence of contrast emphasis in dramatic dialogue, and he should always handle the words so the contrast is clearly made. A few examples, from both contemporary and classic plays, will further clarify this usage:

Respect what *other people see* and touch even if it's the opposite of what *you see* and touch![9]

An investigation of *my* affairs would lead to an investigation of *his* affairs.... [10]

ALICE: Kurt, we're *leaving.*
EDGAR: You're *staying.*[11]

I pray you, father, *being* weak, *seem* so.[12]

I have *hope* to *live,* and am *prepar'd* to *die.*[13]

And let my *liver* rather *heat* with *wine*
Than my *heart cool* with mortifying *groans.*[14]

Let that fool *kill hisse'f.* Ain't no call for *you to he'p him.*[15]

OL' CAP'N: Who's been putting these integrationary ideas in my boy's head? Was it you—I'm asking you a question, dammit! Was it *you?*
IDELLA: Why don't you ask *him?*[16]

Find in the plays you are reading ten examples of contrast emphasis.

EXERCISE

In Chapter 9 we discussed the technique of relating to images or pictures that the actor supplies from his imagination. Dramatists also make extensive use of images in their dialogue, and communicating these images to the audience through the dramatist's words is one of the actor's major tasks in handling language. Peter Brook explained:

**SHARING
THE
IMAGERY**

> The exchange of impressions through images is our basic language: at the moment when one man expresses an image at that same instant the other man meets him in belief. The shared association is the language—if the association evokes nothing in the second person, if there is no instance of shared illusion, there is no exchange.... The vividness and the fullness of this momentary illusion depends on his [the speaker's] conviction and skill.[17]

Laurence Perrine defined imagery as "the representation through language of sense experience." And of course, sensory experience is one of the pleasures derived from going to the theatre. Perrine's definition continues:

> The word *image* perhaps most often suggests a mental picture, something seen in the mind's eye—and visual imagery is the most frequently occurring kind.... But an image may also represent a sound; a smell; a taste; a tactile experience, such as hardness, wetness, or cold; an internal sensation, such as hunger, thirst, or nausea; or movement or tension in the muscles or joints.[18]

Images are either *literal* or *figurative,* although they both serve the same purpose of providing a vivid sensory experience. A figurative image expresses something in terms ordinarily used for expressing something else; thus, some comparison is either stated or implied. A literal image is a direct description couched in terms intended to stimulate a sensory response. "The russet dawn colors the eastern sky" and "She talks about her secret as she sleeps upon her pillow" are literal images. But in *Hamlet* and *Macbeth,* Shakespeare says in figurative language:

> But look, the morn in russet mantle clad,
> Walks o'er the dew of yon high eastward hill,

and

> Infected minds
> To their deaf pillows will discharge their secrets.

The terminology relating to imagery can be very complex; indeed, more than two hundred kinds of figurative speech have been identified. It is neither necessary nor desirable for the actor to become entangled in such subtlety. It is essential, however, that for both literal and figurative images he appreciate the sensory experience the dramatist is expressing. For figurative language, he must also understand the aptness of the comparison. Most important of all, he must respond to imagery with all his senses before he can communicate it to an audience. Sam Shepard's description in *Red Cross* of swimming in the rain provides a rich example:

JIM: ... Your body stays warm inside. It's just the outside that gets wet. It's really neat. I mean you can dive under water and hold your breath. You stay under for about five minutes. You stay down there and there's nothing but water all around you. Nothing but marine life. You stay down as long as you can until your lungs start to ache. They feel like they're going to burst open. Then just at the point where you can't stand it any more you force yourself to the top. You explode out of the water gasping for air, and all this rain hits you in the face. You ought to try it.[19]

Shakespeare is an imagist par excellence. Consider this example from *Macbeth:*

> Now does he feel
> His secret murders sticking on his hands.

and from *King Lear:*

> Thou art a bile,
> A plague-sore, an embossed carbuncle,
> In my corrupted blood.

Imagery has particular power to affect the emotions of both the actor and his audience. Consider Constance's moving lament for her lost son in *King John:*

> Grief fills the room up of my absent child,
> Lies in his bed, walks up and down with me,
> Puts on his pretty looks, repeats his words,
> Remembers me of all his gracious parts,
> Stuffs out his vacant garments with his form.

Imagery can be beautiful, as in Romeo's rhapsody when he first sees Juliet:

> O, she doth teach the torches to burn bright.
> It seems she hangs upon the cheek of night
> As a rich jewel in an Ethiop's ear.

It can be folksy, as in O'Casey's *The Shadow of a Gunman:*

MRS. HENDERSON: I'm afraid he'll never make a fortune out of what he's sellin'.... Every time he comes to our place I buy a package o' hairpins from him to give him a little encouragement. I 'clare to God I have as many pins now as ud make a wire mattress for a double bed.[20]

It can be earthy, as in Davis's *Purlie Victorious:*

OL' CAP'N: You don't know, boy, what a strong stomach it takes to stomach you. Just look at you sitting there—all slopped over like something the horses dropped; steam, stink and all![21]

---

(1) Find examples of imagery in the roles you are studying, and try to communicate as fully as possible the sensory experience the playwright intended to evoke.

(2) Work on several of the following speeches, exploring the language and using it fully to communicate the meaning. Do whatever research is necessary to understand the words, the structures, and the images.

a. First Voice in *Under Milk Wood,* a Play for Voices, by Dylan Thomas

(The Voice is describing a small town in Wales.)

FIRST VOICE: *(Very softly.)* It is Spring, moonless night in the small town, starless and bible-black . . . courters'-and-rabbits' wood limping invisible down to the sloeblack, slow, black, crowblack, fishingboat-bobbing sea. The houses are blind as moles (though moles see fine to-night in the snouting, velvet dingles) or blind as Captain Cat there in the muffled middle by the pump and the town clock, the shops in mourning, the Welfare Hall in widows' weeds. And all the people of the lulled and dumbfound town are sleeping now.

Hush, the babies are sleeping, the farmers, the fishers, the tradesmen and pensioners, cobbler, school-teacher, postman and publican, the undertaker and the fancy woman, drunkard, dressmaker, preacher, policeman, the webfoot cocklewomen and the tidy wives. Young girls lie bedded soft or glide . . . down the aisles of the organplaying wood. The boys are dreaming wicked or of the bucking ranches of the night and the jollyrodgered sea. . . . You can hear the dew falling, and the hushed town breathing.[22]

b. Carol in *Red Cross,* by Sam Shepard

(She stands on the bed and acts out the speech as though she were skiing on a mountain slope.)

CAROL: . . . I'll be at the top of this hill and everything will be all right. I'll be breathing deep. In and out. Big gusts of cold freezing air. My whole body will be warm and I won't even feel the cold at all. I'll be halfway down and then I'll put on some steam. A little steam at first and then all the way into the egg position. The Europeans use it for speed. I picked it up when I was ten. I'll start to accumulate more and more velocity. The snow will start to spray up around my ankles and across my face and hands. My fingers will get tighter around the grips and I'll start to feel a little pull in each of my calves. Right along the tendon and in front, too. Everything will be working at once. All my balance and strength and breath. The whole works in one bunch. There'll be pine trees going past me and other skiers going up the hill. They'll stop and watch me go past. I'll be going so fast everyone will stop and look. They'll wonder if I'll make it. I'll do some jumps and twist my body with the speed. They'll see my body twist, and my hair, and my eyes will water from the wind hitting them. My cheeks will start to sting and get all red. I'll get further and further into the egg position with my arms tucked up. I'll look down and see the valley and the cars and house and people walking up and down. I'll see all the cabins with smoke coming out the chimneys.[23]

c. Bynum Walker in *Joe Turner's Come and Gone,* by August Wilson

(Bynum, a conjure man, is giving Jeremy Furlow some advice about women.)

BYNUM: Alright. Let's try it this way. Now, you take a ship. Be out there on the water traveling about. You out there on that ship sailing to and from. And then you see some land. Just like you see a woman walking down the street. You see that land and it don't look like nothing but a line out there on the horizon. That's all it is when you first see it. A line that cross your path out there on the horizon. Now, a smart man know when he see that land, it ain't just a line setting out there. He know that if you get off the water to go take a good look . . . why, there's a whole world right there. A whole world with everything imaginable under the sun. Anything you can think of you can find on that land. Same with a woman. A woman is everything a man need. To a smart man she water and berries. And that's all a man need. That's all he need to live on. You give me some water and berries and if there ain't nothing else I can live a hundred years. See, you just like a man looking at the horizon from a ship. You just seeing a part of it. But it's a blessing when you learn to look at a woman and see in maybe just a few strands of her hair, the way her cheek curves . . . to see in that everything there is out of life to be gotten. It's a blessing to see that. You know you done right and proud by your mother to see that. But you got to learn it. My telling you ain't gonna mean nothing. You got to learn how to come to your own time and place with a woman.[24]

d. Claire in *A Delicate Balance,* by Edward Albee

(Claire is telling her brother-in-law, Tobias, what it is like when an alcoholic hits bottom.)

CLAIRE: ...Pretend you're very sick, Tobias, like you were with the stomach business, but pretend you feel your insides are all green, and stink, and mixed up, and your eyes hurt and you're half deaf and your brain keeps turning off, and you've got peripheral neuritis and you can hardly walk and you hate. You hate with the same green stinking sickness you feel your bowels have turned into... yourself, and *everybody*. Hate, and, oh, God!! you want love, l-o-v-e, so badly—comfort and snuggling is what you really mean, of course—but you hate, and you notice—with a sort of detachment that amuses you, you think—that you're more like an animal every day...you snarl, and grab for things, and hide things and forget where you hid them like not-very bright dogs, and you wash less, prefer to *be* washed, and once or twice you've actually soiled your bed and laid in it because you can't get up...pretend all that. No, you don't like that, Tobias?[25]

e. Juliet in *Romeo and Juliet,* by William Shakespeare

(To prevent her having to marry Paris, Friar Laurence has given Juliet a potion that will make her appear as dead. She will then remain in the family vault until Romeo comes from banishment to rescue her. She has said good night to her mother and her nurse and is now alone realizing she must drink the potion.)

JULIET: Farewell! God knows when we shall meet again.
I have a faint cold fear thrills through my veins
That almost freezes up the heat of life.
I'll call them back again to comfort me.
Nurse!—What should she do here?
My dismal scene I needs must act alone.
Come, vial.
What if this mixture do not work at all?
Shall I be marry'd then tomorrow morning?
No, no! this shall forbid it, lie thou there.

(Laying down a dagger)

What if it be a poison which the Friar
Subtly hath minister'd to have me dead,
Lest in this marriage he should be dishonor'd
Because he marry'd me before to Romeo?
I fear it is, and yet methinks it should not,
For he hath still been tried a holy man.
How if, when I am laid into the tomb,
I wake before the time that Romeo
Come to redeem me? There's a fearful point!
Shall I not then be stifled in the vault,

To whose foul mouth no healthsome air breathes in,
And there die strangled ere my Romeo comes?
Or if I live, is it not very like
The horrible conceit of death and night
Together with the terror of the place—
As in a vault, an ancient receptacle,
Where for this many hundred years the bones
Of all my buried ancestors are pack'd,
Where bloody Tybalt yet but green in earth
Lies fest'ring in his shroud, where as they say
At some hours in the night spirits resort—
Alack, alack! is it not like that I
So early waking—what with loathsome smells
And shrieks like mandrakes torn out of the earth,
That living mortals hearing them run mad—
O if I wake, shall I not be distraught,
Environed with all these hideous fears,
And madly play with my forefathers' joints
And pluck the mangled Tybalt from his shroud
And, in this rage with some great kinsman's bone
As with a club dash out my desp'rate brains?
O look! methinks I see my cousin's ghost
Seeking out Romeo that did spit his body
Upon a rapier's point. Stay Tybalt, stay!
Romeo, Romeo, Romeo! Here's drink—I drink to thee.

(Falls upon the bed)[26]

f. Romeo in *Romeo and Juliet,* by William Shakespeare

(Romeo, believing Juliet is dead, comes to the tomb to say farewell and to die at her side.)

ROMEO: How oft when men are at the point of death
Have they been merry—which their keepers call
A lightning before death. O! how may I
Call this a lightning? O my love, my wife!
Death, that has suck'd the honey of thy breath
Hath had no power yet upon thy beauty.
Thou art not conquer'd—Beauty's ensign yet
Is crimson in thy lips and in thy cheeks,
And Death's pale flag is not advanced there.
Tybalt, ly'st thou there in thy bloody sheet?
O what more favor can I do to thee
Than with that hand that cut thy youth in twain
To sunder his that was thine enemy?
Forgive me, cousin. Ah dear Juliet,

Why art thou yet so fair? shall I believe
That unsubstantial Death is amorous
And that the lean abhorred monster keeps
Thee here in dark to be his paramour?
For fear of that I still will stay with thee
And never from this pallet of dim Night
Depart again, here, here will I remain
With worms that are thy chambermaids, O here
Will I set up my everlasting rest
And shake the yoke of inauspicious stars
From this world-weary'd flesh. Eyes look your last,
Arms take your last embrace, and, lips (O you
The doors of breath) seal with a righteous kiss
A dateless bargain to engrossing Death!
Come bitter conduct, come unsavory guide,
Thou desp'rate pilot, now at once run on
The dashing rocks thy seasick weary bark.
Here's to my love! *(He drinks)* O true apothecary,
Thy drugs are quick. Thus with a kiss I die. *(Falls)*[27]

NOTES

1. Edward Bond, *Early Morning* (London: Calder and Boyars, 1968), pp. 21–22.

2. Jerzy Grotowski, *Towards a Poor Theatre* (New York: Simon & Schuster, 1968), p. 171.

3. George Bernard Shaw, *Complete Plays with Prefaces* (6 vols.; New York: Dodd, Mead, 1962), vol. I, p. 347. Italics ours.

4. Arthur Kopit, *Indians* (New York: Hill and Wang, 1969), p. 9. Italics ours.

5. James Baldwin, *Blues for Mister Charlie* (New York: Dial Press, 1964), p. 63. Italics ours.

6. Christopher Fry, *The Lady's Not for Burning; A Phoenix Too Frequent; and an Essay "An Experience of Critics"* (New York: Oxford University Press, 1977), p. 54.

7. Sean O'Casey, *Three Plays* (New York: Macmillan, 1960), pp. 42–43.

8. Kopit, *Indians,* p. 47.

9. Luigi Pirandello, *Right You Are If You Think You Are,* trans. Eric Bentley (New York: Columbia University Press, 1954), p. 19. Italics ours.

10. Friedrich Duerrenmatt, *Play Strindberg,* trans. James Kirkup (Chicago: The Dramatic Publishing Company, 1952), p. 57. Italics ours.

11. Duerrenmatt, *Play Strindberg,* p. 58. Italics ours.

12. William Shakespeare, *King Lear* (New Haven, CT: Yale University Press, 1947), p. 71. Italics ours.

13. William Shakespeare, *Measure for Measure* (New Haven, CT: Yale University Press, 1954), p. 46. Italics ours.

14. William Shakespeare, *The Merchant of Venice* (New Haven, CT: Yale University Press, 1923), p. 4. Italics ours.

15. Charles Gordone, *No Place to Be Somebody* (Indianapolis: Bobbs Merrill, 1969), p. 12. Italics ours.

16. Ossie Davis, *Purlie Victorious* (New York: Samuel French, 1961), p. 31. Italics ours.

17. Peter Brook, *The Empty Space* (New York: Atheneum, 1968), pp. 77–78.

18. Laurence Perrine, *Sound and Sense* (New York: Harcourt Brace Jovanovich, 1956), p. 40.

19. Sam Shepard, *Chicago and Other Plays* (New York: Urizen Books, 1981), p. 115.

20. O'Casey, *Three Plays,* p. 101.

21. Davis, *Purlie Victorious,* p. 31.

22. Dylan Thomas, *Under Milk Wood* (New York: New Directions, 1954), pp. 1–2.

23. Shepard, *Chicago and Other Plays,* pp. 101–2.

24. August Wilson, *Joe Turner's Come and Gone* (New York: New American Library, 1988), p. 46.

25. Edward Albee, *A Delicate Balance* (New York: Atheneum, 1966), p. 23.

26. William Shakespeare, *Romeo and Juliet* (New Haven, CT: Yale University Press, 1917), pp. 101–3.

27. Shakespeare, *Romeo and Juliet,* pp. 120–21.

CHAPTER 15

AUDITIONING FOR THE PLAY

The actor's first encounter with the director is usually at that nerve-racking experience, the audition. Michael Shurtleff, whose book on auditioning has become the bible of the subject, warns, "In order to act, it is necessary to audition.... All the training in the world can go for naught if the actor in the reading situation can't convince the auditors he can perform the role."[1] This statement not only reinforces the importance of the audition, but also it implies that the audition is a process requiring certain skills the actor can develop and train.

Because the audition is such a defining moment in the life and career of an actor, in this chapter we shall talk about useful principles that will help you face this task. When you audition, you will need to find a way to allow the director to see the depth and breadth of your talent and your mastery of technique. We hope to help you achieve that goal.

From a director's point of view, the audition is a simple, time-saving way to become familiar with numerous actors and to attempt to identify those who most closely resemble his concept of the characters in the play being cast. The director uses the audition to find an actor who has the talent and the technique to play a certain part, who is physically right for the part, and who will blend well with the other cast members. Of course, if the audition is for a repertory company or a stock company, the director is also looking for versatility and perhaps other theatrical skills, since members of these companies often must do technical work during a portion of the season. The actor often conjures up images of the director as an ogre, eager to help young aspirants get started on a nontheatrical career. Exactly the opposite is the case. The director wants to mount a successful production of the play, and to do so he needs the right actors. At the start of the audition, at least, he hopes you will be the one for which he is searching; he is pulling for you, not against you.

In most auditions, whether for college, stock, repertory, or professional productions, an actor reads a scene from the play being cast. Often actors receive the scene when they arrive for the audition and have only a short time to look it over. At other times, they simply may be interviewed by the director or asked to do a monologue or scene prepared for the occasion.

It has become customary at many auditions attended by representatives from various companies that actors be allotted a total of three minutes, during

A scene from the New York Shakespeare Festival production of *A Chorus Line,* book by James Kirkwood and Nicholas Dante; setting by Robin Wagner, costumes by Theoni V. Aldredge; lighting by Tharon Musser. In this internationally acclaimed musical, dancers compete in a grueling audition in order to secure a place in the chorus line of a Broadway musical. (Photo by Martha Swope.)

which they present one dramatic and one comedic piece prepared prior to their arrival. At the Southeast Theatre Conference Auditions for summer theatres, however, the actor is allowed only one minute to perform prepared material and then given thirty seconds to sing. After hearing the prepared auditions, companies call back for further readings and interviews actors who have impressed them with their potential. No doubt your teacher receives many notices of auditions and will be glad to share them with you. Check each carefully for the time allotted for prepared material.

Usually, however, actors will audition for a particular production of a particular play. Most directors have their own system for holding auditions, and an actor should not be alarmed at one who uses unusual methods to determine a performer's suitability for a role. In *A Chorus Line,* a musical about dancers auditioning for a Broadway musical, the "director" asks each dancer to talk about himself or herself as well as to dance. Some of the dancers rise to the occasion; others do not.

PREPARING FOR THE AUDITION

Whether you are participating in one of the large "cattle-call" auditions attended by several companies or reading for a single role in a play, you will want to be ready to present one or more prepared monologues. Selecting this material is at the same time the most difficult and the most important task the auditioner faces. Guidelines and cheap advice about what works and what does not work are plentiful, but because directors vary so greatly in their taste and their needs, no definitive scheme exists. A few suggestions may help:

1. Select something you like. You will be living with the piece for a considerable period of hard work. Do not add to the drudgery of it by starting with something you hate.

2. Use material well within your grasp and understanding. Although "type casting" has developed a bad connotation, all actors should realize the range of roles for which they are best suited. Those roles constitute your "type." It is unwise to select an audition piece from material outside this range. The director may eventually cast you for a part that demands a considerable stretch in age and temperament, but you will show yourself best in roles that are close to what you believe to be your best aptitudes.

3. Unless the director specifically requests them, avoid dialects. Mastering and using them will needlessly complicate your preparation.

4. Try to select material that will not be performed twenty times by other actors at the same audition. You cannot be clairvoyant, but new material will give you a distinct advantage. When several actors perform the same piece, the director not only tires of hearing it but also has an opportunity that would not otherwise be feasible to make a direct comparison between you and the other actors. It is more difficult to avoid the old standard "warhorses" from

the classics than it is from the modern repertoire, but even here the actor should seek fresh material.

5. Always be prepared to do more than one piece. Most actors try to have at least four: a comic modern piece, a comic classic piece, a serious modern piece, and a serious classic piece. Although you should focus on straight roles, you should probably be prepared to do at least one character part that you believe to be well within your performance range.

Nearly anything you select to prepare as audition material will need to be "cut" to fit the playing time you are likely to be allotted at the audition. Even if the director asks you to perform a piece without the constraints of a specific time limit, three to five minutes will be plenty. Unlike cutting a program for performance before an audience, telling the story is not the prime factor to consider. Joan Finchley suggests asking the following questions:

1. What fascinates me about what the character says?

2. What part(s) of the speech do I personally connect with?

3. Which parts of the speech provide the best dramatic possibilities?

4. Which parts best reveal information about the character's intentions and feelings?[2]

Of course, you will want to read the entire script and analyze the actions and intentions of the character exactly as you would if you were preparing to perform the role in a production.

At some point in your preparation, you will want to seek help from either trusted acting teachers or friends. Ask them whether you are presenting the material in a manner that will demonstrate your best qualities. Have them check your audibility and your visibility, and ask them questions calculated to validate your communication of the character's actions and intentions.

Preparing to read "cold" from the script of a play requires a different kind of effort. Most directors would certainly prefer that actors not memorize any parts of the text, but you certainly may, and should, read the script if it is available before attending the auditions. The director will not expect a fully developed characterization in a cold reading. He will expect you to be able to perform well under pressure and to show that you can quickly focus on an intention and perform it well enough to bring your words to life. One of the reasons directors use cold readings is that they allow more of "the real you" to come through the audition, so attempts to externalize the character will be futile and uncalled for.

If you are allowed to hear other auditioners read, be wary of the tendency either to copy an effective reading or to try too hard to be different. Another warning: Do not attempt to guess what the director wants. Center your energies on understanding the script well enough to give an intelligent reading that shows you can make defensible choices. Believing is a part of auditioning, too. You must be able to believe in your abilities and in the words you are speaking.

PHOTOGRAPHS AND RÉSUMÉS

Directors will usually expect you to give them a picture of yourself and a résumé of your experience. Your picture should be a black-and-white, eight-by-ten, head-and-shoulder shot. Some actors like to provide composites, also, but they should always be used as supplements to the standard photo. The picture should be recent and natural, showing yourself as nearly as possible like you look on the day you audition.

Sample résumé prepared by a student actress to use in conjunction with auditions for summer jobs at professional or semiprofessional theatres. Although the needs of various producing organizations vary, the auditioner should present his or her training and experience in the best possible light without overstating the case. Names and phone numbers of people who can vouch for your abilities are also useful. The photograph of the actress would usually be pasted to the back of the résumé. (Résumé printed by permission of Keili Lefkovitz.)

Keili Elizabeth Lefkovitz
AFTRA

CURRENT ADDRESS & PHONE:
612 S. 4th Street Apt. A
Columbia, MO 65201
(314) 443-2352

HEIGHT: 5'5-1/2"
WEIGHT: 135
HAIR: Brown
EYES: Brown
AGE: 21

THEATRE AND MUSIC

Bye Bye Birdie	chorus	1991	KC
Steppin' Out	Sylvia	1993	MU
Sexual Perversity in Chicago (In Repertory)	Deb	1993	MU
Duck Variations (In Repertory)	Emil	1993	MU
Pippin	chorus	1993	MU
JoNell Johnson and Ruthie Mapes	Ruthie	1993	MU
ACTF First Alternate at Kennedy Center in Washington, D.C.			
The Love of the Nightingale	Philomele	1994	MU
The Good Doctor	ensemble	1994	Professional Summer Repertory Theatre
Some Enchanted Evening	Nellie	1994	Professional Summer Repertory Theatre

AWARDS
JoNell Johnson and Ruthie Mapes;ACTF - Best Actress (Ruthie Mapes); Best Ensemble Cast
Tom Berenger Acting Scholarship

SELECTED RADIO & TELEVISION COMMERCIALS
McDonald's
Wal-Mart
Commerce Bank
Cystic Fibrosis PSA
World's of Fun "Night Magic"
Coat and Sportswear Outlet
Holiday Promo for KSHB-TV
Crown Center
Kansas City Zoo "A Home for K.C., the Elephant"
Seville Square
Sietz Bologna

TRAINING & SPECIAL SKILLS
Alan Nichols (Kansas City, MO); Acting
Bryan Young Full Circle Co. (Kansas City, MO); Acting, singing, dance
University of Missouri, Department of Theatre (Columbia, MO); acting, voice

Gymnastics, karate, stage combat, singing, javelin, swimming, cheerleading.

technical resume available upon request

KEILI

The prime purpose of the picture is to remind the auditors of who you are. They will decide if they can make you look like a different character. In fact, most directors discount, or actually resent, attempts on your part to stimulate their imagination. Having your name printed on your photograph, or affixing a one-page summary of your résumé to its back, is a good idea, as résumés and photos can get separated in the shuffle of a large casting call.

Your résumé should contain the history of your theatrical life. At the most basic level, it should contain personal, descriptive information: age, height, weight, and color of hair. It must tell the producer or director about your training and your experience and about the people who you have worked with, the kinds of theatres and productions in your background, and your union affiliations (SAG, AFTRA, Equity), if any. The résumé serves as the chief source of information about you. The information should be accurate and arranged so it is easy to find and comprehend. Most of all, it should contain an up-to-date address and telephone number.

Your résumé, like your picture, must give as truthful a view of you as possible. Auditors are simply not fooled by padded lists of roles you have performed in acting class. Do not be ashamed of who you are. Approach the audition with pride. Believe in yourself, and present yourself as one who wants to be seen, to be heard, and to work.

When the day for the audition arrives, use your techniques for relaxation to control your nervousness. Remember that relaxation involves the state of both mind and body. You must be able to remove at will any condition that blocks your intellectual thought process or your ability to command your voice and body to perform at their full range of flexibility. Actors employ a variety of methods to achieve total relaxation. For some, yoga or transcendental meditation provide the answer. Others prefer a vigorous routine of physical exercise. Find a method that works for you.

AUDITIONING

Stanislavski often recommended complete attention or absorption in a sound, smell, feeling, or object as a method of relaxation. Such an exercise can be practiced anywhere and under almost any circumstance. Learn to turn this state of total concentration into a means of relaxing every part of your body.

EXERCISE

Prior to auditions, you may want to work especially on your face. Concentrate on the muscles at the corners of the eyes and the muscles that control the bridge of the nose, the cheeks, and the two corners of your mouth. Remember that self-consciousness is the cause of most tension. You must be able to banish the self-doubt that lingers in your mind and focus your energies on the problem at hand.

If possible, examine beforehand the room where the audition is to take place. Get a friend to check your audibility. Make sure every word you are going to speak can be heard in every part of the room. Check the light also. If you have a choice, decide the best place to stand so your face is clearly visible.

Dress comfortably. Your clothing should be clean and simple and permit ease of movement. Neatness counts. Tyrone Guthrie was fond of saying that people who dress like slobs very nearly always turn out to be slobs. Some actors like to dress in a manner suggestive of the role for which they are auditioning. If you choose to do so, make your selection subtle so your "costume" will not overpower your performance. The director wants to meet you, to check on the condition of your "tools," and to observe your imagination at work. He has probably already engaged a costume designer. For general auditions, leotards and skirts for women and comfortable trousers with loose shirts for men are usually appropriate.

Warm up before your time comes or your name is called. The actor should be in the habit of never performing without an adequate warm-up, period! Your pre-audition routine should begin the moment you arrive and should be a part of everything you do prior to the audition, whether in the privacy of the warm-up room or in the "holding" area where you await your call. Roger Ellis, author of another outstanding handbook on auditioning, believes any routine you are comfortable with is all right so long as you are

(1) Shedding the tribulations of your personal life outside the rehearsal hall

(2) Increasing your awareness of your physical, emotional, and intellectual power

(3) Raising the energy level in every part of your body, especially your voice (volume, breath support, and articulation)

(4) Running over the particular physical and vocal demands in your prepared pieces

(5) Listening for your name to be called by the stage manager (*very* important)[3]

When you get your call, you should walk briskly to the stage or the front of the audition room, clearly say your name (or number if required), flash a friendly smile, take a moment to center your concentration, and begin. If you are performing prepared material, place your eye contact forward so the people listening to your audition can see your face. If you are asked to read something you have never seen before, ask for a few minutes to look it over. Usually your auditors will grant such a request. If you are reading with another actor, assume a shared position, three-quarter front. Do not be afraid to make eye contact with the other actor. Share the scene in every sense of the word; listen to the other actor, and try to respond to whatever characterization he or she is giving to the role. Thank your listeners when you are finished, repeat your name if given the opportunity, and confidently and quickly leave the stage.

In some situations, directors hold a second round of auditions known as *call backs*. In this way they narrow the field to those actors, sometimes as few as two per role, broadly suitable for their needs. If you receive a call back, try to take the time to do additional work on the script. Approach the call back with the same kind of energy and enthusiasm you brought to the original audition. Directors, above all else, are looking for actors who want to work and who appear to have the ability to tap their talent and apply their resources to the role. Look on a call back as a new opportunity to show the director that you know how to take a chance, to communicate with the audience and with another actor, and to imagine possibilities for developing the role.

Sound advice that will cover all contingencies is impossible, but the preceding tips should place you in a proper frame of mind for the audition and should help you prepare material that will show your talents to the best of your ability. Remember to be honest. Be ready to improvise. Do not, to repeat, try to anticipate "what they want." Most important, do not blame yourself if you do not get the part. At most auditions, the competition is staggering for even the smallest part. Contrary to what many actors believe, directors nearly always have a vision of the play. Their choices, therefore, are rarely whimsical. Although you should always try to improve your audition techniques, remember that failure to wn the role is not necessarily a reflection of how you auditioned or of your ability to act.

If you do get the part, be properly sympathetic with those who were not so fortunate. Begin immediately to do your prerehearsal homework, for you are now ready to commence the intense preparation period that will lead to the opening night we anticipated at the beginning of this book.

EXERCISE

(1) Start a file of scenes you believe would serve you well as audition pieces. Make certain to select them from both classic and modern plays and from both comedies and serious dramas. Present your file to your instructor for criticism.

(2) Prepare and perform in class a three-minute audition containing two pieces: one comic and one serious, and one from a classic and one from a modern play.

(3) Examine résumés of actors currently looking for employment. Begin a theatrical résumé of your own, and update it regularly as you achieve additional training and experience.

NOTES

1. Michael Shurtleff, *Audition: Everything an Actor Needs to Know to Get the Part* (New York: Walker, 1978), p. 1.

2. Joan Finchley, *Audition!* (Englewood Cliffs, NJ: Prentice-Hall, 1984), p. 4.

3. Roger Ellis, *An Audition Handbook for Student Actors* (Chicago: Nelson-Hall Publishers, 1986), p. 93. Italics in the original.

CHAPTER 16

SHOW TIME!
REHEARSING AND PERFORMING

Once the actor has survived an audition and starts rehearsals for a production, he has the advantage of working under the guidance of a director. The director, equipped with a thorough knowledge of the values of the play and of the technical resourcefulness to realize them on the stage, helps individual actors shape their characterizations so they will make the greatest possible contribution to the play's total meaning. He will be eager to help the actor create a character that is true to the dramatist's intentions as he has interpreted them for that particular production.

The director's interpretation becomes the foundation for his master plan—a plan often intricately complicated in its detail—for coordinating all aspects of the production into an artistic whole. Each actor's characterization is a vital part of that plan, and much of the rehearsal time is spent on its development and its relationship to the other characters in the play. To bring the actor to "performance level," the director will also devote rehearsal time to gaining clear speech, good projection, precise movement, rhythm, and energy.

The prerehearsal period—after you are cast and before rehearsals begin—is a time for you to learn about your role and the structure of the play as a whole. It is a time to read about the period of the play and, if appropriate, to study the art and general history of the period. Do not be in a hurry to memorize lines, even though you must take this responsibility seriously and complete it by the time you are asked to be "off book," a moment that varies from director to director.

Prior to rehearsals is a good time to study the play's structure. Discover how each character's action relates to the whole drama. Take a while to examine the play with fresh eyes—as if you had no role in it at all. Being flexible toward your role early in rehearsals is just as important as being solidly and comfortably prepared when rehearsals end.

During the rehearsal period, you will join a team that consists of the director, the stage manager, the other actors, and, finally, of the various production crews. All of these people strive for a single objective: the creative and artistic expression of the play's total meaning. Although the actor is expected to analyze his role on his own, he must relate his performance to the director's concept for expressing the play to the audience. He must also learn how to use all the elements of modern theatre to reinforce his character, including lights, scenery, costumes, sound, and many more. He must learn to keep a cool head in a demanding and often pressure-packed group enterprise. Producing a play is a fine example of cooperative effort—a process described by Harold Clurman as "the relating of a number of talents to a single meaning."[1]

Although they often are not sharply defined and they may considerably overlap, five principal phases make up the process of rehearsal:

1. Finding the meaning

2. Developing the characters

3. Creating the form

4. Making technical adjustments

5. Polishing for performance

FINDING THE MEANING

If a production is to realize its possibilities, if it is to be the "relating of a number of talents to a single meaning," everyone working on the production must understand what that single meaning is. And everyone must understand how his particular part, small or large as it may be, contributes to the expression of it. Indeed, the final success or failure of the production will rest in all likelihood on that part of the rehearsal period devoted to finding the meaning of the play.

The director, the actors, and the designers may come to an agreement about the meaning of the play in a number of ways. Often their understanding results from group discussions, in which each person, having analyzed the play beforehand, stands ready to present his interpretation but willing to modify it if necessary. In other instances, the production team depends on the director to possess a more thorough knowledge of the play than anyone else and to teach his interpretation to the others. Even more frequently, the contributing artists reach agreement through a combination of these approaches. Usually, the schedule will call for a number of "reading rehearsals," in which actors sit in a circle reading aloud their individual parts and discussing the play with the director and with each other. Other members of the production team will often be invited to these sessions.

Today, an actor may have the opportunity to work in a wide variety of performance spaces and theatres. The Tony Award-winning Oregon Shakespeare Festival presents an eight-month (February-October) season of eleven plays performed in repertory in three theatres. The Festival is one of the oldest and largest professional regional theatre companies in the United States. Pictured is the Allen Pavilion of the Elizabethan Theatre, the oldest existing full-scale Elizabethan stage in the Western Hemisphere. (Photo by Gregory N. Leiber.)

The important thing is that everyone clearly understands what the play means. Until this common understanding has been reached, the group is likely to be working at cross purposes, and the rehearsals cannot proceed effectively.

Once the interpretation is set, each actor begins to search for the basic motivating desire of the character he is playing and its relationship to the total meaning. Here again agreement between the actor and the director is necessary, and the reading rehearsals usually produce this understanding. At the same time, the actor begins to consider the problem of line interpretation—of relating the lines to the character's motivating desire and to the meaning of the play as a whole.

The time given to finding the meaning through reading and discussion may vary from as little as one rehearsal to as much as a third of the entire rehearsal period, depending on the practice of the director and the subtleties of the play. In fact, the process is rarely finished, as new and deeper meanings are certain to reveal themselves during all kinds of rehearsals and, indeed, during performances.

Although the actor and director are teammates, sharing the goal of excellence, they have different responsibilities. The director is the team captain, who ultimately decides which particular actions move the play toward the desired effect. The director also interacts with other team members—set designer, lighting designer, costume designer, property master—and, most of all, with the playwright, either directly or through the play. A play is not just an imitation of an action but is also a work of art, requiring unity, structure, and focus that a director must create. The director guides actors in much the same way an acting teacher guides an acting class—supervising the production; inspiring an actor's own analysis, growth, and development; and serving as a formal friend.

College actors tend to expect directors to give them too much direction. Actors are creators. In addition to learning their roles, showing up at rehearsals, and adapting to different directorial methods and to their fellow actors, they should be self-reliant. The truly professional actor understands that the director's perspective on the total production is predominate and that his or her word is final. The actor has a right to expect the director to help with problems of nuance, style, and motivation but not to teach acting or suffer tantrums from actors with bruised egos.

DEVELOPING THE CHARACTER

With the meaning of the play in mind, the actor is ready to concentrate on characterization. At this time most actors find their greatest satisfaction as creative artists, and, as we have seen, the temptation is great to rush to this phase before the proper groundwork has been established. In this series of rehearsals, the actor explores his inner resources to discover how he can use his experiences to understand the problems of the character. He uses his imagination to supply additional circumstances to round out the character's background and to aid him in believing the action. He observes people and objects to find helpful details. He continues to read, study paintings, and listen to music if he needs to enlarge his experience in order to understand any aspect of the play.

By this time, the actor has completed the task of breaking his role down into beats. He knows the intention of each beat and can relate it to the character's motivating desire. He devises a score of physical actions through which he can realize his intentions, and he experiments with various ways of playing each beat, both at home by himself and at rehearsals with the other actors.

At the same time, the actor is determining the motivation behind each line, discovering its subtext and verbal action, and relating it to the character's motivating desire. If the background of the character's speech differs from his own, he has the added task of learning to reproduce it believably by listening to speakers with a similar background or to recordings. Chances are that the actor will be called on during these rehearsals to have completed the memorization of his lines and cues.

Many consider memorizing lines to be an unpleasant task, and professional actors go about accomplishing it in different ways and at different times. For example, the late Lynn Fontanne preferred to memorize her lines before she began rehearsals so she would be free to concentrate on problems of character development. In contrast, Alla Nazimova claims to have never memorized her lines but "absorbed" them as she developed her character. She believed this approach allowed her to understand her role so thoroughly that she could think the lines as the playwright had written them without having actually committed them to memory.[2]

Both of these practices are extremes. We have already seen that many directors do not like actors to memorize the lines before the rehearsals begin. Without an actor having had the opportunity to discuss the play with the director and other members of the cast, directors know that the actor runs the risk of forming incorrect opinions or, at least, opinions at odds with the interpretation the group formulates. They also know from experience that once the actor has learned the lines, it may be difficult to modify established speech patterns. Gradual absorption, on the other hand, is a time-consuming process. Anyone with a less superb technique than Nazimova's can hardly rely on coming to think the lines without having memorized them—admirable as the theory may be. Granted adequate time for rehearsal, it is best not to memorize until you have completed your score—until you know your intentions, your physical and verbal actions, your structural units, your subtext, your inner monologues, and your images.

Incidentally, accurate memorization is another of the actor's responsibilities. He owes it to the dramatist, who is dependent on the actor for the truthful representation of his work, and he owes it to his fellow players, whose own lines must be motivated by what has gone before.

As a general practice, the actor may safely adopt a policy of memorization somewhere between the two extremes represented by the practices of Fontanne and Nazimova. Jim Donohue, in an excellent article discussing techniques of memorization, identified three objectives that the actor needs to achieve with this task: "(1) learning lines at the same time as memorizing them, (2) doing all this easily and quickly, and (3) ensuring one hundred percent recall without help."[3]

After the actor is familiar with the meaning of the play and with the motivating desire of his character, he is less likely to establish incorrect interpretations when he memorizes his lines. After blocking rehearsals, associating the lines with the movement helps clarify their meaning and make memorization easier. In fact, most actors like to speak the lines out loud as they memorize them. The kinesthetic memory of the feeling of the sound in the mouth and the tension or relaxation of the muscles used to make the word makes its repetition easier to remember.

As we have noted, most directors will expect lines to be memorized at about the halfway point of the rehearsal period. This schedule allows the actor to gain advantage from the earlier rehearsals, and he certainly needs to be free from the burden of memorization during the final stage of preparation.

CREATING THE FORM

In its narrowest and most practical application, creating the form means blocking the movement and inventing the business. Once the creative excitement of first discovery is past, the actor's job in this process consists mainly of mechanical repetition. The actor must stay sharp and alert during this potentially boring work, and he can do so if he remembers that what is being invented and repeated will eventually be the external embodiment of his inner characterization. Without it, the actor cannot convey either the dramatist's meaning or his own. Every actor at every performance has the obligation not only to bring inner life to his characterization but also to externalize this experience in a concrete, artistically valid form. It is not enough that the form simply be lifelike, although in many plays that is an important goal; it also must be theatrically effective—interesting. To bore the audience in the name of realism is a cardinal error.

Creating the form is a rewarding, and sometimes agonizing, process. It does not spring full grown from the imaginations of either the actors or the director but grows slowly. It comes in bits and pieces and cannot be forced. Although parts of it may need to be "grafted on from the outside," as Stanislavski said in his supplement to *Creating a Role,* it cannot be wholly imposed in this fashion. It comes from the combined imaginations of the actors and the director, stimulated initially by the playwright and later by the responses of the actors to one another and to the products of other artists—props, settings, costumes, and lights, for example. It must develop organically as the character develops. Form grows out of character and character out of form, so, enigmatic as it sounds, what a character is determines what he does, and what he does determines what he is.

Most of the time, the ground plan determines the actor's large movements (entrances and exits, crosses from one area to another). The director and designers think these out before rehearsals begin, aware that the most important consideration in making the ground plan is the movement it will impose on the actors. The large movements become apparent as soon as the ground plan is explained, and the actors accept these new conditions and motivate them. In fact, the blocking, the ground plan, the director's concept, the scenic design, the costume design, the prop design, and the lighting design all join the playwright's words as part of the actor's given circumstances.

Some movements and other physical activities are inherent in the lines. Examples are crossing to answer the doorbell or telephone, serving tea, or less obvious indications such as Petruchio's threat to Katharina (*The Taming of the Shrew*): "I swear I'll cuff you, if you strike again"; or Juliet's plea to Romeo: "Wilt thou be gone? It is not yet near day." Most acting editions of plays also describe physicalization in their stage directions, but the actor must examine this material carefully. In all likelihood it will relate to a ground plan and set of circumstances entirely different from those of the current production, and the director often may tell the actors to ignore it entirely. Even including all these sources, it is necessary to invent additional movement and physical activity. Remember that physical objectives help the actor believe in the character and express the desires of the character in ways the audience can see and understand. During this part of the rehearsal period, often called *working rehearsals,* the actor and director constantly use their imaginations to devise movement and business that will give outer form to inner characterization.

The actor also uses these rehearsals as a testing ground for what externals of manner, dress, action, and so forth he can use to reinforce the characterization. These externals are vital because, as we recall from earlier chapters, doing is believing. The actor is likely to believe the character to the extent he can translate the character's desires into action. Such small things as using a handkerchief, eating a sandwich, turning on a light, or writing down an address provide physical objectives on which the actor can concentrate his attention.

Determining the amount and nature of the physical activity is a matter to be settled between actor and director. Good directors frequently make suggestions, but the actor has both the opportunity and the responsibility for originating small actions that will help create form. Nowhere is the quality of the actor's imagination more evident than in this phase of his work. Of course, in order to claim the stage, all business must be justified in terms of the total meaning of the play and the production.

Costumes and properties are vastly important in creating the form of both the role and the production. Properly related to, they become in themselves excellent "actors," and they are essential to the creation of physical image. Stanislavski wrote:

> A costume or an object appropriate to a stage figure ceases to be a simple material thing, it acquires a kind of sanctity for an actor.... You can tell a true artist by his attitudes towards his costume and properties.[4]

Somewhere toward the end of the rehearsal period, the actors will begin to work in the setting, with the properties that will be used in performance, in costume, and under the lights. At this time, adjustments are always necessary. The furniture may take up more space than the small chairs and tables with which the actors have been working. Opening and closing actual doors may require more time than the actors have been allowing in pantomime. The position of a piano may have to be changed to improve the sight lines for the audience. The manipulation of the costumes may require more care than anticipated. A climactic scene may have to be played farther downstage in order that it may be lighted effectively. Such adjustments are an inevitable part of rehearsal. The experienced actor recognizes the need for these changes and immediately finds ways (sometimes by inventing additional "circumstances") to motivate them in terms of his character's desires.

During "technical rehearsals" certain actions may have to be repeated over and over to allow the lighting and sound crews to coordinate their timing with that of the actors. The actor is responsible for handling these hardworking rehearsals calmly and pleasantly. Although it may appear that the development of the production has come to a standstill or actually regressed, the actor must remember that he has now had several weeks of rehearsals and that the technical production crews are attempting to catch up in one or two nights. The experienced actor recognizes that the technical crew will catch up quickly. He also knows that only through these rehearsals can the entire company become the smooth-working team it will take to make the production a success.

MAKING TECHNICAL ADJUSTMENTS

The final rehearsals, including the dress rehearsals, are devoted to polishing for performance. At this time experimentation ceases, and feelings of tentativeness must disappear. During the earlier rehearsals, the actor has had an opportunity to try different ways of bringing his character to life. He has experimented (always under the guidance and subject to the approval of the director) with details of business, movement, and line reading. Throughout the entire period, he has perfected details that will allow him to believe his character. These rehearsals are, in fact, a continual process of selection and rejection. But by the time the play is ready for polishing, his choices must be firm. During the final rehearsals, the actor needs to have confidence in his characterization and in the technical support for the production, as only then can he be comfortable and assured in his performance.

Much attention in the polishing rehearsals turns to *timing* and *projection*, although both will have been anticipated earlier.

Timing is a matter of pace and rhythm, pertaining to the tempo at which lines are spoken and business and movement are executed and to the rapidity at which cues are picked up. As long as the actors feel uncertain about the details of their performance, they cannot establish and maintain a tempo.

POLISHING THE PERFORMANCE

A sense of timing is one of the most subtle elements of stage technique. For its development, an actor must have experience before an audience. Too slow a tempo will not hold interest, but too fast a tempo will obscure the meaning. Too consistent a tempo will become monotonous; too varied a tempo will seem jerky and illogical. If actors are slow to pick up cues, their rhythm will falter between speeches. The actor must be both physically and mentally alert to his cues. Physical readiness is largely a matter of breathing. The actor must inhale before his partner has finished speaking so he will have the necessary breath to begin his line. Otherwise, the time required to take a breath will destroy the rhythm of the dialogue. If the actor is too fast in speaking his lines—often a problem with beginners—their meaning will be blurred. To the expert ear, this blurring clearly indicates that an actor is not using his lines to accomplish a verbal action. Maintaining too constant a tempo identifies an actor who is not hearing and feeling different tempo-rhythms for varying structural units.

An important consideration in timing is the use of the pause. Many beginning actors tend to use the pause for their own convenience (because they are not breathing correctly, because they are not thinking fast enough, because they are not sure of what they are doing) without regard to dramatic effect. The pause should be used sparingly, and *only when silence is more effective than speech*. The pause is often an effective way to mark a transition from one structural unit to another.

Some playwrights are so conscious of the need to use the pause effectively that they take great pains to indicate the proper place for silence in their scripts. Actors performing in the plays of Harold Pinter, for example, will find pauses to be as much a part of the dialogue as the words themselves.

Timing varies from play to play, from scene to scene, from character to character, and from audience to audience. The thought-provoking play requires a slower tempo than does the farce, and expository scenes at the beginning require a slower tempo than do climactic scenes at the end. One character moves and speaks more slowly than another, and one audience is quicker at grasping meanings than another. During the final rehearsals, the director will guide the cast in establishing effective tempos for the play, for different scenes, and for different characters. The actors alone have the responsibility to feel out the audience and make necessary adjustments from performance to performance.

Projection is another variable element. A constant requirement of the theatre is that the audience hear and understand the lines. This requirement may be satisfied in a variety of voice levels, ranging from a shout to a whisper. Projection does not mean talking loud but describes the actor's effort to share every moment of the play with the audience. The degree of loudness that is most suitable will be determined by the play, the scene, the character, and the size and acoustical qualities of the auditorium. Again, variety is necessary. Nothing is more tiresome than listening over a period of time to an unvaried voice. Unmotivated, abrupt changes, on the other hand, are likely to startle the audience and attract undue attention.

Visual projection is equally important. The audience must see the action as clearly as they can hear the lines. Three requirements of movement, business, and gesture are

1. They must be suitable to the character, the scene, the play, and the general style of the production.

2. They must be clearly seen.

3. Their significance to the total meaning must be readily comprehensible.

At final rehearsals, actors turn much of their attention to auditory and visual projection. The director carefully checks their effectiveness, but the final test can be made only by performing before an audience. To ensure that the actors will meet the test on opening night, producers and directors have preview performances or invite an audience to the final "run-throughs."

WORKING AT REHEARSALS

For a talented actor, well trained in techniques of his art, rehearsals are a happy time, though they are not always filled with fun. Preparing a play for production is at best hard work, often fraught with frustration. But during rehearsals the actor has the greatest opportunity for creative accomplishment. He should begin rehearsals resolved to use all of his resources for the good of the production. What is best for the production should be the single criterion for choices, and nothing makes for a happier atmosphere than sharing this resolve with all members of the cast.

Rehearsals will proceed best if the actor establishes a relationship to the director and to the other actors based on mutual respect. The director determines the working methods, the rehearsal schedule, and the distribution of rehearsal time among the different acts and scenes. The actor respects both the method and the schedule and cooperates with the director in his way of working. Needless to say, he attends rehearsals regularly and punctually. He is ready to work at the scheduled time, which means that he arrives fifteen to thirty minutes early, warms up, and prepares for his first scene. He has an obligation to keep himself healthy, rested, and in good spirits, so sickness, fatigue, or personal problems do not interfere. To the other actors, he is generous and demanding: demanding that they give their best, generous in giving his best to them.

At the first opportunity, the actor will also want to get to know the stage manager, to understand his importance to the production and to respect his authority. Although his specific duties vary from theatre to theatre and company to company, the stage manager is the person who, according to Lawrence Stern, "accepts responsibility that the rehearsals and performances run smoothly on stage and backstage."[5] Establishing the proper relationship with this individual is absolutely critical to a productive rehearsal and performance period.

Throughout each rehearsal, the actor is alert and committed to the work at hand. He gives his entire attention to what is going on, both when he is in the scene and when he is waiting for an entrance. He marks directions in his script or in a notebook. Once blocking or business has been given by the director or worked out by the actor and director at rehearsal, the actor is responsible for retaining it. He brings a supply of pencils (with erasers) to rehearsal with him and records all movements in the margin of his script at the time they are blocked, using standard abbreviations. Drawing diagrams in the margin is a practical way of recording complicated blocking. The actor does more, though, than keep track of his blocking. He writes down his beats, intentions, subtext, comments, and interpretations until his copy of the script becomes a complete score for the playing of his role. That score becomes an invaluable source of reference during later rehearsals and performances. He takes careful notes on his director's oral critiques and refers to them before the next time he rehearses the scene for which they were given. He studies, absorbs, experiments, probes, watches, listens, and creates.

Rehearsals constitute a fluid process during which the production gradually emerges. For the actor, the process offers a chance to explore every facet of the character he is portraying. Layer by layer the actor develops the character and relates it to the performances of the rest of the company and the production as a whole. The actor recognizes that early rehearsals must progress in bits and pieces; therefore, he is cautious of going too fast. Each moment of the play must be explored and the problems solved through trial and error. Early decisions can be only tentative; preliminary ideas about a character may actually be reversed as rehearsals progress. The production must develop organically. Without change at each rehearsal, satisfactory progress toward the final shape of the production bogs down. Only late in the rehearsal period can the actor begin to think of solutions as "set."

Rehearsal expectations vary from company to company, but the work habits of all good actors reflect an attitude toward the theatre that is conducive to creativity and free from serious "acting traps" that shackle their efforts. What are these traps? Joseph Slowik has pinpointed four on which Grotowski regularly concentrated while Slowik was observing his company. They are *impatience, half-heartedness, poor work ethics,* and *substitution.*[6]

Impatience leads to a lack of technique, because it causes the actor to look for shortcuts that disrupt and emasculate his work. Stanislavski called this trap taking the "line of least resistance" in creating a character. The impatient actor relies on tricks, on work that has been successful in a previous characterization, or on actions that have been neither sufficiently grounded in the play's given circumstances nor properly articulated with the other performances.

Half-heartedness means giving less than maximum effort during rehearsals. Good actors simply do not work with anything less than their entire being. They know that truth and believability are difficult to achieve under any circumstances and that without maximum effort they simply will not appear.

Poor work ethics inevitably lead to a rehearsal atmosphere in which creativity cannot take place, in which actors will be afraid to take a chance. Sure signs of poor work ethics are resentment, back biting, buck passing, and unconstructive criticism, all mortal enemies of the trust necessary for success in the theatre.

Substitution is the most pervasive trap of all, but also the most difficult to define. Slowik said:

> Anything less than [a] preciously recognizable human response is a substitute. It is something behind which the actor hides when he is empty. When audiences seem to be satisfied with less than the "real thing" actors continue to hide behind substitution, building their careers on one of the most destructive enemies of creativity.[7]

WORKING AT HOME

All the actor's work cannot be accomplished at rehearsals. "Homework" is too often neglected by the beginner. A creative actor uses rehearsals as an opportunity to test for the director and with the other actors what he has worked out by himself. Dividing his role into beats, discovering and stating the intentions, finding additional circumstances, setting the sensory tasks, and writing the subtext all are problems for the individual actor, subject to the guidance of the director. The actor can also work by himself on many of the specific problems that arise during rehearsal. Referring often to the notes he took at the oral critique, he works on the suggestions associated with his role and brings a fresh approach to the next rehearsal.

PLAYING THE PART

We have seen that the actor's first major concern during rehearsals is discovering the total meaning of the play by studying the script, examining other sources, and discussing the interpretation with the director and the other actors. In the kind of play that constitutes the great body of Western drama, both classic and contemporary—the kind of play in which the dramatist expresses his meaning by creating characters involved in some sort of conflict—the actor must next give immediate attention to understanding the character he is playing and to believing the character's speech and actions. In later rehearsals, he becomes increasingly concerned with projecting the character to the audience, and he continues to focus on these concerns during the entire run of the play. He must bring the character newly to life at every performance, confident that he is not only performing "natural" actions but also creating a theatrically effective form.

As the play is repeated in performance, the core—the superobjective, motivating desires, intentions of the beats, externals of character, and physical form of the production—stays the same. Keeping it the same is one of the actor's responsibilities. He is required to perform the play as rehearsed, and the Actors' Equity Association fines and ultimately suspends professionals who fail to respect their obligation. Of course, this requirement does not mean that creativity ceases and that the robotlike actor repeats from memory what has been "set" in rehearsal. Rather, he commits himself at each performance to accomplishing the character's objectives and to establishing relations with objects and other actors *as if it were for the first time.* Performance demands continual and fresh adjustment to the stage life going on around him. To keep a performance the same, it must always be subtly different; mechanical repetition does not retain vitality.

Concentration is the keynote to success, but you must recall the earlier lesson in which we concluded that concentration for the actor must take place on two levels. Let us review this important, if sometimes confusing, duality.

On one level, he directs his attention to satisfying the desires of the character. He uses his speech and actions to get what the character wants and attempts to influence the behavior of the other characters as he tries to satisfy his objective. By concentrating on this objective, he is able to believe his actions. They, in turn, produce feelings similar to the feelings the character would have if the situations were real. The actor's imagination also allows him to use the feelings that arise from his relationship to the other actors.

On another level, the actor concentrates on expressing the character in theatrical terms. The audience must hear the lines and see the actions. A tempo must be maintained that will be suitable to the play, stimulating to the audience, and dramatically effective. The actor does his part to create enough variety in the performance to ensure a continual renewal of the audience's interest. In order to maintain this level of concentration, the actor must develop what Lynn Fontanne called an "outside eye and ear" to guide him in playing his role. He has the dual function of being both character and interpreter.[8]

In some contemporary works, the creation of character in imaginary circumstances is a minimal part of the actor's responsibility. He expresses his or the playwright's meaning to the audience in his own person. In these instances the audience becomes a part of the given circumstances of the play, and the actor's task is to find every way possible to communicate with them directly, clearly, and forcefully.

The actor must serve his function with ease and authority. The audience experiences no pleasure watching a performer who is tense and strained and no comfort watching one who does not appear confident in his ability to perform with some degree of credit to himself. Concentration, again, is the keynote to relaxation. When the actor can turn his full attention to doing a job he knows he is prepared to do, he forgets his fears and his self-consciousness.

Although many of the suggestions we have made about performing a role are universal, conditions will certainly vary with the experience of the company, the sophistication of the audience, and whether or not the play is presented for a limited run, for a long run, or in repertory. These distinctions are too complex for inclusion in this introductory text, but you should be prepared to seek advice from your instructor, your director, your stage manager, or a colleague who has experienced the particular conditions under which you will be performing. Keeping a role fresh during a long run is a particularly difficult problem and one that will tax your ability to generate anew exciting intentions and actions every time you step on stage. Naturally, each audience must believe you are performing the role for the first time and, for them, you are. Any reasonably accomplished actor can get excited about opening night; it is the fifth, or seventy-fifth, or 375th performance of the same role that taxes your technique.

One of the final tasks of the actor is to learn to handle criticism, both positive and negative, that results from his performance. Although it would be foolish to say actors should pay no attention to criticism from the press or their friends, it is important for the young actor to establish the habit of acting for his fellow actors and his director rather than for the critics. Negative criticism is depressing and inevitably affects a show adversely. Praise or flattery usually adds fuel to the fires of self-esteem, a conflagration from which the actor's enemies all too often emerge. Acting is a frightening art, the only one in which the moment of its final creation is also the moment of its acceptance or rejection by the public. The actor often suffers because the audience, on which he is dependent for his success, does not appear to view his art with the same respect it has for other artists. Uta Hagen explained the phenomenon this way:

> More than in the other performing arts the lack of respect for acting seems to spring from the fact that every layman considers himself a valid critic. While no lay audience discusses the bowing arm or stroke of the violinist or the palette or brush technique of the painter, or the tension which may create a poor entre-chat, they will all be willing to give formulas to the actor.... And the actor listens to them, compounding the felonious notion that no craft or skill or art is needed in acting.[9]

This book has been dedicated to the purpose of helping the actor believe in his craft, his skill, and his art. *Believe* is the operative word, the linchpin, of its message. Without a believable foundation for character; believable actions; believable intentions; believable vocal, physical, and emotional technique; and above all, a belief in the script and one's fellow artists, the actor is doomed to failure. With them, the actor has a chance to create magic, to move an audience to a deeper understanding of the mystery and the majesty—as well as the failures and the foibles—of humankind.

NOTES

1. Harold Clurman, *The Fervent Years* (New York: Knopf, 1945), p. 41.

2. See Morton Eustis, *Players at Work* (New York: Theatre Arts Books, 1937).

3. Jim Donohue, "Learning Lines with Meaning; a Method for Memorizing," *Dramatics*, January 1988, p. 30.

4. Constantin Stanislavski, *An Actor's Handbook,* ed. Elizabeth Reynolds Hapgood (New York: Theatre Arts Books, 1963), p. 43.

5. Lawrence Stern, *Stage Management: A Guidebook of Practical Techniques,* 3rd ed. (Boston: Allyn and Bacon, Inc., 1987), p. 4.

6. Joseph Slowik, "An Actor's Enemies," paper delivered to the Mid-America Theatre Conference, Omaha, Nebraska, March 16, 1984.

7. Slowik, "An Actor's Enemies," p. 6.

8. Lewis Funke and John E. Booth, *Actors Talk About Acting: Fourteen Interviews with Stars of the Theatre* (New York: Random House, 1961), p. 67.

9. Uta Hagen with Haskel Frankel, *Respect for Acting* (New York: Macmillan, 1973), p. 3.

HELLO OUT THERE

BY WILLIAM SAROYAN

CHARACTERS

YOUNG MAN

THE GIRL (EMILY)

THE MAN

THE WOMAN

ANOTHER MAN

THIRD MAN

Scene: *There is a fellow in a small-town prison cell, tapping slowly on the floor with a spoon. After tapping half a minute, as if he were trying to telegraph words, he gets up and begins walking around the cell. At last he stops, stands at the center of the cell, and doesn't move for a long time. He feels his head, as if it were wounded. Then he looks around. Then he calls out dramatically, kidding the world.*

YOUNG MAN: Hello—out there! *(pause)* Hello—out there! Hello—out there! *(long pause)* Nobody out there. *(still more dramatically, but more comically, too)* Hello—out there! Hello—out there!

(A GIRL'S VOICE is heard, very sweet and soft.)

THE VOICE: Hello.

YOUNG MAN: Hello—out there.

THE VOICE: Hello.

YOUNG MAN: Is that you, Katey?

THE VOICE: No—this here is Emily.

YOUNG MAN: Who? *(swiftly)* Hello out there.

THE VOICE: Emily.

YOUNG MAN: Emily who? I don't know anybody named Emily. Are you that girl I met at Sam's in Salinas about three years ago?

THE VOICE: No—I'm the girl who cooks here. I'm the cook. I've never been in Salinas. I don't even know where it is.

YOUNG MAN: Hello out there. You say you cook here?

THE VOICE: Yes.

YOUNG MAN: Well, why don't you study up and learn to cook? How come I don't get no Jell-O or anything good?

THE VOICE: I just cook what they tell me to. *(pause)* You lonesome?

YOUNG MAN: Lonesome as a coyote. Hear me hollering? Hello out there!

THE VOICE: Who you hollering to?

YOUNG MAN: Well—nobody, I guess. I been trying to think of somebody to write a letter to, but I can't think of anybody.

THE VOICE: What about Katey?

YOUNG MAN: I don't know anybody named Katey.

THE VOICE: Then why did you say, Is that you, Katey?

YOUNG MAN: Katey's a good name. I always did like a name like Katey. I never *knew* anybody named Katey, though.

THE VOICE: *I* did.

YOUNG MAN: Yeah? What was she like? Tall girl, or little one?

THE VOICE: Kind of medium.

YOUNG MAN: Hello out there. What sort of a looking girl are you?

THE VOICE: Oh, I don't know.

YOUNG MAN: Didn't anybody ever tell you? Didn't anybody ever talk to you that way?

THE VOICE: What way?

YOUNG MAN: You know. Didn't they?

THE VOICE: No, they didn't.

YOUNG MAN: Ah, the fools—they should have. I can tell from your voice you're OK.

THE VOICE: Maybe I am and maybe I ain't.

YOUNG MAN: I never missed yet.

THE VOICE: Yeah, I know. That's why you're in jail.

YOUNG MAN: The whole thing was a mistake.

THE VOICE: They claim it was rape.

YOUNG MAN: No—it wasn't.

THE VOICE: That's what they claim it was.

YOUNG MAN: They're a lot of fools.

THE VOICE: Well, you sure are in trouble. Are you scared?

YOUNG MAN: Scared to death. *(suddenly)* Hello out there!

THE VOICE: What do you keep saying that for all the time?

YOUNG MAN: I'm lonesome. I'm as lonesome as a coyote. *(a long one)* Hello —out there!

(THE GIRL appears, over to one side. She is a plain girl in plain clothes.)

THE GIRL: I'm kind of lonesome, too.

YOUNG MAN: *(turning and looking at her)*: Hey—No fooling? Are you?

THE GIRL: Yeah—I'm almost as lonesome as a coyote myself.

YOUNG MAN: Who *you* lonesome for?

THE GIRL: I don't know.

YOUNG MAN: It's the same with me. The minute they put you in a place like this you remember all the girls you ever knew, and all the girls you didn't get to know, and it sure gets lonesome.

THE GIRL: I bet it does.

YOUNG MAN: Ah, it's awful. *(pause)* You're a pretty kid, you know that?

THE GIRL: You're just talking.

YOUNG MAN: No, I'm not just talking—you *are* pretty. Any fool could see that. You're just about the prettiest kid in the whole world.

THE GIRL: I'm not—and you know it.

YOUNG MAN: No—you are. I never saw anyone prettier in all my born days, in all my travels. I knew Texas would bring me luck.

THE GIRL: Luck? You're in jail, aren't you? You've got a whole gang of people all worked up, haven't you?

YOUNG MAN: Ah, that's nothing. I'll get out of this.

THE GIRL: Maybe.

YOUNG MAN: No, I'll be all right—*now.*

THE GIRL: What do you mean—now?

YOUNG MAN: I mean after seeing you. I got something now. You know for a while there I didn't care one way or another. Tired. *(pause)* Tired of trying for the best all the time and never getting it. *(suddenly)* Hello out there!

THE GIRL: Who you calling now?

YOUNG MAN: You.

THE GIRL: Why, I'm right here.

YOUNG MAN: I know. *(calling)* Hello out there!

THE GIRL: Hello

YOUNG MAN: Ah, you're sweet. *(pause)* I'm going to marry *you.* I'm going away with *you.* I'm going to take you to San Francisco or some place like that. I *am,* now. I'm going to win myself some real money, too. I'm going to study 'em real careful and pick myself some winners, and we're going to have a lot of money.

THE GIRL: Yeah?

YOUNG MAN: Yeah. Tell me your name and all that stuff.

THE GIRL: Emily.

YOUNG MAN: I know that. What's the rest of it? Where were you born? Come on, tell me the whole thing.

THE GIRL: Emily Smith.

YOUNG MAN: Honest to God?

THE GIRL: Honest. That's my name—Emily Smith.

YOUNG MAN: Ah, you're the sweetest girl in the whole world.

THE GIRL: Why?

YOUNG MAN: I don't know why, but you are, that's all. Where were you born?

THE GIRL: Matador, Texas.

YOUNG MAN: Where's that?

THE GIRL: Right here.

YOUNG MAN: Is this Matador, Texas?

THE GIRL: Yeah, it's Matador. They brought you here from Wheeling.

YOUNG MAN: Is that where I was—Wheeling?

THE GIRL: Didn't you even know what town you were in?

YOUNG MAN: All towns are alike. You don't go up and ask somebody what town you're in. It doesn't make any difference. How far away is Wheeling?

THE GIRL: Sixteen or seventeen miles. Didn't you know they moved you?

YOUNG MAN: How could I know, when I was out—cold? Somebody hit me over the head with a lead pipe or something. What'd they hit me for?

THE GIRL: Rape—that's what they *said*.

YOUNG MAN: Ah, that's a lie. *(amazed, almost to himself)* She wanted me to give her money.

THE GIRL: Money?

YOUNG MAN: Yeah, if I'd have known she was a woman like that—well, by God, I'd have gone on down the street and stretched out in a park somewhere and gone to sleep.

THE GIRL: Is that what she wanted—money?

YOUNG MAN: Yeah. A fellow like me hopping freights all over the country, trying to break his bad luck, going from one poor little town to another, trying to get in on something good somewhere, and she asks for money. I thought she was lonesome. She *said* she was.

THE GIRL: Maybe she was.

YOUNG MAN: She was *something*.

THE GIRL: I guess I'd never see you, if it didn't happen, though.

YOUNG MAN: Oh, I don't know—maybe I'd just mosey along this way and see you in this town somewhere. I'd recognize you, too.

THE GIRL: Recognize me?

YOUNG MAN: Sure, I'd recognize you the minute I laid eyes on you.

THE GIRL: Well, who would I be?

YOUNG MAN: Mine, that's who.

THE GIRL: Honest?

YOUNG MAN: Honest to God.

THE GIRL: You just say that because you're in jail.

YOUNG MAN: No, I mean it. You just pack up and wait for me. We'll high-roll the hell out of here to Frisco.

THE GIRL: You're just lonesome.

YOUNG MAN: I been lonesome all my life—there's no cure for that—but you and me—we can have a lot of fun hanging around together. You'll bring me luck. I know it.

THE GIRL: What are you looking for luck for all the time?

YOUNG MAN: I'm a gambler. I don't work. I've *got* to have luck, or I'm a bum. I haven't had any decent luck in years. Two whole years now—one place to another. Bad luck all the time. That's why I got in trouble back there in Wheeling, too. That was no accident. That was my bad luck following me around. So here I am, with my head half busted. I guess it was her old man that did it.

THE GIRL: You mean her father?

YOUNG MAN: No, her husband. If I had an old lady like that, I'd throw her out.

THE GIRL: Do you think you'll have better luck, if I go with you?

YOUNG MAN: It's a cinch. I'm a good handicapper. All I need is somebody good like you with me. It's no good always walking around in the streets for anything that might be there at the time. You got to have somebody staying with you all the time—through winters when it's cold, and springtime when it's pretty, and summer time when it's nice and hot and you can go swimming—through *all* the times—rain and snow and all different kinds of weather a man's got to go through before he dies. You got to have somebody who's right. Somebody who knows you, from away back. You got to have somebody who even knows you're wrong but likes you just the same. I know I'm wrong, but I just don't want anything the hard way, working like a dog, or the *easy* way, working like a dog—working's the hard way and the easy way both. All I got to do is beat the price, always—and then I don't feel lousy and don't hate anybody. If you go along with me, I'll be the finest guy anybody ever saw. I won't be wrong any more. You know when you get enough of that money, you *can't* be wrong any more—you're right because the money says so. I'll have a lot of money and you'll be just about the prettiest, most wonderful kid in the whole world. I'll be proud walking around Frisco with you on my arm and people turning around to look at us.

THE GIRL: Do you think they will?

YOUNG MAN: Sure they will. When I get back in some decent clothes, and you're on my arm—well, Katey, they'll turn around and look, and they'll see something, too.

THE GIRL: Katey?

YOUNG MAN: Yeah—that's your name from now on. You're the first girl I ever called Katey. I've been saving it for you. OK?

THE GIRL: OK.

YOUNG MAN: How long have I been here?

THE GIRL: Since last night. You didn't wake up until late this morning, though.

YOUNG MAN: What time is it now? About nine?

THE GIRL: About ten.

YOUNG MAN: Have you got the key to this lousy cell?

THE GIRL: No. They don't let me fool with any keys.

YOUNG MAN: Well, can you get it?

THE GIRL: No.

YOUNG MAN: Can you *try?*

THE GIRL: They wouldn't let me get near any keys. I cook for this jail, when they've got somebody in it. I clean up and things like that.

YOUNG MAN: Well, I want to get out of here. Don't you know the guy that runs this joint?

THE GIRL: I know him, but he wouldn't let you out. They were talking of taking you to another jail in another town.

YOUNG MAN: Yeah? Why?

THE GIRL: Because they're afraid.

YOUNG MAN: What are they afraid of?

THE GIRL: They're afraid these people from Wheeling will come over in the middle of the night and break in.

YOUNG MAN: Yeah? What do they want to do that for?

THE GIRL: Don't *you* know what they want to do it for?

YOUNG MAN: Yeah, I know all right.

THE GIRL: Are you scared?

YOUNG MAN: Sure I'm scared. Nothing scares a man more than ignorance. You can argue with people who ain't fools, but you can't argue with fools—they just go to work and do what they're set on doing. Get me out of here.

THE GIRL: How?

YOUNG MAN: Well, go get the guy with the key, and let me talk to him.

THE GIRL: He's gone home. Everybody's gone home.

YOUNG MAN: You mean I'm in this little jail all alone?

THE GIRL: Well—yeah—except me.

YOUNG MAN: Well, what's the big idea—doesn't anybody stay here all the time?

THE GIRL: No, they go home every night. I clean up and then I go, too. I hung around tonight.

YOUNG MAN: What made you do that?

THE GIRL: I wanted to talk to you.

YOUNG MAN: Honest? What did you want to talk about?

THE GIRL: Oh, I don't know. I took care of you last night. You were talking in

your sleep. You liked me, too. I didn't think you'd like me when you woke
up, though.

YOUNG MAN: Yeah? Why not?

THE GIRL: I don't know.

YOUNG MAN: Yeah? Well, you're wonderful, see?

THE GIRL: Nobody ever talked to me that way. All the fellows in town—*(pause)*

YOUNG MAN: What about 'em? *(pause)* Well, what about 'em? Come on—tell
me.

THE GIRL: They laugh at me.

YOUNG MAN: Laugh at *you?* They're fools. What do they know about anything?
You go get your things and come back here. I'll take you with me to Frisco.
How old are you?

THE GIRL: Oh, I'm of age.

YOUNG MAN: How old are you?—Don't lie to me! Sixteen?

THE GIRL: I'm seventeen.

YOUNG MAN: Well, bring your father and mother. We'll get married before
we go.

THE GIRL: They wouldn't let me go.

YOUNG MAN: Why not?

THE GIRL: I don't know, but they wouldn't. I know they wouldn't.

YOUNG MAN: You go tell your father not to be a fool, see? What is he, a farmer?

THE GIRL: No—nothing. He gets a little relief from the government because he's
supposed to be hurt or something—his side hurts, he says. I don't know
what it is.

YOUNG MAN: Ah, he's a liar. Well, I'm taking you with me, see?

THE GIRL: He takes the money I earn, too.

YOUNG MAN: He's got no right to do that.

THE GIRL: I know it, but he does it.

YOUNG MAN: *(almost to himself)*: This world stinks. You shouldn't have been
born in this town, anyway, and you shouldn't have had a man like that for
a father, either.

THE GIRL: Sometimes I feel sorry for him.

YOUNG MAN: Never mind feeling sorry for him. *(pointing a finger)* I'm going to
talk to your father some day. I've got a few things to tell that guy.

THE GIRL: I know you have.

YOUNG MAN: *(suddenly)*: Hello—out there! See if you can get that fellow with
the keys to come down and let me out.

THE GIRL: Oh, I couldn't.

YOUNG MAN: Why not?

THE GIRL: I'm nobody here—they give me fifty cents ever day I work.

YOUNG MAN: How much?

THE GIRL: Fifty cents.

YOUNG MAN: *(to the world)*: You see? They ought to pay money to *look* at you. To breathe the *air* you breathe. I don't know. Sometimes I figure it never is going to make sense. Hello—out there! I'm scared. You try to get me out of here. I'm scared them fools are going to come here from Wheeling and go crazy, thinking they're heroes. Get me out of here, Katey.

THE GIRL: I don't know what to do. Maybe I could break the door down.

YOUNG MAN: No, you couldn't do that. Is there a hammer out there or anything?

THE GIRL: Only a broom. Maybe they've locked the broom up, too.

YOUNG MAN: Go see if you can find anything.

THE GIRL: All right. *(She goes.)*

YOUNG MAN: Hello—out there! Hello—out there! *(pause)* Hello—out there! Hello—out there! *(pause)* Putting me in jail. *(with contempt)* Rape! Rape? *They* rape everything good that was ever born. His side hurts. They laugh at her. Fifty cents a day. Little punk people. Hurting the only good thing that ever came their way. *(suddenly)* Hello—out there!

THE GIRL: *(returning)*: There isn't a thing out there. They've locked everything up for the night.

YOUNG MAN: Any cigarettes?

THE GIRL: Everything's locked up—all the drawers of the desk, all the closet doors—everything.

YOUNG MAN: I ought to have a cigarette.

THE GIRL: I could get you a package maybe, somewhere. I guess the drug store's open. It's about a mile.

YOUNG MAN: A mile? I don't want to be alone that long.

THE GIRL: I could run all the way, and all the way back.

YOUNG MAN: You're the sweetest girl that ever lived.

THE GIRL: What kind do you want?

YOUNG MAN: Oh, any kind—Chesterfields or Camels or Lucky Strikes—any kind at all.

THE GIRL: I'll go get a package. *(She turns to go.)*

YOUNG MAN: What about the money?

THE GIRL: I've got some money. I've got a quarter I been saving. I'll run all the way. *(She is about to go.)*

YOUNG MAN: Come here.

THE GIRL: *(going to him)*: What?

YOUNG MAN: Give me your hand. *(He takes her hand and looks at it, smiling. He lifts it and kisses it.)* I'm scared to death.

THE GIRL: I am, too.

YOUNG MAN: I'm not lying—I don't care what happens to me, but I'm scared nobody will ever come out here to this godforsaken broken-down town and find you. I'm scared you'll get used to it and not mind. I'm scared you'll never get to Frisco and have 'em all turning around to look at you. Listen —go get me a gun, because if they come, I'll kill 'em! They don't understand. Get me a gun!

THE GIRL: I could get my father's gun. I know where he hides it.

YOUNG MAN: Go get it. Never mind cigarettes. Run all the way. *(pause, smiling but seriously)* Hello, Katey.

THE GIRL: Hello. What's *your* name?

YOUNG MAN: Photo-Finish is what they *call* me. My races are always photo-finish races. You don't know what that means, but it means they're very close. So close the only way they can tell which horse wins is to look at a photograph after the race is over. Well, every race I bet turns out to be a photo-finish race, and my horse never wins. It's my bad luck, all the time. That's why they call me Photo-Finish. Say it before you go.

THE GIRL: Photo-Finish.

YOUNG MAN: Come here. *(THE GIRL moves close and he kisses her.)* Now, hurry. Run all the way.

THE GIRL: I'll run. *(THE GIRL turns and runs. The YOUNG MAN stands at the center of the cell a long time. THE GIRL comes running back in. Almost crying)* I'm afraid. I'm afraid I won't see you again. If I come back and you're not here, I—

YOUNG MAN: Hello—out there!

THE GIRL: It's so lonely in this town. Nothing here but the lonesome wind all the time, lifting the dirt and blowing out to the prairie. I'll stay *here*. I won't let them take you away.

YOUNG MAN: Listen, Katey. Do what I tell you. Go get that gun and come back. Maybe they won't come tonight. Maybe they won't come at all. I'll hide the gun and when they let me out you can take it back and put it where you found it. And then we'll go away. But if they come, I'll kill 'em! Now, hurry—

THE GIRL: All right. *(pause)* I want to tell you something.

YOUNG MAN: OK.

THE GIRL: *(very softly)*: If you're not here when I come back, well, I'll have the gun and I'll know what to do with it.

YOUNG MAN: You know how to handle a gun?

THE GIRL: I know how.

YOUNG MAN: Don't be a fool. *(takes off his shoe, brings out some currency)* Don't be a fool, see? Here's some money. Eighty dollars. Take it and go to Frisco. Look around and find somebody. Find somebody alive and halfway human, see? Promise me—if I'm not here when you come back, just throw the gun away and get the hell to Frisco. Look around and find somebody.

THE GIRL: I don't want to find anybody.

YOUNG MAN: *(swiftly, desperately)*: Listen, if I'm not here when you come back, how do you know I haven't gotten away? Now, do what I tell you. I'll meet you in Frisco. I've got a couple of dollars in my other shoe. I'll see you in San Francisco.

THE GIRL: *(with wonder)*: San Francisco?

YOUNG MAN: That's right—San Francisco. That's where you and me belong.

THE GIRL: I've always wanted to go to *some* place like San Francisco—but how could I go alone?

YOUNG MAN: Well, you're not alone any more, see?

THE GIRL: Tell me a little what it's like.

YOUNG MAN: *(very swiftly, almost impatiently at first, but gradually slower and with remembrance, smiling, and THE GIRL moving closer to him as he speaks)*: Well, it's on the Pacific to begin with—ocean water all around. Cool fog and seagulls. Ships from all over the world. It's got seven hills. The little streets go up and down, around and all over. Every night the foghorns bawl. But they won't be bawling for you and me.

THE GIRL: What else?

YOUNG MAN: That's about all, I guess.

THE GIRL: Are people different in San Francisco?

YOUNG MAN: People are the same everywhere. They're different only when they love somebody. That's the only thing that makes 'em different. More people in Frisco love somebody, that's all.

THE GIRL: Nobody anywhere loves anybody as much as I love you.

YOUNG MAN: *(shouting, as if to the world)*: You see? Hearing you say that, a man could die and still be ahead of the game. Now, hurry. And don't forget, if I'm not here when you come back, get the hell to San Francisco where you'll have a chance. Do you hear me?

(THE GIRL stands a moment looking at him, then backs away, turns and runs. The YOUNG MAN stares after her, troubled and smiling. Then he turns away from the image of her and walks about like a lion in a cage. After a while he sits down suddenly and buries his head in his hands. From a distance the sound of several automobiles approaching is heard. He listens a moment, then ignores the implications of the sound, whatever they may be. Several automobile doors are slammed. He ignores this also. A wooden door is opened with a key and closed, and footsteps are heard in a hall. Walking easily, almost casually and yet arrogantly, a MAN comes in.)

YOUNG MAN: *(jumps up suddenly and shouts at THE MAN, almost scaring him)*: What the hell kind of a jailkeeper are you, anyway? Why don't you attend to your business? You get paid for it, don't you? Now, get me out of here.

THE MAN: But I'm not the jailkeeper.

YOUNG MAN: Yeah? Well, who are you, then?

THE MAN: I'm the husband.

YOUNG MAN: What husband you talking about?

THE MAN: You know what husband.

YOUNG MAN: Hey! *(pause, looking at THE MAN)* Are you the guy that hit me over the head last night?

THE MAN: I am.

YOUNG MAN: *(with righteous indignation)*: What do you mean going around hitting people over the head?

THE MAN: Oh, I don't know. What do you *mean* going around—the way you do?

YOUNG MAN: *(rubbing his head)*: You hurt my head. You got no right to hit anybody over the head.

THE MAN: *(suddenly angry, shouting)*: Answer my question! What do you mean?

YOUNG MAN: Listen, you—don't be hollering at me just because I'm locked up.

THE MAN: *(with contempt, slowly)*: You're a dog!

YOUNG MAN: Yeah, well, let me tell you something. You *think* you're the husband. You're the husband of nothing. *(slowly)* What's more, your wife—if you want to call her that—is a tramp. Why don't you throw her out in the street where she belongs?

THE MAN: *(draws a pistol)*: Shut up!

YOUNG MAN: Yeah? Go ahead, shoot—*(softly)* and spoil the fun. What'll your pals think? They'll be disappointed, won't they. What's the fun hanging a man who's already dead? *(THE MAN puts the gun away.)* That's right, because now you can have some fun yourself, telling me what you're going to do. That's what you came here for, isn't it? Well, you don't need to tell me. I *know* what you're going to do. I've read the papers and I know. They have fun. A mob of 'em fall on one man and beat him, don't they? They tear off his clothes and kick him, don't they? And women and little children stand around watching, don't they? Well, before you go on *this* picnic, I'm going to tell you a few things. Not that that's going to send you home with your pals—the other heroes. No. You've been outraged. A stranger has come to town and violated your women. Your pure, innocent, virtuous women. You fellows have got to set this thing right. You're men, not mice. You're homemakers, and you beat your children. *(suddenly)* Listen, you—I didn't know she was your wife. I didn't know she was anybody's wife.

THE MAN: You're a liar!

YOUNG MAN: Sometimes—when it'll do somebody some good—but not this time. Do you want to hear about it? *(THE MAN doesn't answer.)* All right, I'll tell you. I met her at a lunch counter. She came in and sat next to me. There was plenty of room, but she sat next to me. Somebody had put a nickel in the phonograph and a fellow was singing *New San Antonio Rose.* Well, she got to talking about the song. I thought she was talking to the waiter, but *he* didn't answer her, so after a while I answered her. That's how I met her. I didn't think anything of it. We left the place together and started walking. The first thing I knew she said, This is where I live.

THE MAN: You're a dirty liar!

YOUNG MAN: Do you want to hear it? Or not? *(THE MAN does not answer.)* OK. She asked me to come in. Maybe she had something in mind, maybe she didn't. Didn't make any difference to me, one way or the other. If she was lonely, all right. If not, all right.

THE MAN: You're telling a lot of dirty lies!

YOUNG MAN: I'm telling the truth. Maybe your wife's out there with your pals. Well, call her in. I got nothing against her, or you—or any of you. Call her in, and ask her a few questions. Are you in love with her? *(THE MAN doesn't answer.)* Well, that's too bad.

THE MAN: What do you mean, too bad?

YOUNG MAN: I mean this may not be the first time something like this has happened.

THE MAN: *(swiftly)*: Shut up!

YOUNG MAN: Oh, you know it. You've always known it. You're afraid of your pals, that's all. She asked me for money. That's all she wanted. I wouldn't be here now if I had given her the money.

THE MAN: *(slowly)*: How much did she ask for?

YOUNG MAN: I didn't ask her how much. I told her I'd made a mistake. She said she would make trouble if I didn't give her money. Well, I don't like bargaining, and I don't like being threatened, either. I told her to get the hell away from me. The next thing I knew she'd run out of the house and was hollering. *(pause)* Now, why don't you go out there and tell 'em they took me to another jail—go home and pack up and leave her. You're a pretty good guy, you're just afraid of your pals.

(THE MAN draws his gun again. He is very frightened. He moves a step toward the YOUNG MAN, then fires three times. The YOUNG MAN falls to his knees. THE MAN turns and runs, horrified.)

YOUNG MAN: Hello—out there! *(He is bent forward.)*

(THE GIRL comes running in, and halts suddenly, looking at him.)

THE GIRL: There were some people in the street, men and women and kids—so I came in through the back, through a window. I couldn't find the gun. I looked all over but I couldn't find it. What's the matter?

YOUNG MAN: Nothing—nothing. Everything's all right. Listen. Listen, kid. Get the hell out of here. Go out the same way you came in and run—run like hell —run all night. Get to another town and get on a train. Do you hear me?

THE GIRL: What's happened?

YOUNG MAN: Get away—just get away from here. Take any train that's going—you can get to Frisco later.

THE GIRL: *(almost sobbing)*: I don't want to go any place without you.

YOUNG MAN: I can't go. Something's happened. *(He looks at her.)* But I'll be with you always—God damn it. Always!

(He falls forward. THE GIRL stands near him, then begins to sob softly, walking away. She stands over to one side, stops sobbing, and stares out. The excitement of the mob outside increases. THE MAN, with two of his pals, comes running in. THE GIRL watches unseen.)

THE MAN: Here's the son of a bitch!

ANOTHER MAN: OK. Open the cell, Harry.

(The THIRD MAN goes to the cell door, unlocks it, and swings it open.)

(A WOMAN comes running in.)

THE WOMAN: Where is he? I want to see him. Is he dead? *(Looking down at him, as the MEN pick him up.)* There he is. *(pause)* Yeah, that's him.

(Her husband looks at her with contempt, then at the dead man.)

THE MAN: *(trying to laugh)*: All right—let's get it over with.

THIRD MAN: Right you are, George. Give me a hand, Harry.

(They lift the body.)

THE GIRL: *(suddenly, fiercely)*: Put him down!

THE MAN: What's this?

SECOND MAN: What are you doing here? Why aren't you out in the street?

THE GIRL: Put him down and go away.

(She runs toward the MEN.)

(THE WOMAN grabs her.)

THE WOMAN: Here—where do you think *you're* going?

THE GIRL: Let me go. You've no right to take him away.

THE WOMAN: Well, listen to her, will you? *(She slaps THE GIRL and pushes her to the floor.)* Listen to the little slut, will you?

(They all go, carrying the YOUNG MAN's body. THE GIRL gets up slowly, no longer sobbing. She looks around at everything, then looks straight out, and whispers.)

THE GIRL: Hello—out—there! Hello—out there!

CURTAIN

BIBLIOGRAPHY

These books and articles, representing much of the modern theory of acting, should provide informative and interesting reading. (*Note:* Various transliterations of Constantin Stanislavski's name can prove confusing. In the body of the text, we opt for the spelling used in the preceding sentence. In the Bibliography, we use the spelling selected by the author we are citing.)

Boal, Augusto. *Games for Actors and Non-Actors*. Translated by Adrian Jackson. London and New York: Routledge, 1992.

Described as a "book for all those who are interested in the theatre as a force for change," this collection of exercises and improvisations is extremely useful as a supplement to the exercises in *Acting Is Believing.*

Brook, Peter. *The Empty Space*. New York: Atheneum, 1968.

An influential director and experimentalist discusses what makes theatre vital and what makes it deadly. Throughout are many penetrating comments about the art and craft of acting.

Brown, Richard P. (ed.). *Actor Training*. Vols. 1–3. New York: Drama Book Specialists, 1968–1976.

This series deals with approaches to acting through group improvisation, through emphasis on performer rather than on character, and through attempts to objectify subjective experience.

Chaikin, Joseph. *The Presence of the Actor*. New York: Atheneum, 1972.

A valuable aid to the understanding of self-exploration as a means of breaking away from convention and cliché.

Chekhov, Michael. *To the Actor*. New York: Harper & Row, 1953.

A creative approach by a student of Stanislavski and a one-time member of the Moscow Art Theatre. The concepts, especially the "psychological gesture," are imaginative. The exercises are stimulating, providing excellent problems in improvisation.

Cole, Toby (ed.). *Acting: A Handbook of the Stanislavski Method*. New York: Lear Publishers, 1947.

A group of articles describing principles and practices derived from Stanislavski. I. Rapoport, "The Work of the Actor," is particularly useful.

_____ and Helen Krich Chinoy (eds.). *Actors on Acting*. New York: Crown Publishers, 1949.

The long subtitle is significant: *The Theories, Techniques, and Practices of the Great Actors of All Times As Told in Their Own Words*. A selection of material by and about actors from Plato to José Ferrer.

Duerr, Edwin. *The Length and Depth of Acting*. New York: Holt, Rinehart and Winston, 1962.

An account of acting and actors from the Greeks to the present. Of value both as history and as analysis of the actor's problems and objectives, but Duerr's apparent anti-Stanislavski bias damages the book's usefulness.

Funke, Lewis, and John E. Booth. *Actors Talk About Acting*. New York: Random House, 1961.

Taped interviews with fourteen "stars of the theatre": John Gielgud, Lynn Fontanne and Alfred Lunt, Helen Hayes, José Ferrer, Maureen Stapleton, Katharine Cornell, Vivien Leigh, Morris Carnovsky, Shelley Winters, Bert Lahr, Sidney Poitier, Paul Muni, and Anne Bancroft. The interviews provide some understanding of these actors' creative processes.

Gordon, Mel. *The Stanislavsky Technique: Russia; A Workbook for Actors*. New York: Applause Theatre Book Publishers, 1987.

A compendium of the actor-training systems of Stanislavski, Vakhtangov, and Michael Chekhov. Gordon arranges the material both chronologically and topically, so the reader can see how the techniques the United States imported from Russia evolved and compare the subtle differences in approach of the three most famous theorists.

Grotowski, Jerzy. *Towards a Poor Theatre*. New York: Simon & Schuster, 1968.

Articles by and about the famous Polish innovator. They describe a theatre devoid of commercialism, demanding the ultimate in personal dedication and rigorous physical and vocal training.

Hagen, Uta, with Frankel, Haskel. *Respect for Acting*. New York: Macmillan, 1973.

Distinguished both as actress and teacher, Hagen talks about acting in both conceptual and practical terms. A stimulating and rewarding book for the serious student.

Hethmon, Robert H. (ed.). *Strasberg at the Actors Studio*. New York: Viking, 1965.

Tape-recorded sessions at the Actors Studio, giving Lee Strasberg's comments and criticisms of scenes and exercises presented by studio members. The comments reveal remarkable understanding of the actor's problems and offer much practical help, especially in inducing relaxation and freeing the imagination.

Lewis, Robert. *Method—Or Madness?* New York: Samuel French, 1958.

Eight witty and illuminating lectures explaining Stanislavski's principles and describing their use and misuse by American actors.

Magarshack, David. *Stanislavsky on the Art of the Stage*. New York: Hill and Wang, 1961.

Includes a posthumous collection of Stanislavski's lectures under the title "The System and Method of Creative Art." The introduction is a clear summary of the so-called Stanislavski system.

Marowitz, Charles. *The Act of Being*. New York: Taplinger Publishing, 1978.

This lively book takes a historical look at acting from Stanislavski to Grotowski, in search of a workable acting theory for the present-day actor. It is especially useful for its explorations of the changing actor/director/playwright/audience relationships.

_____ *Stanislavsky and the Method*. New York: Citadel Press, 1964.

Helpful application of Stanislavski's principles to various acting problems, including the playing of Brecht and Shakespeare.

Parke, Lawrence. *Since Stanislavski and Vakhtangov; the Method as a System for _Today's_ Actor*. Hollywood, CA: Acting World Books, 1985.

Although Parke's approach is more esoteric than most, his step-by-step method of preparing the actor for performing a role is solidly based on Stanislavski's tradition. His concept of obstacles is a particularly useful addition to the methodology favored by this text.

Samuels, Steven (ed.). *Theatre Profiles 10: The Illustrated Reference Guide to America's Nonprofit Professional Theatre*. New York: Theatre Communications Group, 1992.

This semiannual publication attempts to document the world of the nonprofit professional theatre. This edition features listings for 229 theatres across America and includes important names of people to contact for information about employment and other operational aspects. *Theatre Profiles 11* should be available by the time this edition of *Acting Is Believing* goes to press.

Shurtleff, Michael. *Audition: Everything an Actor Needs to Know to Get the Part*. New York: Walker, 1978.

In our discussion about auditioning, we referred to this book as the bible of all books on the subject. In his chatty, informative style, Shurtleff takes the actor through the entire process of auditioning, defines the kinds of auditions the actor is likely to encounter, and gives tips about how the actor can give himself the best chance to be successful.

Stanislavski, Constantin. *An Actor's Handbook*. Edited and translated by Elizabeth Reynolds Hapgood. New York: Theatre Arts Books, 1963.

Described accurately on the title page as "an alphabetical arrangement of concise statements on aspects of acting." The statements have been selected from the whole body of Stanislavski's writings.

_____ *An Actor Prepares*. Translated by Elizabeth Reynolds Hapgood. New York: Theatre Arts Books, 1936.

The most widely known in England and America of Stanislavski's works. It sets forth the principles of the "inner technique" and describes the concepts of sensory recall, emotion memory, relaxation, concentration, units and objectives, superobjectives, communion, adaptation, and through-line-of-action.

_____ *Building a Character*. Translated by Elizabeth Reynolds Hapgood. New York: Theatre Arts Books, 1949.

Less well known than *An Actor Prepares* but vital to an understanding of Stanislavski's principles. It is concerned with developing an "outer technique" and is a necessary supplement to the earlier work.

_____ *Creating a Role*. Translated by Elizabeth Reynolds Hapgood. New York: Theatre Arts Books, 1961.

How to work on a role from a first reading through various necessary stages of development.

Tulane Drama Review 9: 1 and 2 (Fall and Winter 1964).

These issues, entitled "Stanislavski and America," marked the one hundredth anniversary of Stanislavski's birth. They contain articles and interviews about Stanislavski's principles and their uses by prominent actors, directors, and teachers.

ADDITIONAL SOURCES

Aaron, Stephen. *Stage Fright: Its Role in Acting*. Chicago: University of Chicago Press, 1986.

Adler, Stella. *The Technique of Acting*. New York: Bantam Books, 1978.

Artaud, Antonin. *The Theater and Its Double*. Translated by Mary Caroline Richards. New York: Grove Press, 1961.

Balk, H. Wesley. *The Complete Singer-Actor: Training for Music Theater*. Minneapolis: University of Minnesota Press, 1985.

Ball, David. *Backwards & Forwards: A Technical Manual for Reading Plays*. Carbondale: Southern Illinois University Press, 1983.

Barton, John. *Playing Shakespeare*. London and New York: Methuen, 1984.

Barton, Robert. *Acting: Onstage and Off*. Second Edition. Fort Worth: Harcourt Brace Jovanovich, 1993.

Benedetti, Robert L. *The Actor at Work*. Fifth Edition. Englewood Cliffs, NJ: Prentice-Hall, 1990.

Blum, Richard A. *American Film Acting: The Stanislavski Heritage* (Studies in Cinema no. 28). Ann Arbor, MI: UMI Research Press, 1984.

Blunt, Jerry. *Stage Dialects*. San Francisco: Chandler Publishing, 1967.

Boleslavsky, Richard. *Acting: The First Six Lessons*. New York: Theatre Arts Books, 1933.

Bruder, Melissa, et al. *A Practical Handbook for the Actor*. New York: Vintage Press, 1986.

Cohen, Robert. *Acting One*. Palo Alto, CA: Mayfield Publishing, 1984.

_____ *Acting Professionally: Raw Facts About Careers in Acting*. Second Edition. Palo Alto, CA: Mayfield Publishing, 1990.

Cole, David. *Acting as Reading: The Place of the Reading Process in the Actor's Work*. Ann Arbor: University of Michigan Press, 1992.

Corrigan, Mary (ed.). "Casting: A Survey of Directors' Viewpoints." *Theatre News*, January–February 1983, pp. 6-7.

Corson, Richard. *Stage Makeup*. Sixth Edition. Englewood Cliffs, NJ: Prentice-Hall, 1981.

Donohue, Jim. "Learning Lines with Meaning: A Method for Memorizing." *Dramatics,* January 1988, pp. 28-36.

Ellis, Roger. *An Audition Handbook*

for Student Actors. Chicago: Nelson-Hall Publishers, 1986.

Finchley, Joan. *Audition!* Englewood Cliffs, NJ: Prentice-Hall, 1984.

Goldman, Michael. *The Actor's Freedom*. New York: Viking, 1975.

Grote, David. *Script Analysis: Reading and Understanding the Playscript for Production*. Belmont, CA: Wadsworth, 1985.

Hagen, Uta. *A Challenge for the Actor*. New York: Charles Scribner's Sons, 1991.

Harrop, John, and Sabin R. Epstein. *Acting with Style*. Second Edition. Englewood Cliffs, NJ: Prentice-Hall, 1990.

Hobbs, Robert L. *Teach Yourself Transatlantic: Theatre Speech for Actors*. Palo Alto, CA: Mayfield Publishing Company, 1986.

Hull, S. Loraine. *Strasberg's Method As Taught by Lorrie Hull: A Practical Guide for Actors, Teachers and Directors*. Woodbridge, CT: Ox Bow Publishing, Inc., 1985.

Hunt, Gordon. *How to Audition*. New York: Harper & Row, 1977.

Johnstone, Keith. *Impro: Improvisation and the Theatre*. London: Faber and Faber, 1979.

Kahan, Stanley. *Introduction to Acting*. Third Edition. Boston: Allyn & Bacon, 1991.

King, Nancy. *A Movement Approach to Acting*. Englewood Cliffs, NJ: Prentice-Hall, 1981.

Lessac, Arthur. *Body Wisdom: The Use and Training of the Human Body*.

New York: Drama Book Specialists, 1981.

_____ *The Use and Training of the Human Voice*. New York: Drama Book Specialists, 1967.

Levin, Irina and Igor. *Working on the Play and the Role: The Method for Analyzing the Characters in a Drama*. Chicago: Ivan R. Dee, 1992.

Lewis, Robert. *Advice to the Players*. New York: Harper & Row, 1980.

Linklater, Kristin. *Freeing the Natural Voice*. New York: Drama Book Specialists, 1976.

Lounsberry, Warren C. *Theatre Backstage from A to Z*. Seattle: University of Washington Press, 1967.

Machlin, Evangeline. *Dialects for the Stage*. New York: Theatre Arts Books, 1975.

McTigue, Mary. *Acting Like a Pro: Who's Who, What's What, and the Way Things Really Work in the Theatre*. White Hall, VA: Betterway Publications, 1992.

Manderino, Ned. *The Transpersonal Actor*. Los Angeles, CA: Manderino Books, 1985.

Markus, Thomas. *The Professional Actor from Audition to Performance*. New York: Drama Book Specialists, 1978.

Martinez, J. D. *Combat Mime: A Non-Violent Approach to Stage Violence*. Chicago: Nelson-Hall, 1982.

Matson, Katinka. *The Working Actor: A Guide to the Profession*. New York: Viking, 1976.

Meisner, Sanford, and Dennis Longwell. *Sanford Meisner on Acting*. New York: Vintage Books, 1987.

Miles-Brown, John. *Acting: A Drama Studio Source Book*. London: P. Owen, 1985.

Moore, Sonia. *Training an Actor*. New York: Penguin, 1979.

Morris, Eric. *Being and Doing: A Workbook for Actors*. Los Angeles: Spelling Publications, 1981.

Moston, Doug. *Coming to Terms With Acting: An Instructive Glossary : What You Need to Know to Understand It, Discuss It, Deal With It and Do It*. New York: Drama Book Publishers, 1993.

Novak, Elaine Adams. *Performing in Musicals*. New York: Schirmer Books, 1988.

Olivier, Laurence. *On Acting*. New York: Simon and Schuster, 1986.

Pisk, Litz. *The Actor and His Body*. New York: Theatre Arts Books, 1975.

Rendle, Adrian. *So You Want to Be an Actor?* London: A. C. Black, 1986.

Richardson, Don. *Acting Without Agony: An Alternative to the Method*. Boston: Allyn and Bacon, 1988.

Rizzo, Raymond. *The Total Actor*. Indianapolis: The Odyssey Press, 1975.

Rolfe, Bari. *Movement for Period Plays*. Oakland, CA: Personabooks, 1985.

Russell, Douglas. *Period Style for the Theatre*. Boston: Allyn & Bacon, 1980.

Schechner, Richard. *Environmental Theatre*. New York: Hawthorn Books, 1973.

Spolin, Viola. *Improvisation for the Theatre*. Evanston, IL: Northwestern University Press, 1963.

Stern, Lawrence. *Stage Management: A Guidebook of Practical Techniques*. Third Edition. Boston: Allyn and Bacon, Inc., 1987.

Strasberg, Lee. *A Dream of Passion: The Development of the Method*. Edited by Evangeline Morphos. Boston: Little, Brown, 1987.

Swift, Clive. *The Job of Acting: A Guide to Working in Theatre*. London: Harrap, 1976.

Taylor, John Russell. *The Penguin Dictionary of the Theatre*. Baltimore: Penguin, 1966.

Thomas, James. *Script Analysis for Actors, Directors and Designers*. Boston: Focal Press, 1992.

Woods, Leigh. *On Playing Shakespeare: Advice and Commentary from Actors and Actresses of the Past*. New York: Greenwood Press, 1991.

Yakim, Moni. *Creating a Character: A Physical Approach to Acting*. New York: Back Stage Books, 1990.

THEATRES AND GROUPS

MAJOR RESIDENT THEATRES

Actors Theatre of Louisville
316-320 West Main St.
Louisville, KY 40202-2916

ATL is perhaps the leading American company in the development and production of new plays by American writers. Its Humana Festival of New American Plays has spawned several plays that have moved quickly into the national scene. ATL also emphasizes an interdisciplinary approach to the classical theatre through their Classics in Context Festival. Acting apprenticeships are available at ATL.

Alley Theatre
615 Texas Ave.
Houston, TX 77002

The Alley Theatre is one of the oldest professional repertory theatres in the nation, founded by Nina Vance in 1947. The current focus of the Alley is on newly interpreted classics, new American plays, and contemporary works from other countries.

The American Conservatory Theatre
450 Geary St.
San Francisco, CA 94102

ACT has long been one of the nation's largest and most active repertory companies. Its major produc-

tions have ranged from classics to contemporary works.

The Arena Stage
6th and Maine Ave. S.W.
Washington, D.C. 20024

Now under new direction, The Arena Stage has regularly provided the most dependable source of lively theatre for the people of the Washington metropolitan community. Its repertoire has ranged from important American and international premieres to thoughtful explorations of classical drama.

Dallas Theatre Center
3636 Turtle Creek Blvd.
Dallas, TX 75219-5598

This theatre, founded in the late fifties by the legendary Paul Baker, has been the proving ground for such dramatists as Mark Medoff and Preston Jones.

Guthrie Theatre
Vineland Place
Minneapolis, MN 55403

The Guthrie, which opened its doors in 1963, has recently returned to a commitment to producing the greatest plays of the world repertoire after a period during which it experimented with different approaches and styles. Named for its noted British founding director, it is a handsome, 1,437-seat auditorium with a thrust stage.

The Hartford Stage Company
50 Church St.
Hartford, CT 06013

Under the artistic direction of Mark Lamos, this important regional theatre devotes fully half of each season to world premieres or to second productions of new plays by U.S. writers. It also has been the home for outstanding reinterpretations of texts from the past.

The Long Wharf Theatre
222 Sargent Dr.
New Haven, CT 06511

An international flavor has been the hallmark of the twenty-five years of this important theatre, with many of its productions moving on to Broadway, Off Broadway, and television. It also enjoys a long-standing reputation as an actor's theatre.

Mark Taper Forum
135 North Grand Ave.
Los Angeles, CA 90012

Founded in 1967, the Mark Taper Forum serves a broad audience in both its main-stage series and its laboratory theatre. It, too, has achieved a reputation for the development of new plays.

Trinity Repertory Company
201 Washington St.
Providence, RI 02903

Trinity continues to strive toward the laudable goal of a permanent artistic company engaging its audience as participants rather than spectators. Remaining committed to developing original works, it also produces innovative treatments of world classics.

OTHER SELECTED MAJOR RESIDENT THEATRES

Alabama Shakespeare Festival (Montgomery, AL)

Alliance Theatre Company (Atlanta, GA)

Arizona Theatre Company (Tucson, AZ)

Arkansas Repertory Theatre (Little Rock, AR)

Asolo Center for the Performing Arts (Sarasota, FL)

Baltimore Theatre Project (Baltimore, MD)

Barter Theatre (Abingdon, VA)

Berkeley Repertory Theatre (Berkeley, CA)

California Theatre Center (Sunnyvale, CA)

Circle Repertory Company (New York City, NY)

The Cleveland Playhouse (Cleveland, OH)

Denver Center Theatre Company (Denver, CO)

Goodman Theatre (Chicago, IL)

Indiana Repertory Theatre (Indianapolis, IN)

Manhattan Theatre Club (New York City, NY)

Milwaukee Repertory Theatre (Milwaukee, WI)

Missouri Repertory Theatre (Kansas City, MO)

Nebraska Theatre Caravan (Omaha, NE)

New Dramatists (New York City, NY)

New York Shakespeare Festival (New York City, NY)

Old Globe Theatre (San Diego, CA)

Oregon Shakespeare Festival (Ashland, OR)

The Repertory Theatre of St. Louis (St. Louis, MO)

Seattle Repertory Theatre (Seattle, WA)
Steppenwolf Theatre Company (Chicago, IL)
Trinity Repertory Company (Providence, RI)

WPA Theatre (New York City, NY)
Yale Repertory Theatre (New Haven, CT)

THEATRE ORGANIZATIONS OF INTEREST TO ASPIRING ACTORS

Actors' Equity Association (165 W. 46th St., New York City, NY 10036)
American College Theatre Festival (The Kennedy Center, Washington, D.C. 20566)
Association for Theatre in Higher Education (P.O. Box 15282, Evansville, IN 47716)
Theatre Communications Group (355 Lexington Ave, New York City, NY 10017)

INDEX

Page numbers in italics refer to photographs and diagrams.